Mediaeval Academy Re

1

Mediaeval Academy Reprints for Teaching

HEINRICH FICHTENAU

The Carolingian Empire

MEDIAEVAL ACADEMY REPRINTS FOR TEACHING

HEINRICH FICHTENAU
Translated by Peter Munz

The Carolingian Empire

Published by University of Toronto Press
Toronto Buffalo London
in association with the Mediaeval Academy of America

Translated from *Das karolingische Imperium* published by
Fretz und Wasmuth Verlag A.G. Zürich
Translation first published 1957 in the series Studies in
Mediaeval History edited by Geoffrey Barraclough and
published by Basil Blackwell Publisher Oxford
This edition reprinted from the 1968 printing by arrangement
with Basil Blackwell Publisher

CONTENTS

LIST OF ABBREVIATIONS

AS	Jahrbücher des fränkischen Reiches unter Karl dem Grossen, by S. Abel, continued by B. Simson, 2 vols., Berlin, Halle, Leipzig, 1866, 1883; 2nd edition revised by B. Simson, 1st vol., Leipzig, 1888.
BM	Regesta Imperii, 2nd Ed. edd. J. F. Böhmer and E. Mühlbacher, Innsbruck, 1899–1908.
EHR	English Historical Review.
MGH	Monumenta Germaniae Historica.
	Auct. Scriptores: Auctores Antiquissimi.
	Cap. Leges (in quart size), Sectio II: Capitularia Regum Francorum.
	Conc. Leges (in quart size), Sectio III: Concilia.
	Dip. Diplomata Karolinorum, 1st vol.: Die Urkunden Pippins, Karlmanns und Karls des Grossen, ed. E. Mühlbacher.
	Epp. Epistolae (in quart size).
	For. Leges (in quart size), Sectio V: Formulae Merovingici et Karolini Aevi, ed. K. Zeumer.
	Ger. Scriptores Rerum Germanicarum in usum scholarum separatim editi.
	Leg. Leges (in quart size), Sectio I: Leges nationum Germanicarum.
	Mer. Scriptores Rerum Merovingicarum.
	Poet. Poetae Latini Medii Aevi: Poetae Latini Aevi Carolini.
	Script. Scriptores Rerum Germanicarum (in folio size).
MIÖG	Mitteilungen des Instituts für österreichische Geschichtsforschung.
MPL	Patrologiae Cursus Completus, Series Latina, ed. J. P. Migne.
ZSSRg	Zeitschrift der Savigny-Stiftung für Rechtsgeschichte, Germanistische Abteilung.
ZSSRk	Zeitschrift der Savigny-Stiftung für Rechtsgeschichte, Kanonistische Abteilung.

AUTHOR'S PREFACE

This book deals with the heyday of Frankish rule in Europe, but it does not claim to be a complete history of that rule. Its precise object is to render an account of the attempt to give an inner unity and solidity to the newly founded Frankish state. The prospects for the success of this attempt depended on two things : the formation of a class of officials to make centralized government possible ; and the force of an idea, the idea of the Christian Empire, to justify the exercise of power.

In the days of the Roman empire there had existed an autocratic and centralized imperial government ; and in those days few people had doubted that that government was not only a political but also a theological, divinely ordained necessity. Byzantium was the only real competitor of the Franks for power in Europe, and there the Emperor's claim to exercise power over all Christians had survived. In the west, however, it had become very doubtful whether it would be possible to put forward a similar claim. People there realized that, at best, it would be necessary to compromise between such a claim to universal lordship and the totally different spiritual, political and social conditions that obtained in western Europe. The question we have to ask, therefore, is whether such a compromise had any chance of success or whether the conditions were such that there was no hope of translating the ideal of a unitary Christian state into practice.

If we put the question in this way, we avoid treating the history of ideas as if it were something apart and devoid of practical consequences. The historian of ideas should always relate ideas to realities, especially when the gulf between the two is as great as it was in the reign of Charles the Great. As I have approached the period from this angle, it has become necessary for me to speak more of the negative aspects of Carolingian civilization than has been customary. As a result my picture is a corrective of those presentations in which Charles's reign is allowed to shine in the most dazzling light. It has been my intention to supplement these presentations, not to set them aside. Although I have stressed this in the preface to the German edition of this book, many of my critics have charged me with being one-sided. There is no doubt that historians are justified in celebrating the achievements of Charles the Great; but these achievements are not necessarily belittled if one traces their natural limitations. The study of history is not concerned with the worship of heroes, but with the search for truth. A richer and truer picture of the period will emerge if one emphasizes its disappointing aspects which have been persistently underestimated by historians. Unless one emphasizes these disappointing aspects of Charles's reign, one will never be able to avoid the error of attributing the downfall of an allegedly flourishing Empire to the incompetence of Louis the Pious and his contemporaries. Already under Charles the Great there were very strong political and social tensions in the structure of the Frankish state; and even during his reign Christianity was scarcely capable of veiling the ruthlessness with which Charles's subjects pursued their selfish interests. Although these disruptive forces did not become completely obvious until after Charles's death, the decay of the Frankish monarchy must be attributed to them.

At the present time men are anxious to rediscover the political and intellectual foundations of Europe, and there is much talk about Charles the Great and his Empire. Among scholars, especially in Germany, there is a lively debate about the facts and the ideas that led to the imperial coronation of 800, and since the writing of this book there have appeared a number of new studies—including one of my own—of this problem. Although the new material has led me to rewrite part of Chapter II, the fundamental conception of the book stands unaltered.

For a bibiliography of works on Charles the Great and his age, I would refer the reader to the forthcoming book by Professor F. L. Ganshof. Until then, the references in the present book, together with the bibliography in L. Halphen's *Charlemagne et l'Empire Carolingien* must suffice.

I would like to express my heartfelt thanks to Professor G. Barraclough (Liverpool), to Dr. Peter Munz (Wellington, New Zealand), and to the publishers for their help in making possible an English translation of this book.

H. FICHTENAU.

Vienna,
The University.

TRANSLATOR'S INTRODUCTION

The great French historians of the last generation were unanimous in their estimate of the importance of the reign of Charles the Great for the subsequent course of European history. F. Lot wrote that although the empire of Charles had broken up thirty years after his death, the impression it left was so strong that in the institutions, the law, the ecclesiastical organization, and the culture of each of the new states, there subsisted enough common elements for a European civilization to maintain itself throughout the Middle Ages. This European civilization, the French scholar concluded, was made possible through the reign of Charlemagne. A. Kleinclausz observed that the contemporary poet who called Charles the lighthouse of Europe, was not mistaken, and that the generations which followed him were not the victims of an illusion when they saw in him the sovereign and emperor, king and master, of all his subjects, who exercised his power from the Rhineland where he had wisely fixed his residence ; a power exercised in the west over the old kingdom of the Franks, in the east over Germany, and, beyond the Alps, over Italy. Under his aegis the peoples of a new Europe drew together.

The crucial importance of Charles the Great's reign has never been questioned ; and as a result there is a long series of portraits, descriptions, histories, legends, epics, and even of hagiography, dealing with Charles. The series began with Einhard's famous Life. Professor Fichtenau's book, *Das karolingische Imperium*, of which the following chapters are a partial translation, is only the latest of a long series. The long history of the history of Charles is itself, of course, a tribute to his importance and proof of the fact that he made a profound impression on the European imagination. But it is more : it is, in a sense, a barometer of the fluctuations of the European intellect, of its political and religious passions and prejudices. In this sense Charles the Great can well be compared with Magna

Carta, for the history of the history of that document too, is an index of the political and social attitudes and outlooks of English historians, and the treatment it has received from the thirteenth century to the twentieth reflects the history of each successive age in turn.

The history of the history of Charles began with Einhard's Life. There is much solid history in Einhard and it is inconceivable that any historian of Charles's reign could ever think of dispensing with his work. But even Einhard is already sensitive to considerations other than brute facts: he had educational and literary ambitions and thus there crept into his work a certain amount of stoicism and a number of views culled from his literary model, Suetonius. And one may surmise that when he placed the responsibility for some of Charles's atrocities upon Queen Fastrada, he really intended a warning to Louis the Pious against his own queen, Judith.

The next important document is the work written by the monk of St. Gall. Based, in parts, on good tradition, it is also a very obvious attempt to glorify Charles for political reasons and to tell the clergy, who were becoming so troublesome to Charles the Bald, that in the days of Charles the Great they had been subject to the king; and everybody had been very contented in those days. From this point onwards there is a veritable flood of Carolingian legend, the content of which, as is easily recognizable, often goes not only beyond historical truth, but also beyond the limits of plausibility. The growth of this literature was first systematically traced in the great work of Gaston Paris, *Histoire poetique de Charlemagne*, and it has recently been dealt with more fully, so far as the Germanic lands are concerned, in the scholarly work of R. Folz, *Le Souvenir et la légende de Charlemagne dans l'empire germanique medièvale* (Paris, 1950).

The story thus unravelled is indeed fascinating. In the French parts of the Carolingian empire there is, of course, the long and splendid tradition of Carolingian epic poetry, but there is also Charles's role in the political debates conducted among the French people throughout its history. One need only refer to the way in which Philip Augustus appealed to the memory of Charles when he set out for his crusade; or to the long controversy about the origins of class distinction and of the national assembly in Carolingian France; or to the impact of Napoleon which prompted Guizot's treatment of Charles; or to Michelet's famous portrait of Charles as the priest-ridden king. This subject has been surveyed recently, though unfortunately not very exhaustively, by G. Pepe in his essay, *Un problema storico : Carlo Magno* (Florence, 1952).

In Germany, too, the reign of Charles was considered a matter of vital importance, at least during the days of the medieval empire. Otto I followed in Charles's footsteps and directed the German monarchy along the path of Carolingian theocracy. Otto III compared himself with Charles; Wipo considered his master, Conrad II, a reincarnation of Charles; and in the reign of Henry III the theocracy of Charles seemed once more to have become a reality. The significance of Charles's coronation was explored vigorously by both sides during the Investiture Contest; and Frederick Barbarossa's appeal to the example of Charles is too well known to need emphasis. The figure of Charles played its part during the struggle between Otto of Brunswick and Philip of Suabia; and Innocent III considered the events of the year 800 to have had a normative significance—needless to say, of course, favourable to his cause. Charles the law-giver, Charles the protector of local rights and charters, Charles as an ancestor of the Habsburgs, and Charles even as a saint : these conceptions show how much of the vital debates on the political and religious destiny of the German people turned upon his influence and his achievements.

The rise of the monarchies and of the national states tended somewhat to obscure the real importance of Charles. Modern Germans, for instance, are often undecided as to whether Charles was a German or not. But to look at him from this angle is to do violence to history. His great significance consisted, after all, in the fact that he ruled over western Christendom, and that his reign was the most formative period of European civilization —as distinct from the local civilizations of France, Italy and Germany. One needs 'to call a mist over the face of time' and remember that in Charles's day, in spite of disruptive and centri-fugal tendencies, it was by no means a foregone conclusion that

Europe was to be divided politically and religiously into separate and distinct units. Marc Bloch's remark is therefore very apposite: in order to place the history of the ' posthumous glory ' of Charles the Great in perspective, one must pursue one's studies on both sides of the Franco-German frontier, and from a point of view appropriate to Aix-la-Chapelle as well as to St. Denis.

In modern times historians have, of course, been intent upon distinguishing between the legend and ' what really happened '. Nobody can deny the crucial importance of Charles's reign ; but only serious and meticulous historical research is capable of arriving at an understanding of what that importance was.

In one sense it might seem that it would not be too difficult a task to arrive at some idea of what really happened in the reign of Charles. The source-material for the period is readily available in print in the *Monumenta Germaniae Historica*. The documentary evidence, supplemented by a number of archaeological finds and by the artistic productions of the period, is limited. In that sense the study of Charles the Great and his time is a more manageable undertaking than the study of many a later period for which the source material is so ample that no historian can hope to know it all. As far as the age of Charles is concerned, it is humanly possible to acquaint oneself with all the extant material. There are, of course, gaps : a natural lack of information on all sorts of things ; at times even wilful destruction of vital evidence, as in the case of the letter sent to Alcuin from Rome informing him of the causes of pope Leo III's troubles. Alcuin wrote back to say that the letter had shocked him so deeply that he had burnt it lest an unauthorized person read it. It is difficult to say whether he would have considered a modern historian an unauthorized person or not. But one must suppose that that was the kind of issue on which Alcuin could not afford to take risks.

In spite of the manageable proportions of the evidence, and in spite of the fact that practically all of it has been known for several centuries, there is wide disagreement among scholars on some of the fundamental issues of the period. G. Pepe, in the little volume mentioned above, has surveyed the field. Some of the disagreements are obviously due to different approaches conditioned by the cultural and religious preconceptions of the scholars concerned. Nevertheless it is by no means possible to account for all of them in this way. Many of the disagreements depend on the interpretation of the evidence, and some on the admissibility of the sources. L. Halphen, for instance, was adamant in his rejection of the book by the monk of St. Gall. Professor Fichtenau concedes that the monk may not be wholly accurate but insists that much of the *Gesta* is quite trustworthy. Again there is the famous controversy between Dopsch and Pirenne about the economic conditions of the period, and the equally famous debate about the significance and meaning of the imperial coronation of Charles.

As a result of these disagreements the secondary material about Charles has grown until it has become almost unmanageable. Many scores of special articles and monographs as well as a formidable library of books on the general history of the period show how many different interpretations can be put upon, and how many inferences drawn from, a limited quantity of primary material. And yet no major work on the period has appeared in English since the publication of the biographies of Charlemagne by Thomas Hodgkin and H. W. C. Davis in 1897 and 1900, and of C. J. B. Gaskoin's book on Alcuin, which appeared in 1904. Miss Duckett's later volume on Alcuin, published in 1951, has many solid qualities, but it does not add substantially to the debate on Charles. There are therefore good reasons why one of the most recent additions to the debate should be made available in an English version.

The special qualities of Professor Fichtenau's study can best be picked out by comparison with two other post-war works on Charles, the one by J. Calmette and the other by L. Halphen.[1] Both French works are systematic accounts of the period : that of Halphen is based on meticulous scholarship, while that of Calmette is more discursive in style and contains a lucid and level-headed discussion of the famous controversies between Dopsch, Inama-Sternegg and Pirenne on the economic conditions of the age and a lively chapter on Charles's personality. Both Calmette and Halphen describe the system of government under Charles

---

[1] J. Calmette, *Charlemagne. Sa vie et son oeuvre* (Paris, 1945) ; L. Halphen, *Charlemagne, et l'empire carolingien* (Paris, 1947).

the Great, but omit to examine the tensions and stresses within
that system. From this point of view the present book may be
considered a supplement to the more textbook-like treatment of
the two French scholars. It presents less a picture than an argument ; and its full value will be most apparent if it is read in
conjunction with these French works and the older systematic
studies of A. Kleinclausz.

Professor Fichtenau's work has been considered by many
reviewers of the German edition to be less precise and cautious
than that of Halphen. Probably the author himself would concede
that. His book has been chosen for publication in this series
because it is a fine example of the way in which solid scholarly
work can be combined with a vigorous concern for human
problems, religious, social and cultural. There is no systematiza-
tion, no attempt to portray the age in terms of a well-ordered
whole. The picture which emerges is plastic and is more concerned with the strains and stresses in Carolingian society and
the conflicts that arose from them than with a systematic enumeration of all the known details.

The author's theme is the social, economic, political, and
religious problems which Charles the Great and his advisers
failed to solve. This failure is not glossed over, or excused on
account of the ' spirit of the age ' or other such nebulous factors.
The responsibility is squarely placed on the men of the time, and
not only on them personally but also on the equipment they had
and the use they could make of it. As a result there emerges little
that would justify us in talking about the splendour of the Carolingian age or the great achievements of the so-called Carolingian
Renaissance. The author brings out the limitations of the men
of the period and instead of hero-worship he sees their ' human,
all too human ' aspects. It is in this that the main significance
of the book may be thought to lie. Our picture of Charles the
Great was far removed, long before Professor Fichtenau wrote,
from medieval legends and epics; but historians, with a few
notable if isolated exceptions, have continued to identify the
importance of Charles for the subsequent development of
Europe with the concrete results he is alleged to have achieved.
Professor Fichtenau's book is realistic in that it denies most of

the alleged achievements without failing to bring out the importance of the age. It is the author's conclusion that the Carolingian empire was the first great conception of a young Europe and that it was really no more than a programme for the future. It proved to be a failure because of the speed with which it was improvised and because it was no more than an external form. It was bound to be a failure, because the people who lived in it and directed it were not fully mature, because they had not yet learnt to combine submission to law with liberty. Men in all ages tend to lack the ability to combine submission with liberty, and society is usually protected from degenerating into disorder only by the force of tradition and by the grooves men move in. Professor Fichtenau's argument is that this universal inability had particularly devastating results in the Carolingian age because the protective bonds of the old society had disappeared and the new religion had so far failed to establish new ones.

The programme Charles the Great attempted to realize was therefore bound to prove a failure. And yet Professor Fichtenau is no determinist. He is alive to the fact that the outstanding personality of Charles left a very marked imprint on the period ; he considers that many institutions which seemed unworkable in themselves, were made to work by Charles's powerful determination and his unusual physical and mental powers ; and he attributes great importance to Charles's common sense and his massive, if simple piety. The importance of this purely human factor in the history of the era is rated very highly, and the chapter on Charles the man is therefore an integral part of the story rather than a mere prying into the Emperor's private life.

Ranke once said that every age stands in an absolute relation to God. He presumably meant by this statement to stress that we should not think of history as a story of progress and that we cannot find in history an ever progressive and ever more perfect solution of human problems. Unfortunately, there are too many historians who have given a different sense to Ranke's statement. They write history as if every age found its solution to human problems and thus embodied a set of values of its own. Thi approach to history is hardly realistic for it ignores what we ca observe so readily in our own age and what is, presumably, the case in every other age—namely the fact that the history of an age is not the history of a solution of a number of problems, but the history of the struggle between several possible solutions, and of the way in which men working towards certain solutions are constantly deflected from their paths by other men working for other solutions. Historical realism, as opposed to the purely institutional and formal approach, is the outstanding merit of Porfessor Fichtenau's description of the Carolingian age.

The standpoint from which the age is approached is, however, a religious one. The freshness and the stimulus of the book owe much to the special religious sensibility of the author. This sensibility, I would imagine, is not itself the result of historical study; and there is no point in inquiring into its origins. But it may be as well to say at the very outset what it consists of.

The author recognizes two diametrically opposed forms of the religious life. The one is the religious life as exemplified in Paul, the life of inwardness, of the conscience, the ultimate goal of which is the regeneration of the old Adam. The other life is the life of belief in the magical power of external works, in the healing power of relics, in the importance of an organized mass effort to serve the King of the Heavens in fealty. Professor Fichtenau is not the only recent historian who has seen the conflict between these two extremes exemplified in the history of the transition from the so-called Dark Ages to the high Middle Ages. Mr. Southern, also has drawn our attention to it.[1] He associates the contrast between the spiritual climate of the eleventh and that of the twelfth century with the decline of the one form and the emergence of the other. Professor Fichtenau sees the Carolingian era very much as an example of the first form of religious life; but he draws a telling and convincing picture of the growth of the reform party and of the stirrings of the Christian conscience even in Alcuin and Charles the Great himself.

Approaching his subject with these concepts in mind the author was the better able to appreciate some of the inner weaknesses of the Carolingian state and some of its more questionable policies. He was also able to understand more fully than had

[1] *The Making of the Middle Ages* (London, 1953).

been done before, the lack of public spirit, the extent and real
consequences of corruption, and the futility of so many religious
policies and practices which were based on rank superstition.
Some of these things had been noted before. I think it is to
Fustel de Coulanges, for instance, that we owe the first real
estimate of the extent of corruption among the Carolingian
nobility. And Harnack was by no means unaware of the significance of the trade in, and worship of, relics in the era. But
Harnack was a liberal Protestant and he could not appreciate
that the worship of relics could be associated with a certain form
of religious life. He saw in it a ruthless financial exploitation of
the stupidity of the lower orders. No doubt there may have been
occasional ' enlightened ' financiers, who availed themselves of
widespread superstition to line their pockets. Yet it seems to
me that Professor Fichtenau comes nearer the truth when he sees
in the worship of relics rather another form of the religious life.
His interpretation of the facts is the more plausible when we
remember what we have learnt, since the days of Harnack, from
anthropology.

Professor Fichtenau's approach is, in some respects, reminiscent of the outlook developed by anthropologists in their study
of primitive society. There can be no question that Frankish
society in the eighth and ninth centuries was not primitive in the
sense in which anthropologists to-day use that word. But there
can also be little doubt that there were many similarities ; and
Charles the Great's effort to govern Frankish society, to reform
it in the light of his understanding of the duties of a Christian
ruler, shows similarities with the attempts of certain western
governments to guide the steps of non-European societies which
have already begun to shed their native tribal structure under the
impact of western attitudes. The historian of these early ages of
Europe, can, therefore learn much from the anthropologist.

Professor Fichtenau is, of course, a historian and not an
anthropologist. But there is no doubt that in some places he has
abandoned the traditional historian's approach and has used the
sources in order to attempt a realistic estimate of, e.g., the
' authority-structure ' of the kind of society with which he is
dealing. The traditional historical approach was always through

legal concepts—legal concepts weighted heavily in favour of modern notions of authority and sovereignty. There is, for example, an air of unreality in the statement of U. Stutz that the tendency of legislation in the period 750–820 was to deprive the manorial lord of the power of dismissing the clergy of his private church, or of appointing them without the bishop's assent, and of checking the presentation to churches of unfree clerks. Professor Fichtenau's treatment of the purposes and effects of this legislation is sociologically more convincing. Similarly it is very difficult to paint a realistic picture of the era if one sees in the social and political conflict of the times nothing but conflicts arising out of the clash between Charles's law-making authority and the indigenous legal traditions of his subjects. Therefore, one may well question the value, except for extremely limited purposes, of the picture that emerges in the first part of H. Mitteis' *Der Staat des hohen Mittelalters* (Weimar, 1948). If, on the other hand, one reads Professor Fichtenau's account of the political problems of the age, one cannot but be impressed by the similarity of his findings with the generalizations of the anthropologist. ' Indigenous chiefs,' Professor Gluckman writes, ' are caught between the pressure of the Western Government whose servants they are, and the pressure of the people whom they represent against the Government. Where there are no indigenous chiefs, the Government has no machinery to work through, since it cannot handle the allegiances of kinship groups and of religious congregations. Where Governments appointed their own chiefs, these were not restrained by indigenous sanctions and often became rank exploiters of their fellows . . . '[1]

There is one other important respect in which the author could well appeal to an anthropological outlook in defence of his method. Critics have chided him for not resisting the temptation to postulate the existence of an intimate connection between the various manifestations of public and private activity in a given historical field. It is certainly true that if historical method is defined as the use of texts and if a historian is not supposed to assert anything for which he cannot produce texts, this is a very unhistorical method. But in this case, one might argue, a

[1] *The Institutions of Primitive Society*, Oxford, 1954, p. 80.

narrowly defined historical method is not helpful in telling us much about society ; and it may therefore be quite legitimate to draw inferences, e.g. from the absence of dialectics or from Charles's architectural activities, for the general make-up of society. There is no need to justify this method by anything but an appeal to common sense ; and one need not have recourse to such vague concepts as the spirit of the age, in order to understand its validity. Whether the author's particular inferences are, in fact, justified, is, of course, another matter ; and there has indeed been room for legitimate criticism. Nevertheless, the method itself is not necessarily unsound because it cannot be summed up in terms of conventional historical method.

In respect of the problem of what was involved in Charles's coronation as emperor, Professor Fichtenau has done well to heed the wise words recently written by Professor Schramm : the coronation must have meant different things to different people and any attempt to say what it meant to all people is, in fact, unhistorical. There is no doubt that much light can be thrown on some of these meanings ; and it is gratifying to see the large measure of agreement between the views of Professor Fichtenau and those of Professor Ganshof, as expressed in his lecture on the *Imperial Coronation of Charlemagne* (Glasgow, 1949) and in his impressive essay on *La fin du règne de Charlemagne.*[1] In both these studies Professor Ganshof, with great sensitivity and by a minute study of the sources, has been able to pin-point some of the policies connected with the imperial dignity and to identify them with certain characters. Professor Fichtenau's conclusions, in spite of one notable disagreement, corroborate those of Professor Ganshof in many respects. He sees in the events of December 25th, 800, the culmination of a development that can be traced as early as the time of the council of Frankfort in 794. With regard to the immediate preparations he agrees with Professor Ganshof in taking very seriously the testimony of the *Annales Laureshamenses* about the Roman Synod. Earlier historians have often considered this document to be not altogether trustworthy ; but Professor Fichtenau has been able to advance compelling reasons for believing that the author of these

[1] *Zeitschrift fur schweizerische Geschichte*, XXVIII (1948).

Annales was none other than Richbod, the bishop of Trier, himself.[1]

The argument over the meaning of empire for Charles has invariably been connected with the meaning of the *Civitas Dei* of St. Augustine, with which we know Charles to have been acquainted. A. Kleinclausz, L. Halphen, L. Levillain and H. Hirsch believed that Charles's empire was meant to be something like a prefiguration on earth of the City of God. This view has been contested ; but whatever one's opinion may be on the matter, it is important to point out that it is by no means clear what St. Augustine had in mind, and that, therefore, it is not at all clear what Charles thought St. Augustine meant, even if it could be proved with certainty that Charles's aims were derived from St. Augustine. Here again, Professor Fichtenau's religious sensibility enables him to give a plausible and reasonable estimate of the influence of St. Augustine's ideas and to show that it is doubtful whether, e.g. Alcuin's understanding of the ideas of St. Augustine was a correct one. This whole question is of considerable importance in view of the fact that, since the appearance of H.-X. Arquillière's essay entitled *L'Augustinisme politique* (Paris, 1934), it has become customary to describe the theocratic trend in medieval political thinking as *political Augustinianism*. According to Professor Fichtenau, St. Augustine's City of God was meant to contain the just in heaven as well as on earth. It was a spiritual community, the membership of which depended on an inner attitude, to be contrasted with the tangible political communities on earth. Alcuin, on the other hand, was not able to see in such an inner attitude the criterion of distinction between the two kinds of community ; and, misunderstanding St. Augustine, he identified the City of God with Christendom and the City of the Devil with the heathen. St. Augustine's City of God had no tangible boundaries ; but Alcuin's had, and, moreover, they almost coincided with the actual dominions of Charles. Whether Alcuin's interpretation of St. Augustine was really at fault may be a matter of doubt, but there can be little doubt that Alcuin's ideas on the matter do not correspond to what

[1] *Karl der Grosse und das Kaisertum*, MIÖG, LXI (1953), which forms a valuable supplement to Chapter II of the present book.

Arquillière has described as *political Augustinianism*. The essence of *political Augustinianism*, according to Arquillière, is the absorption of nature by supernature. Professor Fichtenau's analysis, however, shows that in Charles's empire there was no absorption of nature by supernature any more than there was an absorption of supernature by nature. These arguments, therefore, seem to show that Arquillière was wrong in believing Charles's empire to have been a decided triumph of political Augustianism, i.e., something like the City of God. On Professor Fichtenau's reading of the facts one cannot conclude, as Arquillière did, that all that remained to be done for a complete ecclesiastico-spiritual victory, was the substitution of the Pope for the Emperor as the head of the City of God.

It is much more realistic to see in the Carolingian political system an attempt to construct a replica of the Byzantine political system. In the Carolingian system, as in Byzantium, there was no clear division between the secular and the spiritual spheres of life and of authority ; and the secular sphere could therefore not be subjected to the spiritual sphere or be absorbed by it any more than the spiritual sphere could be subjected to the secular sphere. The distinction between the two spheres is, in fact, of much later origin and reflects very clearly the heightened sensibility and the increasing use of dialectical arguments characteristic of a later age. Christopher Dawson has made us familiar with the similarities between the Carolingian state and Byzantium. Professor Fichtenau's arguments move in the same direction. It is only fair to point out, however, that the latter is more alive than Dawson to the important distinctions between the Byzantine conception of the imperial dignity and the Carolingian conception. The Carolingians, indeed, waged some kind of propaganda warfare against the Byzantine tendency to deify the emperor and against the description of the emperor as *isoapostolos*. Professor Fichtenau is careful to explain, against both J. Calmette and A. Kleinclausz, that Charles, though ruling by divine appointment, never claimed what eastern Christians readily conceded to their rulers.

But in spite of these important, if subtle, distinctions, it appears from the present book, that Charles's empire, like the

Byzantine empire, was something like a 'sacred empire', a state and a church at the same time. And Charles, the head of that empire, considered it his duty to safeguard the religious as well as the political welfare of his subjects. E. Troeltsch, following the work of K. Müller and of A. Hauck, realised the social importance of this system. He argued that Charles had set human and concrete ends to the church, and had used it in order to civilise mankind. Charles appears thus as something like a revolutionary in that he put the religious idea at the service of the state and of its educative tasks. It is not certain that Charles was really a revolutionary in that sense. He merely did for the west what Roman emperors had done earlier for the east. What is important is that Professor Fichtenau, always sensitive to the transcendental aims of religion, is very doubtful as to the genuine qualities of this 'sacred empire', and that, unlike Troeltsch, he therefore does not rate Charles's achievements in the sphere of civilisation and education very highly. Against Dawson, and in agreement with H. Pirenne, he arrives at a relatively low estimate of the so-called Carolingian Renaissance and has no illusions as to the real quality of the 'sacred empire'. 'The old tribal structure', he writes, 'was gone—but apart from Charles's powerful personality, there was nothing to keep men together. Christianization was but skin-deep and therefore the famous peace of the empire was nothing more than a temporary lull in the armed combat.'

The author is therefore able to approach the rise of the spiritual reform party, represented by such men as Agobard of Lyons and Benedict of Aniane, with genuine understanding and sympathy. And as for the political consequences of Charles's 'sacred empire', he sounds an ominous warning: for he sees in the foundation of the imperial bishoprics the origin of the conditions that made the Investiture Contest necessary: that Contest was caused by Gregory VII in protest against the 'sacred empire'. It has repeatedly been shown that Gregory VII did not accept the idea of a 'sacred empire' at all and that he was not merely concerned to change its head; he challenged the very foundations of the Carolingian as well as of the Byzantine tradition.

In conclusion, I feel that one further word of explanation is needed in presenting this translation to the English-speaking world. The present book has aroused a certain amount of criticism in German scholarly circles because it is customary for German historians not only to be concerned with the disinterested search for historical truth, but also to regard themselves as the guardians of the ' greatness ' of the historical past. The English scholar, working in a community whose national life has been less frustrated than that of Germany, is less jealous of guarding the elements of so-called greatness in the history of England ; but when reading this book he ought to remember that the author, writing initially for a German public, has, at times, been forced to adopt an apologetic tone when he has been most critical of Charles's achievements. To a reading public accustomed to the traditions of English scholarship, there is less need for the author's insistence that in spite of his obvious shortcomings, Charles ought to be considered great, than there is to a German public. For the English reader there would have been no need for the kind of argument that is to be found, e.g., at the end of Chapters I and III ; for to him the whole German debate as to whether the memory of the medieval *Reich* ought to be treasured or not is irrelevant to historical understanding.

The pages which follow contain a translation of the Introduction and of Chapters I–VI of *Das karolingische Imperium. Soziale und geistige Problematik eines Grossreiches*, Zürich, 1949. The book was revised by the author before the translation was made, and the present edition therefore represents an improved version of the original German text. The revision includes the omission of a number of pages and the complete re-writing of the last part of Chapter II. Chapter VI ends with the author's reflections upon the declining years of Charles. The notes, though copious, have been translated in full so far as they refer to the portions of the book that have been translated. I have, as far as possible, avoided the retention of German expressions and have often preferred to paraphrase them rather than leave them untranslated. I have, however, used a number of Latin expressions, lest a double translation should introduce misunderstanding. My aim was not only to provide an accurate translation but also one which is as readable in English as is possible. Translation can, of course, never be perfect; that is especially the case in a translation from the German, for German is a language which permits certain equivocations and imprecisions that are not permissible in English.

I would like to take this opportunity of thanking the author for the patience and kindness with which he has answered a large number of questions. But above all, I owe a very special debt of gratitude to my friend Professor F. L. W. Wood for the loving and painstaking care with which he has introduced innumerable improvements into the English version. Without his patient help I would not have been able to make the English text as readable as it is.

P.M.

Victoria University College,
Wellington,
New Zealand.

August, 1955.

Chapter I

INTRODUCTION

' The illustrious tribe of the Franks, established by God the Creator, brave in war, faithful in peace, wise in their counsels, of noble body, of immaculate purity, of choice physique, courageous, quick and impetuous, converted to the Catholic faith, free of heresy. . . . Such is the nation which, because they were courageous and strong, shook off the hard yoke of the Romans in battle.'[1]

These are the words which preface the tribal law of the Salian Franks. Who were these people who were so full of their own praise and who spoke of themselves in one breath with the old masters of the Roman empire? They were not a nation; not even in the sense in which the numerous tribes which had moved from the large, sandy basin of the northern plains into the ancient regions of Mediterranean culture, had been nations. They were not like the Marcomans, the Goths or the Scirians, to mention only a few. They were a mere collection of separate groups. The first of these groups comes to our notice in the times of the emperor Julian (361–363 A.D.) in northern Brabant. They were beaten by him and afterwards fought, together with others, sometimes for and sometimes against the Empire. The relatives of the Salian Franks, the Ripuarians, took part in the battle against the Huns on the Catalaunian fields, and settled down, as *ripuarii*, on the banks of the Rhine, where they conquered both Cologne and Trier.

One of the numerous chiefs and minor kings of the Salian Franks, Childerich, ruled in Tournai, close to the modern frontier between Belgium and France. His son Clovis was destined to become the most important contemporary of the Ostrogothic king, Theodoric. He was the first of the many Louis's whose

---

[1] *Lex Salica*, Prologue, i, 4; *Lex Salica* 100 *Titel-Text*, K. A. Eckhardt ed., in: *Germanenrechte*, Neue Folge, *Westgermanisches Recht*, Weimar, 1953, pp. 82 sq. and pp. 88 sq.

history has become the history of France. In those days there was
little left of the Roman yoke that could be shaken off. In the
north of Gaul there still was a provincial governor, but he had
no power left. He was completely surrounded by territory
occupied by Germanic tribes. Clovis eliminated the power of
that governor and then turned his attention to his new neighbours, the Burgundians, the Visigoths and the Alamans. Soon
this man of unscrupulous energy grew into the ruler of a kingdom
of considerable importance and found ways and means of
liquidating not only his rivals among the Salian and the Ripuarian
Franks but also the majority of his own relatives. The kingdom
of the Franks was founded long before there was such a thing as
a Frankish nation.

The process of fusion and unification was speeded up by the
great opportunities that lay ahead of the nobility of this new
monarchy. It was also made easier by the fact that large parts of
the Roman administrative system continued to exist. Very little
that was really new was created. All that happened was that the
masters of the local population of Gaul had changed. These
masters did not cold-shoulder the ' Romans ', as their opposite
numbers in other Germanic kingdoms had done, and mixed
marriages gave them the necessary influx of strength which had
been lacking in the other kingdoms. The only condition was
that the barrier erected by religion between pagans and Christians
should be broken down.

The baptism of Clovis was an historical act which supplemented and perfected all his previous achievements. Legend
was to adorn it later in a fanciful manner. But for Clovis it was
a shrewd political move and little more. Genuine emotion was
of little consequence to this cold calculating politician. For this
very reason he did not embrace that form of Christianity which,
because of the simple intelligibility of its tenets, had appealed so
strongly to other Germanic rulers. In contrast to the other
Germanic kings, Clovis became a Catholic, not an Arian, and
thus the master, not the opponent, of the Catholic Roman
population of Gaul and of their bishops.

From that day forward the words ' free of heresy ' were
freely used to describe the Franks and their rulers. This epithet

was bound to increase the pride of the people who had overnight been transformed from anonymous *foederati* of the Romans and from mere frontier guards into masters of a kingdom of their own. They ascribed the incredible turn their destiny had taken not only to Clovis but above all to the new God who had brought victory to their arms. ' Long live Christ, who loves the Franks ; may he protect the army! '[1] As Catholics they were distinguished from the Germanic tribes who adhered to Arianism by their belief in the full divinity of Christ. It followed that they were the specially chosen race of that God, Christ, and thus in the way customary to the age, their consciousness of their destiny and their pride in being Franks was given a religious foundation. It was in much the same way that the other two heirs of the Roman Empire, the Arabs and the Byzantines, derived from the fact of their orthodoxy both their belief in the special protection of God, and their conviction that they were politically responsible for the whole world.

Such opinions, held by members of the Frankish nobility, became a powerful factor in the further expansion of the kingdom. At a later date, Frankish scholars endeavoured to provide a historical justification for the sense of power and destiny of their people. This historical justification proved an important factor in counteracting the ever-present feeling that the ancient Romans had been far superior to the Franks. First of all, they charged the Romans with the persecution of Christianity, while the Franks had honoured the martyrs and had fought against Germanic paganism and Germanic heresy. But this was not enough. The scholars also wished to find something in the Frankish past to compare with the thousand years of Roman history. For this purpose they invented a myth, much as the Romans themselves, under the influence of Greek civilization, had done before them. They admitted that Aeneas, the legendary ancestor of the Romans, had been a relative of the Trojan king, Priam ; but they themselves, the whole of the Frankish people (so their chronicler Fredegar relates) descended from the Trojans and their kings.[2]

[1] Ibid., pp. 88 sq. The quotation is compressed.
[2] *Chron.* ii, 4 ; iii, 2. MGH, *Mer.*, ii, 45 sq. 93. For the following remarks see E. Zöllner, *Die politische Stellung der Völker im Frankenreich*, Wien, 1950. I am greatly indebted to Dr. Zöllner for many references given to me in conversation.

The time was not yet ripe to derive from their new faith in their own destiny a claim for the entire political inheritance of the old Empire. Clovis was still flattered when an east Roman emperor nominated him consul. He inscribed the Emperor's name on his coins, and his descendants, on the whole, willingly recognized the Empire. In return they rose higher and higher in the scale of honorary titles and dignities which the eastern Empire conferred. Two of the Merovingian kings were even chosen as ' adopted sons ' by Byzantine rulers. The Franks, after all, were needed as a pawn in the game which Byzantium was playing against other barbarian tribes. On the other hand, the Roman intelligentsia inside the Frankish kingdom was bound to serve the ' barbarian ' rulers more willingly, once the relationship of those rulers to the successors of the ancient Emperors had become one of friendly subordination.

Only a relatively small area in the north of the region dominated by the Merovingians had actually been occupied in a thorough-going manner by Frankish settlers. Further south there were the regions of mixed races in which people of Germanic extraction lived side by side with people steeped in Roman culture. These Germanic people were Franks, but further south still they belonged to the Goths, Burgundians and other subjugated tribes. Finally there were large stretches of land in which the Roman character of the ancient, non-Germanic provincial population had remained undiluted. This was the case south of the Loire, in Aquitaine, especially in Auvergne ; but it applied also in the alpine lands of Raetia and elsewhere. Side by side with the urban population, which continued to engage in commerce and manufacture, there were the peasants who paid rent, and the *coloni*. Finally, there were the *villae* owned by aristocratic landlords which contained hundreds of slaves. Members of the privileged families still, and for long hereafter, continued to use the title of senator ; and so far as the ' Senatorial ' class was concerned, there had been little change beyond the fact that there was no longer a senate and that journeys to the court of the king had replaced journeys to Rome. The owners of large estates and the tax-farmers continued to collect the moneys to which they were entitled by Roman law. At times they collected even more. The rich continued to live in luxury and the poor continued to be exploited. The latter looked with secret hope upon the new rulers. ' Where,' they asked, ' except among the Romans, are there to be found such evil conditions? Where is there so much injustice as there is among us? These vices are unknown among the Franks.'[1]

It is true that the Franks, at the time of their settlement in Gaul, did not think of the state as an abstract organism. They could not conceive the notion that the state had paid servants who collected the taxes. Among the Franks all public functions had originally been carried out by the king, the nobility and the assembled army, all of which were held together by the bond of personal fealty. But now the public domains passed to the conqueror, the king of the Franks. The administration of the provinces continued as before and the large sums which were collected as taxes and which had previously been handed over to the governor and the emperor, were paid to him. In addition, the loot of war and the confiscated property of political opponents, a veritable flood of gold, passed into the coffers of the Merovingian king whose power thus rose to unprecedented heights. To the Franks he was the master of the conquered land in which they had come to live. To the Romans, he took the place of the absolute monarch. No order but the king's was valid. The right of the assembled army to take part in the framing of policies and the influence of the magnates over public business was quickly extinguished. Similarly the old Germanic custom of electing the king disappeared. To coming generations it might well seem that the old Germanic institutions had been replaced by Roman forms of government and administration. At any rate, it had become quite clear that the old Germanic practices were hardly capable in the long run of coping with the problems of government in such a large and highly developed country as Gaul.

Members of the senatorial families became faithful followers of the Merovingian ruler. The majority of bishops were appointed from among their ranks. The people of Roman culture were granted equality before the law with the Franks, and soon after

---

[1] Salvian of Marseille, *De gubernatione Dei*, v, 36. MGH, *Auct.*, i, 62.

Clovis's death they also were expected to render military service. The *comes*, originally a Roman military commander, became the successor of the Roman governor. As such he was entrusted in each province with the highest civil authority and became the standard type of higher functionary. The Roman customs system, the tolls, the coinage, and the chancelleries of the higher organs of government, together with their *referendarii*, were all put at the disposal of the king. All these things had been unknown to the Germans.

The institutions themselves, of course, underwent a change. Members of the old senatorial families may have entered the royal service, but a large part of the public administration remained, nevertheless, reserved to the Frankish minority. At the same time, the sober, abstract character of the Roman bureaucracy was replaced more and more by a personal and emotionally conditioned conception of service. The practice of writing down all proceedings disappeared and the *comes* became more and more the count. His office was fused with that of the royal judge and of the commander of the army in the Germanic *pagus*.

Thus the centre of gravity in Clovis's kingdom was slowly shifted and the shift was emphasized by geographical factors. The real core of Frankish settlement was in the farthest north. But in Roman times it had been the south, with its flourishing towns, that had played the most important part. After the Frankish conquest the coast of Mediterranean Gaul was beyond the reach of Clovis's power. The western half of that coast formed the Visigothic province of Septimania and was destined to remain outside the Frankish kingdom proper. Cities like Arles, Narbonne and Marseilles and even the Burgundian towns of Lyons and Vienne, yielded pride of place to Paris, which Clovis had chosen to be his residence. The old merchant families continued to live in the metropolitan cities of the south. Since time out of mind they had controlled the overseas trade between Gaul and Italy, Egypt and Syria. These families consisted of Syrians, Romans, Jews and Greeks. By their origin and by their activities they were the people who maintained the contacts among the imperial lands along the shores of the Mediterranean. The Frankish conquest, however, gravely weakened their position, for there is no doubt that as the exponents of Roman civilization were being pushed into the background by Frankish magnates, the import of luxury goods must have receded. Although these magnates soon learnt to appreciate Roman comfort and although much was spent on ornaments for churches, on reliquaries and clerical garments, overseas trade suffered from the ' barbarization ' of daily customs.[1] This decline of trade must have begun long before the Mediterranean had come to be dominated by Arab fleets.

In the north the king had rewarded his Frankish followers with the estates or *villae* of Roman noblemen. The ordinary Frankish people, too, had exchanged their military occupations for the cultivation of the soil. The Franks had never known such an institution as a closed aristocratic caste. But as people began to feel the increasing importance of large estate-owners as against small peasant proprietors, social differentiation was bound to be accentuated. Moreover, this differentiation was not confined to the economic sphere. The same process began among the Franks as Salvian of Marseilles had already observed among the Romanized population of Gaul : the weaker men ' commend themselves to the magnates so that they may be protected by them. They become the clients (*dediticii*) of the wealthy and place themselves, so to speak, under their jurisdiction and orders '.[2] Formally, the Franks who did this preserved their personal status at law ; they had to remain freemen if they wanted to continue to belong to the nation of freemen (*franci*). But economically, socially, and legally a new situation had been created. Every man who had surrendered to a lord became, in fact, dependent in so far as he was subject to the lord's coercion and the lord's right to exact service from him.[3] The distinction between wealthy and poor, between powerful men and small men in a dependent position, so characteristic of provincial Roman society, invaded the very nation which had been so proud of its aristocratic egalitarianism.

Clovis's successors not only continued his well-night absolute

---

[1] See also H. Pirenne, *Mahomet et Charlemagne*, Paris-Bruxelles, 1937, p. 99.
[2] Salvian, op. cit , v, 38, p. 62.
[3] H. Mitteis, *Leh recht und Staatsgewalt*, Weimar, 1933, p. 30.

government but also divided the kingdom, according to Salian law, as they were wont to divide family property. (Unity was no longer represented by an all-pervading idea of an abstract state but by the fact that the rulers of the several sub-kingdoms were related to each other.) In the old days the Germanic clan and the Germanic family, under the strict leadership of its head, had represented a closed community with a strong will. Clan and family continued to be looked upon as a unit. But the old family discipline of the Merovingians, as well as of other families, was no longer preserved. According to the calculations of one historian, there were twenty-nine feuds between members of the royal family during the single century after Clovis's death.[1] Again and again murders were committed in the closest family circles, and large stretches of land were devastated by armies consisting of vassals of the men concerned. Nevertheless, at least in the beginning, a common line of foreign policy continued to be pursued. Expansion was continued until the majority of the Germanic tribes dwelling in central Europe were united under the dominion of the Merovingian house.

The Alamans, Bavarians, Thuringians, Frisians and Saxons who thus came to be partially or wholly, temporarily or permanently, subject to the Frankish kingdom, created conditions favourable to yet a further removal of the centre of gravity of Frankish dominion. A stable centre, of course, could not be found while the members of the ruling family continued their feuds. But by the side of Neustria, the core of Clovis's power with Paris in its centre, there emerged Austrasia, the home of the Ripuarian Franks. It included the lands along the Moselle, and Alemannia and Hesse, and its ' capital ' was Metz. This city was situated inside the borders of the old Roman empire, but it was even further removed from all Mediterranean contacts than Paris had been. Neustria became more and more Romanized. But Austrasia, in spite of its fairly considerable non-Germanic population, remained a ' barbarous ' country. The most important ruler of this country was Theudebert, a grandson of Clovis. His rule extended even over Bavaria and the lower Rhineland, and it seemed in his day that it might even be possible to establish

[1] F. Dahn, *Die Könige der Germanen*, Leipzig, 1896, vii. 1, p. 66 n. 2.

a continental empire that would revive all the claims of the ancient Mediterranean *imperium*. Theudebert himself wrote to the Byzantine emperor that his rule extended, after the subjection of numerous tribes, from the frontiers of Pannonia to the northern seas. He assumed the imperial title of Augustus and replaced, on the Austrasian gold coins, the name and the portrait of the emperor by his own. He also followed the custom of the emperors in collecting taxes from all the citizens of the empire, that is, from his Frankish fellow-tribesmen as well as from his Roman subjects.

Thus we see a Merovingian king consciously removing the last traces that reminded people of Roman dominion. But these traces were now little more than historical memories, and in obliterating them Theudebert was merely following a development that was conditioned by the times. How distant, after all, was the *pax Romana* in those days of turmoil! Overseas trade was perilous, and scarcely a place was left in which the ancient heritage of learning could be peacefully cultivated. Compared with the general decay of education, especially among the secular nobility, it signified little that one of the Merovingian kings tried his hand at grammar and poetry or that in Toulouse and elsewhere there still existed something like an 'academy' of learned *literati*.[1] Hand in hand with the autonomy of the provinces there grew up a new provincialism in the style of living. The gold which could no longer circulate freely throughout an empire, disappeared into private coffers. Real estate with peasants, houses and live-stock became the most important property.

The counts, originally appointed as the representatives of the king in each province, were drawn more and more into the orbit and interests of the landed magnates of their provinces. The less effective the king's authority became, the more necessary it was for the counts to build up their personal resources and authority in the form of landed property and of manorial influence. In other words, a royal appointment was ineffective unless it was backed by the appointee's own power. The appointee had to be the most powerful man and the wealthiest landowner in the

[1] M. Manitius, *Geschichte der lateinischen Literatur des Mittelalters*, München, 1911, i, pp. 122 sq.

district. It became necessary to choose the count from among the nobility of the province in which he was to exercise his authority. (This mean that he had to be chosen from among the ranks of the very people against whose interests he was often supposed to direct his activities. In this way the king's central administration lost its influence in the provinces.)Its losses were the gains of the magnates. As early as 614 king Chlothar had been obliged to give legal sanction to the prevailing practice. He promised that henceforward the counts would be chosen only from among the ranks of the landed magnates of every province.

Thus the royal authority, once so powerful, was more and more dissipated. It was usurped partly by the magnates, partly by the half-conquered tribes of Austrasia, partly by the Romanized south. The Romanized elements also increased relatively in numbers and recovered a considerable part of the influence over culture and language which they had lost in northern Neustria. The king was no longer the sole source of authority; each province had its own circle of powerful magnates. And some of these magnates endeavoured to dominate the king himself in the royal palace in order to gain ascendancy over their rivals.

Nobody was more likely to succeed in such an attempt than the nobleman who was in charge of the administration of the royal household and of the armed levy in one of the sub-kingdoms. The greater the weakness and incompetence of the dynasty, the more he tended to become the true ruler. In his phase of Frankish history the struggle among the rulers of the sub-kingdoms became more and more a struggle of the 'mayors of the palace' for power throughout the Frankish realm. During one of many such conflicts between Neustria and Austrasia, the Austrasian *maior domus* gained a victory near Tertry in Picardy (687). This was the first great triumph in the history of a family which was destined to rise from the ranks of the provincial aristocracy not only to lordship over the Frankish kingdom but also to rule over Europe. The family was rich in landed property, especially in the country between the Rhine, the Moselle, and the Meuse. Their ancestor, Arnulf, had risen to be bishop of Metz. His property had probably lain in the same diocese. Toward the end

of the sixth century, when he was a young man, Arnulf had been
sent to the Austrasian palace and, seizing his opportunity, had
risen in the service of the king. He was put in charge of six
provinces which had, as a rule, been administered separately.
According to a later source he ruled over these provinces at will
and became the most powerful man at the king's court.[1]

The episcopal dignity did not prevent Arnulf from continuing
his political activities. These were the wildest times of Merovingian history. The weak government of boys on the royal
throne had been replaced by the incredible hardness and determination of a woman, Brunhild, the daughter of a Visigothic
ruler. At this juncture the aristocracy considered the time ripe
for an open rebellion against the central government in Austrasia
which was connected with that of Burgundy. Under the leadership of Arnulf a coalition was formed between the ruler of
Neustria and the Burgundian and Austrasian nobility. Brunchild
was not in a position to resist such a coalition. The woman who
for thirty-eight years had fought for the greatness of the Merovingian house was finally, by royal order, dragged to death by
wild horses. In spite of this, Chlothar II, though nominal ruler
of the entire kingdom, remained little more than a faithful
servant of his powerful followers. Especially in Austrasia the
Neustrian king's power was very limited, and actual power was
wielded by Arnulf and his kinsman, Pepin ' of Landen '. Pepin's
daughter was married to Arnulf's son.

Pepin's son Grimoald, *maior domus* in Austrasia, tried to make
capital out of a manœuvre of his Neustrian colleague. He planned
to remove king Dagobert II and to acquire, in a semi-legal manner,
supreme power for his own family. But Grimoald had underestimated the resistance in Neustria. He paid for his attempt
with his life. His nephew, Pepin ' of Heristal ', was obliged to
begin almost afresh. It was only with great difficulty that he
managed to maintain himself in Austrasia against his Neustrian
competitor Ebroin, for Ebroin had restored order among the
nobility of Neustria with harsh violence and had replaced the
customary anarchy by a centralized authority. But when Ebroin
fell a victim to a reactionary plot and was murdered, Pepin was

[1] BM, i, 1b.

able to enter into his rival's heritage. From the time of the battle of Tertry, in which he captured the Neustrian king, Pepin, with the consent of the nobility, ruled over all three parts of the kingdom.

If the time had been ripe for drawing the Germanic tribes of the east into the orbit of the kingdom, Pepin, the first Carolingian ruler of the whole Frankish kingdom, might have established its greatness and anticipated the achievements of Charles the Great. But the Merovingians had neglected those regions and had failed to spread among them the Franco-Roman conceptions of life and government. In the meantime, owing to the continuous civil wars, their own standards of civilisation had sunk lower and lower. The Frankish church was in a similar state ; its representatives, to judge from their attitude and their beliefs, were more like pagans than like Christians. The result was that when, in the reign of Pepin, the idea of a mission to the Germanic tribes of the east was finally put into execution, it was necessary to call upon Anglo-Saxon missionaries to plan and continue the work that had been begun many years earlier by occasional travelling Irishmen or Franks.

In spite of their work, Pepin's son Charles, later surnamed ' the Hammer' (Martel), found that the newly-converted Frisians were quick to seize the first signs of weakness in the kingdom in order to turn against the Franks. One such weakness arose from Charles's illegitimacy, for Pepin's marriage to Charles's mother had been canonically invalid. Charles therefore had considerable difficulty in maintaining himself against his father's legitimate wife and her grandsons. The Neustrians, also, rose against his government, and it was only in 720 that he was able to restore the original situation. Soon afterwards he again subjugated the Bavarians and Alamans. It was indeed high time to meet, by the concentration of all the forces of the Frankish kingdom, a danger that had become more and more threatening ever since the entry of the Arabs into Spain (711). Aquitaine, long since independent, could not by itself resist the thrust of Arabian cavalry or prevent their advance across the Pyranees into the interior of Gaul. Troops had to be levied several times, even from Austrasia, before the invasion could be halted. In the history of Frankish resistance, the battle of Poitiers (732) was an important landmark. But it would be an over-simplification to believe that this victory alone made Charles the saviour of the Frankish kingdom and of western civilization. In the very year after the battle the old Roman towns of Arles and Avignon fell into the hands of the Saracens. Several cities in Provence were destroyed, and Charles had to fight another battle under the walls of Narbonne before he was master of the situation.

The Mediterranean coast with its ancient centres of culture and commerce had thus become the battlefield between Christianity and Islam, and its importance was reduced more than ever. Indeed, the continental power of the Franks could never hope to wrest control of the Mediterranean from the Arab fleets. Both Provence and Septimania remained defenceless against further raids. The slowly operating Frankish defences often began to function only after the successful completion of a raid. A measure of safety was established only during the heyday of Carolingian rule from the middle of the eighth to the beginning of the ninth centuries. During the subsequent age of decline the old troubles were to recur with even greater vehemence.

Since the Mediterreanean remained closed to Frankish expansion and since the regions on the other side of the Rhine were likely to pose problems rather than yield profits, it was no easy matter for Charles Martel to keep his magnates contented and to reward them for their services according to their expectations. The reserves of the Merovingian monarchy which had been built up during the early years of conquest, had long since been squandered during the civil wars among the followers of the many sub-kings. Moreover, the Frankish nobility had by no means forgotten that Charles himself was one of themselves, and that he lacked the aura of semi-mythical splendour and the thaumaturgic power which rendered the descendants of the Germanic kings, no matter how degenerate, worthy objects of worship. As mayor of the palace, Charles Martel was therefore obliged to reward his faithful followers for their services by using the landed wealth of the Frankish church.

He could do so all the more easily as he had already undermined the independent position of the Frankish bishops through the appointment of ecclesiastics devoted to his interests to the most important sees. He had not allowed canonical regulations to worry him. His nephew Hugh, for instance, administered simultaneously one archbishopric, two bishoprics and two large abbeys. And when Milo, one of Charles's faithful followers, had distinguished himself in warfare at his master's side he obtained the archbishopric of Rheims in addition to that of Trier. It was a far cry from these ecclesiastical princes who remained, in their conduct and in their aims, secular magnates, to the ideal of the spiritual pastor which Gregory the Great had depicted in his *Regula Pastoralis*.

The transfer of church property to laymen, although carried out on the orders of the Merovingian puppet ruler (*verbo regis*), was in reality effected by his *maior domus* in the interest of the power of the state. It made Charles Martel's great task less difficult. At the same time, members of the laity possessed themselves on their own initiative of ecclesiastical property and destroyed the bishop's authority over both the clergy and the property of the parish churches that were situated on their estates. The large domains swallowed churches and monasteries with their clergy as they had swallowed serfs and small farms. All this was well in accord with Germanic conceptions. No synod met to remind people of the rules of Roman canon law. The metropolitan had ceased issuing orders to his bishops, and for decades it became impossible to summon ecclesiastical assemblies. There were bishoprics without bishops, monasteries without abbots—or if there were bishops and abbots, they were laymen. It was an age in which ecclesiastical authority in the Frankish church had sunk to its lowest depth. The moral and spiritual decay was equally great.

The Papacy was in no position to interfere. True, when the Roman empire in the west had begun to dissolve, the Roman provincial population had endeavoured more than ever to preserve their connection with the spiritual head in Rome in order to emphasize that they were neither Arians nor pagans. This endeavour grew in strength as the rise of the tribal kingdoms dissolved the political unity of the Empire, for the new kingdoms had an obvious and disconcerting tendency to organize the clergy on a territorial basis and to make them part and parcel of the king's secular administration. As late as the early seventh century Gregory the Great had actually been the primate over the whole church in the western Mediterranean. Even though this primacy was more a matter of moral authority than of actual administrative power, it was unlikely to survive the growing ' barbarization ' and atomization of the old western Empire for long. Gregory understood this fact well. It was his great achievement, pregnant with significance for the future, that he provided new supports for the church.

Gregory was the first of the popes to realize that his main task was not the preservation of the gradually decaying Romanism of the provinces, but the capture for the catholic faith of pagan and Arian tribes. This matter was forced upon his attention by the Lombards who had established their power over a large part of Italy under the very gates of Rome. The Lombards, however, once they had been converted to Catholicism, simply established, like the Visigoths and the Franks, another new, closed territorial church under the control of their king. Accordingly Gregory's mission to the Anglo-Saxons was of more far-reaching significance; for England was to become the country in which the revival of a universal European church, under the control and direction of Rome, was prepared.

In England, in Gregory's time and for many years after, there was no unified power which sought to turn the bishops into royal functionaries. The Irish monks, moreover, had done valuable work for the moral and spiritual education of the clergy. These facts explain the rapid rise of Catholicism among the Anglo-Saxons. True, the transfer of the scholarly and theological culture of the Roman Empire to the tribal life of the Anglo-Saxons was only partially successful. Nevertheless, the Anglo-Saxon clergy absorbed this culture more deeply than the majority of the German clergy on the continent. When the rulers of the Frankish kingdom, in later years, were looking for men who would be able to lay the foundations of Christianity among the Germanic tribes on the far side of the Rhine and thus link them with the Frankish kingdom, they were to find such missionaries not among their own clergy but in the British Isles.

Charles Martel, for instance, transplanted the Anglo-Saxon Pirmin to Reichenau in Swabia. He also promoted the Anglo-Saxon mission among the Frisians, to whom Pepin had already introduced the Angle Willibrord as missionary. All these foreigners stood in need of Frankish protection. But they had little truck with the Frankish church. When Wynfrith, the most important of the Anglo-Saxon missionaries, arrived on the continent, his first visit was neither to the bishops of the Rhineland, nor to Charles Martel, but to Rome. (He began his work for the conversion to Christianity of central Germany by papal authority and under his new Roman name of Boniface.)

Even where Boniface found undisciplined remnants of Christianity left behind by earlier attempts at conversion, he had to begin anew. Conversion was followed by ecclesiastical organization. Boniface proceeded strictly according to the prescriptions of canon law. As archbishop and papal vicar he himself became the head of the new church organization, although he lacked a fixed metropolitan see. Even Bavaria, where conditions had always been better than in central Germany, came under his headship. In Bavaria there were ancient bishoprics which formed a territorial church similar to that of the Franks. But the direct connections with Rome had never been lost sight of, for the Bavarian dukes had been obliged to seek friends south of the Alps in order to counterbalance the power of the Franks who had tried again and again to absorb their country.

Charles Martel had allowed Boniface to proceed almost as if the matter was of no concern to him. After Charles's death in 741, when the kingdom was divided between his sons Pepin and Carloman, the situation changed. Carloman, who had received the office of mayor of the palace and the inheritance of the eastern half of the kingdom, immediately began to interest himself in the activities of the new archbishop. He summoned Boniface and communicated to him a plan for a reform of the whole Frankish church. Soon afterwards the bishops of the newly founded dioceses (mainly Anglo-Saxons), together with Boniface, met in a synod in which the question of ecclesiastical discipline was discussed. Carloman undertook to enforce the decrees of the synod and incorporated them as capitularies into the laws of the kingdom. A moment of great significance had been reached. Boniface had to suffer the secular ruler to take the initiative in ecclesiastical matters to a degree unprecedented even during the height of Merovingian power. This was the price he had to pay for the advancement of reform and its application to the old Frankish territory.[1]

Thus the alliance, which was to be of such great consequence, between the Frankish state and the bishops of the eastern missionary districts, was forged. The bishops obtained everything they required for their work. They were given rich lands and financial resources, military power and a promise of armed support from the kingdom, no longer with the object of peaceful mission but for violent conversion. They became great lords and weighty supporters of the state. For centuries to come they were more devoted to the kings and emperors than to their spiritual head in Rome. They had little connection with the masses of the people whom they ruled rather than served. The splendour of the empire of the Saxons and of the Salians is inseparable from these imperial prelates; but in the end, their successors were to create the conditions that led to the investiture controversy and to the consequent weakening of central Europe.

Pepin, too, carried out reforms in Neustria, but, like his brother, only to the extent to which they were of advantage to Carolingian rule. Ecclesiastical property was rarely restored to its rightful owners, and the metropolitan organization, though agreed upon, was never established. The voice of the State remained decisive in the filling of episcopal sees. There was nothing Boniface could do to arrest this trend, and during his last years he devoted most of his attention to the establishment, in Fulda, of a model monastery, governed according to the rules of St. Benedict, which was to be independent of the Frankish territorial church and directly connected with Rome. But the idea of forming an *élite* of monks to serve as models for the conduct of the other classes, was only really taken up again

---

[1] H. v. Schubert, *Geschichte der christlichen Kirche im Frühmittelalter*, Tübingen, 1921, pp. 306 sq. Th. Schieffer has recently denied that it is possible to speak of a conflict between the Frankish territorial church and papal claims represented by Boniface. (*Abhandlung der geistes- und sozialwissenschaftlichen Klasse der Mainzer Akademie der Wissenschaften*, 1950, No. 20, pp. 1431 sqq.)

C

two generations later. Then it was revived not in Germany but
by the great Aquitanian reform movement of Aniane.

In 747 Carloman resigned the throne and withdrew to an
Italian monastery. Thus Pepin became sole ruler. So far the
Carolingians had never dared to remove the Merovingian
puppet kings, lest they be held to have usurped the crown of the
Franks. Perhaps it was Boniface who first suggested a solution
of the problem. It was agreed that a papal judgment was to
decide the fate ' of the kings who were living in the kingdom of
the Franks without exercising royal authority '. Pope Zacharias
decreed ' that it was best that those be named kings who exercised
the highest authority '.[1] Thereupon the last of the Merovingians
disappeared into a monastery, and in November 751 the magnates
of the kingdom elected Pepin king. Tradition has it that he was
anointed by Boniface. The anointing of kings was an Anglo-
Saxon custom and had hitherto been unknown among the Franks.
The anointing was supposed to indicate that the king's connection
with the supernatural and the divine, a connection deeply rooted
in pagan conceptions and popularly attributed to the Germanic
kingship of the Merovingians, was not extinguished. The unction
demonstrated that God's grace was with the ruler who had been
appointed by the pope.

Pope Zacharias, through his intervention, had obliged the
new king of the Franks. Two years later this fact was remembered by his successor, Stephen II, when he was threatened by
the king of the Lombards. He travelled across the Alps and met
Pepin in the royal palace of Ponthion on the Marne. The ensuing
discussions established the alliance between the two great powers
of the west and were to have a lasting influence upon the course
of history. The king, under oath, promised Stephen to assist
him especially in the vindication of the rightful claims of the
apostolic see in Rome and in central Italy. As a result the pope,
from then on, addressed Pepin as *patricius Romanorum*, thus
granting him that east-Roman title which the imperial Exarch of
Ravenna, as the representative of the Byzantine emperors, was

---

[1] *Annales Regni Francorum (Einhardi)*, MGH, *Ger.*, **vi**, p. 9. Schieffer, op. cit.,
p. 1455 is of the opinion that Boniface had no part in the deposition of the Merovingian king.

wont to bear. He thus broke with Byzantium, as he had broken with the Lombards. The pope supplemented the political alliance by a ceremonial unction of Pepin and his sons which almost amounted to a spiritual adoption. In Kiersy, near Laon, the king and his magnates agreed to make war on the Lombards and issued a document to Stephen II which probably contained a more exact definition of the territories and of the rights which were to be granted to the papacy after the defeat of the enemy.

Pepin beat the Lombards in two campaigns and secured to the Papacy the dominion over Rome and over the Byzantine provinces of central Italy. A Byzantine protest remained as ineffective as a later attempt to induce the Franks to change sides by fomenting a marriage alliance between Pepin's daughter and an imperial prince. It became increasingly clear that the east was prevented by internal troubles and the theological controversy about the worship of images from seriously defending its ancient claims. Byzantine chroniclers preserved a frosty silence about the Franks. Since Byzantium was not capable of dominating the west, they ignored its rulers.

The closer relations between Pepin and the pope did not result in closer relations between the Frankish church and Rome. The Frankish ruler, now that he had become a king, was even less inclined than he had been before to surrender his authority over the Frankish church. If he reformed the church, he reformed it according to his own lights. When an ecclesiastical assembly stated ' we have decreed . . .', it could well happen that the following sentence read : ' But the lord king says that his will is . . .',[1] and that the ecclesiastical decree was thus annulled. All the same, the ecclesiastical discipline of both the regular and the secular clergy was improved and synods met regularly to discuss complaints. In this way, no doubt, only the grossest abuses were removed. But the result was that soon the activities of the spiritual administrators were comparable to those of the secular officials. Both groups worked under the king's supervision and were responsible to him.

The regulation of ecclesiastical affairs was not the king's only worry. He also had to see to it that the recalcitrant dukes

[1] MGH, *Cap.*, i, p. 34, c. 6 ; Cp. Schubert, op. cit., p. 322.

on the outskirts of the kingdom were kept in firmer control than they had been accustomed to. In particular Aquitaine had to be reconquered. Eight campaigns in eight years, and also the murder of the duke of Aquitaine, were necessary before Pepin gained firm possession of that country. In the end, however, he managed to hold it, together with Septimania, the old Visigothic possession on the Mediterranean coast of Gaul. During one of the eight campaigns, Tassilo, the duke of the Bavarians, had deserted the army in which he was bound to serve as a vassal of the Frankish king. Pepin did not punish him. It was left to his son Charles, twenty years' later, to remember this crime and use it as a pretext for the destruction of the Bavarian duchy.

On his death in 768, Pepin left the kingdom to his two sons. The kingdom was divided as it had been so often before. But this time the dying ruler did not effect the division by separating Neustria from Austrasia. Carloman was given a closed block of territory which stretched from Septimania to the Rhine and to Alemannia. Charles received only a narrow strip of land stretching along the coast of the Atlantic Ocean from the south of Gaul to the estuary of the Rhine. It broadened only in the east of Austrasia so as to include Thuringia. According to this division the palaces and domains which had belonged to the Merovingians, as well as a large part of the old Carolingian family property, went to Carloman, in spite of the fact that he was the younger of the two brothers.[1] It was not surprising, therefore, that Charles felt ill-will towards his brother. And this ill-will found new justification when Carloman refused to assist his brother in the subjection of a new rising in Aquitaine. Carloman himself continued this father's traditional policy in Italy. But Charles soon tried to encircle his brother's possessions through his marriage to the daughter of the Lombard king Desiderius. Charles also came to terms with the duke of Bavaria. This coalition seemed to be the preparation for a violent conflict between the two brothers. But on the eve of the war which everyone regarded as inevitable, Carloman died. Charles the Great soon became the ruler of the whole kingdom. His brother's sons sought shelter with the king of the Lombards.

[1] H. Zatschek, *Wie das erste Reich der Deutschen entstand*, Prague, 1940, pp. 46 sq.

No sooner was Charles in possession of the sole power than he, in turn, continued his father's foreign policy. He vanquished Desiderius after having renounced earlier both marriage and alliance. At Easter 774 the ruler of the Franks entered Rome and was festively received by Pope Hadrian I. Charles renewed Pepin's promises and expressed them this time in a more precise formula: he assumed the duty to protect the Papacy.[1] When Charles was crowned king of the Lombards in Pavia, all danger to the Papacy was removed. The young ruler, however, made quite sure that he, not Hadrian, would inherit the possessions of the Lombards. Later on he succeeded also in reducing the Lombard duchy of Benevento in southern Italy to a state of dependence, as earlier it had been dependent on the kings of the Lombards.

With the expansion of the Frankish kingdom its resources grew, and also the conviction that the subjection of all tribes living on its frontiers was both necessary and justified, especially as they were pagans. Foremost in the latter category were the Saxons, whom both the Merovingians and Charles's own ancestors had vainly tried to incorporate into their dominion. During the war in Lombardy, Saxon raiders had entered Hesse with impunity and had devastated both Frankish settlements and churches. After the conclusion of the Lombard war Charles concentrated the whole strength of his kingdom against the Saxons. He also tried to make capital out of the social tensions in Saxony, by supporting some elements of the Saxon nobility against the lower orders. But every time he thought the country had been subdued, the Saxons rose again as soon as the royal armies had marched away, and sought a bloody revenge. The war, cruelly conducted from the first, developed, in the end, into fantastic excesses of atrocity.

When Charles committed acts of cruelty which were hardly compatible with the honour of a Christian ruler, the scholars in his palace justified their royal master by insisting that the Saxons were not honest enemies but had faithlessly violated pacts they had sworn to observe, and denied the Christian faith to which they had been converted. Among such acts the notorious

[1] P. E. Schramm, in: ZSSRk, 1938, xxvii, p. 206.

blood-bath of Verden on the Aller must be included, although it is possible that the number of victims has been overstated. There was also a mass deportation of Saxons into Frankish territory, and the sons of recalcitrant nobles were forced to attend monastic schools in the kingdom. None of the dignitaries of the Frankish church raised a protest against such methods. Instead, they happily accepted the idea that missionary activity could be promoted by violence rather than by spiritual means. Later, under the Saxon dynasty, bishops were to pursue the same easy path when they tried to Christianize the Slavs. For the time being the methods seemed to be justified by their success. Their dangers were not revealed for centuries.

In 787, two years after the baptism of Widukind, the most important leader of the Saxon risings, Charles marched into Bavaria. Tassilo was forced to make his submission. Soon afterwards, at a general assembly, he was charged with high treason and desertion and was imprisoned in a monastery. The duchy of Bavaria was dissolved and the country was put in charge of Frankish officials. Now the Frankish kingdom stretched as far as the Elbe, the Bohemian forest and the Enns. But Charles was still not satisfied. He wanted to conquer the empire of the Avars, the nucleus of which was situated in the great plains between the Danube and the Theiss. Although it had long since declined from its former greatness, it was still possessed of the fabulous treasures which it had amassed, in the course of centuries, through raids and from tributes paid by east European princes, including even the Byzantine emperor.

The great campaign against the Avars, well planned and initiated by the king himself, was delayed at first by Saxon risings and later by a conspiracy of Frankish magnates. In the end the mere pressure exercised by these preparations was sufficient to heighten the tension in the state of the Avars to the point where its organization collapsed. Charles the Great was therefore able to leave the actual campaign to his son Pepin and to his counts. Thus the whole region of the Danubian plains came under Frankish dominion. Those of the Avars who had neither been killed nor fled into the Balkans, were nominally converted to Christianity and were soon absorbed into the Slav tribes, which hitherto had been under their subjection. The country between Danube and Theiss became the 'Avar desert', and was no more than waste frontier land. Bavarian settlers under the leadership of the archbishops of Salzburg and Aquileia moved eastwards, but were unable to fill the vast, newly-conquered territories.

As a result of these developments, Charles the Great ceased to be merely a Frankish ruler and became the master of the West. Apart from the Arabs in Spain, there was nobody to resist him. He had tried to interfere in Spain also, but after an unsuccessful campaign he had been content to establish a narrow march south of the Pyrenees, sufficient to prevent surprise attacks across the mountain-passes or along the coast. With this measure he had formally fulfilled his obligations towards the Christians of Spain, who did not always prefer Frankish rule to that of the Moors. By making war on Saxons, Avars and Saracens, three mighty pagan nations, the Frankish ruler proved to his contemporaries that he was willing to play his part as the protector of Christendom not only in Italy but everywhere. Would Charles be prepared to content himself with the titles of king and *patricius* when Frankish arms had laid the foundations to far higher claims?

Charles's power and his aims pointed towards a new conception, or rather towards the revival of an ancient conception which still had a shadowy existence : the universal empire of the West. But history never repeats itself ; and when the Frankish king finally became emperor, the dominion of the Franks proved to be very different from the Roman empire. It was a continental state without the Mediterranean. It was a vast, thinly-populated area, not a flourishing, highly-civilized land filled with commercial cities. It was a clumsy body-politic, which held together for a few generations only, and, in the end, dissolved almost without pressure from external forces.

Be that as it may, on Christmas day of the year 800, the decisive act took place. In the church of St. Peter in Rome, pope Leo III placed a crown on the Frankish ruler's head, and Charles was proclaimed emperor. The pope had recently been tortured and imprisoned by his enemies in his own capital. He had been obliged to defend himself against serious charges in a trial before Charles. The situation was hardly auspicious for an imperial coronation.

Nevertheless the coronation was a moment of historical signi-ficance. Those members of the Roman nobility, who attended the ceremony, may well have thought that the Franks were hardly mature enough to enter into the heritage of the *populus Romanus*. But for the Franks themselves it meant the fulfilment of all the things that had been hinted at in the prologue of the Salian law : they were the chosen people, founded by God and ordained to rule Europe.

CHAPTER II

CHARLES THE GREAT

No man's stature is increased by the accumulation of myths, and nothing is detracted from genuine historical greatness by the consideration of a man's purely human side. In order to analyse an epoch it is necessary to analyse the man who was its centre, who determined its character and who was, at the same time, shaped and determined by it. It is therefore not mere curiosity but an endeavour to fulfil the historian's task if we strive to pierce and get behind the myth that has surrounded the figure of Charles. That myth has been built up over a period of centuries and has tended to conjure up in place of a tangible personality, full of vitality, the figure of a timeless hero.

In the case of Charles—and that alone would justify our beginning with him—we can even form a picture of his bodily physique. The bodily appearance of his contemporaries, although we know their names and their works, remains shadow-like for us to-day. But as far as Charles the Great is concerned, we are not only in possession of his bodily remains but also have an exact description of his appearance. It is true that Charles's biographer Einhard borrowed the terms of his description from Suetonius.[1] Nevertheless it was possible for him to choose from among the numerous biographies of the ancient emperors which he found in Suetonius those expressions which were most applicable to his master. Einhard and his contemporaries were especially struck by Charles's bodily size. Ever since the opening of Charles's tomb in 1861 we have know that his actual height was a full 6 feet 3½ inches.[2] It was therefore not poetic licence

[1] E. Bernheim, *Die Vita Karoli Magni*, in : *Hist. Aufsätze f. G. Waitz*, Hannover 1886 ; M. Buchner, *Einhard's Künstler- und Gelehrtenleben*, Bonn, 1922.
[2] E. Mühlbacher, *Deutsche Geschichte unter den Karolingern*, Stuttgart, 1896, i, p. 235. J. Calmette doubts the correctness of Einhard's statement ' septem suorum pedum proceritatem eius . . . habuisse mensuram ', for the seven feet which Einhard attributed to his hero would amount to more than two meters. (*Karl der Grosse*, Wien-Innsbruck, 1948, pp. 175, 326). But Calmette must have overlooked the

when one of the court-poets, describing the royal hunt, remarked :
' The king, with his broad shoulders, towers above everybody
else '.[1]

Einhard noticed two blemishes in Charles's physique : a
thick, short-set neck and a protruding paunch.[2] He was therefore
far from representing the ideal type of Germanic hero that was
to be conceived by later ages. Einhard added, however, that
these characteristics were forgotten in the general impression
created by Charles's well-balanced physique. Charles, on the
whole, seems to have resembled a human type which is well
known among us : the general build weighty, the skull round,[3]
as is shown by the famous small statue which used to be part
of the cathedral treasure of Metz.[4] We must give credence to
Einhard when he speaks of Charles's large, vivacious eyes[5] and
of his joyful countenance.[6] Even a clever artist must have found
it difficult to render these things in bronze. The small statue
may well have been a model for a monument of the emperor
which was never erected.[7] On such a monument it would have
been necessary to emphasize the ruler's dignity and authority,
not his charm.

Charles's appearance was certainly not lacking in dignity and
authority. Only his voice, according to Einhard's report, was
out of character. It seems that it was too highly-pitched.[8] Einhard
also found fault with Charles's spluttering way of speaking which
was too much like loquaciousness.[9] All this belonged to one side

expression *suorum*. It is not permissible to use the equestrian statue, which used to
be in the Musée Carnavalet and which is now in the Louvre, as evidence ; for the
horse, like the sword that has recently been removed, is a modern addition.

[1] MGH, *Poet.*, i, p. 370, v. 172.

[2] Einhard, *Vita Karoli Magni*, MGH, *Ger.*, c. 22 : ' cervix obesa et brevior
venterque proiectior '.

[3] Einhard, loc. cit. ; ' apice capitis rotundo '. Cf. the description of this type of
man by E. Kretschmer, *Körperbau und Charakter*, Berlin, 1940, p. 27.

[4] See note 2, above. It is almost certain that the body is that of Charles the Great
and not, as some scholars have believed, that of Charles the Bald.

[5] Einhard, loc. cit. ; ' oculis praegrandibus ac vegetis '.

[6] Ibid. : ' facie laeta et hilari '.

[7] H. Fichtenau, *Byzanz und die Pfalz von Aachen*, MIÖG, 1951, lix, pp. 49 sqq.

[8] Einhard, loc. cit. ; ' voce clara quidem, sed quae minus corporis formae
conveniret '.

[9] Ibid., c. 25 : ' erat eloquentia copiosus et exuberans poteratque quicquid
vellet apertissime exprimere . . . Adeo quidem facundus erat, ut etiam dicaculus
apparet.'

of Charles's character—to the side that was known by his friends.
He always loved the company of other human beings. Opmistic
and daring, he stimulated them to common enterprises. He was
no theoretician and was not given to pondering. It would be
quite wrong, however, to see nothing but this side. We must
never overlook the tenacity and the hardness which were so
characteristic of him. It was no mean achievement to take the
field, year after year, against the Saxons and to hasten on endless
rides from one frontier of his vast dominions to another. People
had good cause to tremble at the blows of ' iron ' Charles. The
formula of the old oath—' a friend to friends ; an enemy to
enemies '—characterizes Charles's outlook, just as it characterizes
the reaction of young peoples. Side by side with his charming
manner, there was his hardness, even his cruelty. There was
nothing of that well-beloved harmony of character which can
only be the fruit of gradual education, spread over many
generations.

It is a pity that Einhard fails us when he describes Charles's
personality, for his description is entirely conventional. It had
to be conventional, for, although emperors may differ in physical
build, they must all have the same virtues, namely the imperial
virtues without which nobody can be a real emperor. Thus his
description of Charles is couched in Aristotelian and Stoic terms,
such as *temperantia, patientia,* and *constantia animi.*[1] And in so
far as Einhard attributed *magnanimitas* and *liberalitas*[2] to Charles,
we can discern a mingling of ancient and Germanic princely
ideals. When the hospitality shown to foreign guests resulted in
neglect of considerations of public economy, Stoic *magnanimitas*
was imperceptibly transformed into Germanic ' loftiness of
spirit '. For Charles ' found in the reputation of generosity and
in the good fame that followed generous actions a compensation
even for grave inconveniences '.[3]

The Stoic traits in Einhard's picture of Charles are, however,
by no means insignificant. Many of Charles's counsellors must
have drawn his attention to the fact that these traits were ideals

---

[1] *Temperantia,* ibid., c. 19 ; *patientia,* ibid., c. 8 ; *constantia animi,* ibid., c. 7 and c.
18.

[2] *Magnanimitas,* ibid., c. 7 and c. 21   *liberalitas,* ibid., c. 21.

[3] Ibid. ,c. 21.

that had been appropriate to his imperial predecessors and were
therefore appropriate for him. People must have appealed again
and again to his *clementia*,[1] a Stoic concept subsumed under
temperantia, when it was a question of preventing the execution
of conspirators, of liberating hostages, or of returning property
that had been confiscated in punishment for an offence. Stoicism
was, after all, allied with Christianity. A Christian ruler had to
exercise self-control. If he indulged in *crudelitas* and raged against
his enemies he was not far from the very opposite of a good king,
the *rex iniquus* or tyrant.

Charles endeavoured in more than one sense to live up to the
model of Stoic and Christian self-discipline. He could not tolerate
drunkards in his palace. Banquets were held only on important
feast days. Fasting, however, he deeply loathed. He often complained that it impaired his health.[2] When he was an old man he
conducted a long battle with his physicians who never succeeded
in making him eat boiled meat in place of the roast to which he
was accustomed.[3] The fact that Einhard incorporated such stories
in his biography and that a large number of almost humourous
anecdotes, such as were collected later by Notker,[4] were recounted
by his own contemporaries, shows that there was a very real
difference between the late Roman, and especially the Byzantine,
conception of the ruler, on one hand, and the Frankish conception, on the other. Charles did not observe in his court the stiff
dignity and the ceremonious distance that became an emperor.
In this respect he never modelled himself on anyone ; he behaved
naturally and revealed his true self.

There is no evidence that Charles ever withdrew from the
people around him in order to ponder and work out his plans.
He always needed the company of people, of his daughters, of

---

[1] Cf. AS, i (2nd ed.), p. 182 n. 2 ; and also p. 33, n. 4.
[2] Einhard, op. cit., c. 24.   [3] Ibid., c. 22.
[4] *Gesta Karoli* ; MGH, *Script.*, ii, p. 726, Notker, ' the monk of St. Gall ', only
wrote the *Gesta Karoli*, on the basis of narrations of one of Charles's warriors by
the name of Adalbert, in 884. S. Abel, B. Simson, A. Dopsch and others have
accepted him as credible ; L. Halphen, *Études critiques sur l'histoire de Charlemagne*,
Paris, 1921, does not share this view. It may well be true that Notker got many
facts wrong ; but his picture of Charles the man has, in its main outlines, with-
stood all criticism. If there is no historical foundation to his stories, he must have
been an outstanding psychologist to invent such a genuine portrait of Charles's
character.

his friends, and even of his menial retinue. He not only invited to his banquets everybody who happened to be about ; he also gathered people for the hunt and even insisted that his magnates, his learned friends and his bodyguard were to be present when he was having a bath.[1] The author of a poetical description of palace life at Aix-la-Chapelle refers repeatedly to the noisy bustle in the baths. It seems that Charles was happiest among the din of the hunt or in the midst of the building going on at Aix-la-Chapelle.[2]

Charles was the centre of the whole kingdom—not only because it became him as ruler to be the centre, but also because it suited his temperament. Generally receptive, and approaching both science and scholarship with an open mind, he wanted to feel that he was at the centre of everything. It must have been an easy matter for court scholars, like Theodulf of Orléans, to persuade the king that his intellectual faculties were broader than the Nile, larger than the Danube and the Euphrates, and no less powerful than the Ganges.[3] When Alcuin, another of these scholars, wanted to flatter Charles, he questioned him about a complicated problem of the Christian calendar. Charles's authoritative reply to this letter did not prevent Alcuin, whose vanity was hurt, from tactlessly exposing the king. He wrote back that the clergy of the royal palace were the real authors of the reply and that the opinion they had given had betrayed their ignorance.[4]

In spite of such occasional indiscretions, Alcuin flattered Charles by explicitly calling him the first philosopher of his realm. The Franks, he wrote, were happy under his rule ; for had not Plato said that kingdoms ruled by philosophers were happy indeed?[5] This was to be taken not in a pagan, but in a Christian sense ; for the philosopher's *sophia-sapientia* comprised the spheres of both profane and theological knowledge.[6] It was a ruler's supreme duty to be the just judge of his people ; and the office of judge extended far into the realm of the spirit. Charles's ecclesiastical legislation shows how seriously he took

---

[1] Einhard, op. cit., c. 24, for banquets. For hunting, see *Karolus Magnus et Leo papa*, MGH, *Poet.*, i, p. 369 sqq., 137 sqq. ; for bathing, Einhard, op. cit., c. 22.

[2] MGH, *Poet.*, loc. cit., vv, 121 sqq. and 159 sqq.

[3] Ibid., p. 484, vv, 25 sqq.

[4] MGH, *Epp.*, iv, pp. 224 sqq., ep. 143–5.

[5] Ibid., p. 373, ep., 229.   [6] See below, p. 100.

this duty. It is probable, of course, that many of these laws were composed in much the same way as the above-mentioned letter to Alcuin.[1] Charles, however, did not confine his judgments to matters of ecclesiastical discipline. His verdicts extended also to theological doctrines. The *Libri Carolini*, a treatise on the subject of the worship of images, directed against Byzantium,[2] was issued as the ' work of the most enlightened and distinguished and admirable Charles '.[3] For a long time it was believed that the marginal notes in the Vatican manuscript of this work represented the observations made by Charles when the text was read out to him.[4] This belief appears now to have been unfounded.[5] All the same, the work proves clearly that Charles was prepared to play the role which so many emperors and some kings had played before him. He wanted not only to watch over the propagation of the faith and over the organization of the church, but also to decide, as the country's foremost theologian, on matters of dogma.

To claim such a function showed that he had both a high conception of the office of ruler and a strongly developed sense of his own importance. The same sense of the importance of his office is shown in the anecdote, related by Notker,[6] according to which Charles once said : ' Would that I had twelve clerks so learned in all wisdom and so perfectly trained as were Jerome and Augustine! ' Whereupon Alcuin could not refrain from replying : ' The Maker of heaven and earth has not many like to those men and do you expect to have twelve? '[7]

---

[1] In the opinion of recent scholars, Charles's personal part in ecclesiastical legislation was much smaller. Cf. C. de Clerq, *La législation réligieuse Franque*, *Rec. des Travaux d'Histoire et de Philologie de l'Univ. de Louvain*, ii, 38 ; quoted H. Spehr, in : *Arch. f. Kulturgesch.*, 1943, xxxi, 208.   [2] MGH, *Con.*, ii, Suppl.

[3] Ibid., p. 1. The theory that Theodulf of Orléans was the author has been advanced, but so far not proved, by W. von den Steinen and A. Allgeier. Cf. L. Wallach, in : *Traditio*, 1953, ix, p. 144, n. 56. It would appear that Alcuin participated in the redaction of the work, ibid., p. 147.

[4] M. Tangl., in : *Neues Arch. d. Ges. f. ältere dt. Geschichtskunde*, 1911, xxxvi, pp. 752 sqq. ; W. v. d. Steinen, ibid., 1932, il, pp. 207 sqq.

[5] The first doubts were raised by A. Mentz, *Die Tironischen Noten*, Berlin, 1942, pp. 75 sqq. (reprinted in *Archiv f. Urkundenforschung*, 1942, xvii, cf. pp. 262 sq.) The argument of W. von den Steinen has been newly examined by H. Fichtenau, *Karl der Grosse und das Kaisertum*, MIÖG, 1953, lxi. pp. 276 sq.

[6] Notker, op. cit., p. 734, c. 9.

[7] If these words were spoken by Charles (and it seems very probable that they were), they show that he conceived his task to be analogous to that of the Roman

Even on this occasion, it would seem, the only reason why Alcuin put Charles in his place was that he had taken the remark as a criticism of his own, not very significant contribution to theology. It is unlikely that he objected to Charles's remark on grounds of principle. As a rule the courtiers, and Alcuin among them, vied with each other in hiding from the king that there was any difference of quality between the achievements of ancient Christian civilization and their own. A new Rome or Athens was expected to arise in Aix-la-Chapelle,[1] and they were anxious to emphasize their superiority over Byzantium, where government was in the hands of females and theology was riddled with errors. Charles required all the fresh naturalness of his temperament in order to prevent himself from sliding from the realm of practical possibilities into the world of fantastic dreams and illusions in which so many Roman emperors had foundered.

Charles's campaigns as well as his building plans never, in fact, went beyond the limits of reason. It was very rare that he conceived such fantastic projects as the construction of a canal between the Rhine and the Danube for which the technical means then available were totally inadequate.[2] Notker relates that Charles once exclaimed to some Byzantine ambassadors : ' Oh, would that pool [the sea] were not between us ; for then we would either divide between us the wealth of the east, or else we would hold it in common '.[3] If such words were ever really spoken, they must have been due to the high spirits of a banquet rather than an expression of genuine political plans. Charles never expected his Franks to join him on the sort of campaign that Alexander had undertaken with his Macedonians. The arrogance which we can occasionally detect in him ought to be distinguished from megalomania, of which he was never guilty. It was not megalomania, but merely an attempt to brag when,

emperors in whose reign the Fathers of the church had lived. In the same passage Notker described Charles's disappointment at the poor results which his efforts had yielded : ' ad maturitatem patrum praecendentium non pervenire condolens, et plus quam mortale laborans, in hanc tediatus vocem erupit . . . '

[1] Among the frequently quoted passages of this kind I would refer here only to MGH, *Poet.*, i, p. 368, vv, 94 sqq., and p. 386, vv, 39 sq. ; MGH, *Epp.*, iii, p. 279, No. 170. Cf. also note 93.

[2] AS, ii, 56 sq.   [3] Notker, op. cit., p. 743, c. 26.

after his coronation, he obliged pope Leo III to accept a golden
chalice, decorated with precious stones, weighing at least 50 lb.,
and its golden paten that weighed more than 25 lb.[1]

At times Charles's affability, so much praised by Einhard,
gave way to surprising explosions of temper. If we follow the
king with Notker[2] into the palace-school, we find him ' with
fire in his eyes ' uttering terrible words, which ' seemed thunder
rather than human speech ', as he addressed the lazy sons of the
nobility : ' By the King of Heaven, I take no account of your
noble birth. . . .' Was this story part of Notker's propaganda?
It could have been ; but we possess a poem by a pupil of the
school who admits in broken Latin that he had been subjected to
bodily chastisement by Charles himself on account of his mistakes
in grammar.[3]

It would be silly to take very seriously such pedagogic thunderstorms which must have passed over quickly. Without a
reference to such explosions, however, the portrait of Charles's
impulsive and impetuous nature would be incomplete. The
king's ire, which made his contemporaries tremble, was quite a
different matter. It was part of the Germanic, just as it was of
the oriental, conception of a ruler and was contrary to the Stoic
ideal. At the beginning of the legend of Charlemagne there
stands the figure of the ' iron Charles ' as his enemies saw him
approaching—clad from top to toe in iron, and with an iron
soul as well. In confusion they shouted : ' Oh, the iron! Woe,
the iron! '[4] Not only the king's enemies, however, but also his
faithful followers stood in fear of him. Charles's grandson
Nithard wrote with approval that Charles had governed the
nations with ' tempered severity '.[5] Charles was able to control
the warring men and the centrifugal tendencies of his dominions

---

[1] AS, op. cit., ii, 241 n. 3. If the Carolingian pound was heavier than the Roman
pound, the weights quoted must be increased. On the same occasion Charles gave
away two further cups each of which weighed more than 12 kg. For the Carolingian
pound see E. Patzelt, *Die karolingische Renaissance*, Baden-Wien-Leipzig, 1924, p. 144.

[2] Notker, op. cit., p. 732, c. 3.

[3] MGH, *Poet.*, i, p. 77 ; cf. L. Traube, *Einleitung in die lateinische Philologie des
Mittelalters*, in : F. Boll ed., *Vorlesungen und Abhandlungen*, München, 1911, ii, p. 52.

[4] Notker, op. cit., p. 759, c. 17. For a remarkable parallel in the life of Mohammed as described by Mohammed ibn Ishak, see S. Singer, *Germanisch-romanisches
Mittelalter*, Zürich, 1935, pp. 157 sq.

[5] Nithard, MGH, *Script.*, ii, p. 651, c. 1.

because the fear of his personal severity made evil men as gentle as lambs.[1] He had the power to make the ' hearts of both Franks and barbarians ' sink.[2] No amount of official propaganda could produce the same effect as the hardness of Charles's determination. The lack of such determination in Louis, his successor, was among the factors that led to the decay of the empire.

This side of Charles's character, although necessary for the preservation of the kingdom, was well beyond the boundaries laid down by the precepts of Stoicism and of Christianity. Charles himself was probably not aware of this. But Einhard, his biographer, who had much sympathy with both these ideals, felt it deeply. Einhard passed over the much discussed ' bloodbath of Verden '[3] in silence. With reference to the conspiracy between his son Pepin and the Thuringians, however, he was forced to admit that the king had been guilty of injustice and cruelty. He added that Fastrada, the queen, had talked Charles into these acts.[4] But even if we choose to disregard such exceptional events, there is no doubt that Charles's wars of aggression were directed not only against pagans—to attack pagans was not only permitted : it was considered a king's duty[5]—but also against Christians, such as the Basques of Navarre, whom he actually forced into the arms of the Moors.[6]

There was nobody to intimate disapproval or reproof for such things, or for Charles's conduct in his private life, or for the way he behaved towards his family. Charles, in any case, would hardly have been perturbed by disapproval or criticism. It would certainly not have impaired the impetuosity and the self-assurance with which he was accustomed to act. He was the very opposite of his successor Louis who, owing to his different character and to a different education, was tortured, during the latter part of his life, by scruples and by the reproaches of his retinue. Charles thought of himself as a Christian through

---

[1] MGH, *Poet.*, i, p. 367, vv, 41 sqq. [2] Nithard, loc. cit.

[3] K. Bauer's attempt (*Westfälische Zeitschr.*, xcii, 1936, pp. 40 sqq.) to substitute *delocare* for *decollare*, does not seem tenable ; cf. H. Spehr, in : *Archiv f. Kulturgeschichte*, xxxi, 1943, p. 219.

[4] Einhard, op. cit., c. 20.

[5] For the concept of *bellum iustum* see the comprehensive treatment by E. Bernheim, *Mittelalterliche Zeitanschauugen*, Tübingen, 1918, i, p.28.

[6] AS, i, pp. 296 sqq.

D

and through, but he never managed to transcend the limits of
the popular piety of the Franks. After all, even the conceptions
of his clergy were, for the most part, limited in the same way.

The first great impression which Charles as a seven-year-old
boy underwent, was the translation of the relics of St. Germain.
Charles always remembered the occasion because he lost a tooth
that day. But he also remembered it because of the miraculous
events that took place. At first it had been impossible to lift
the coffin. Later the coffin moved of its own accord into the
new tomb and exuded a sweet odour.[1] This account is said to
be based on Charles's own statements. It may well be true, for
Charles used to participate in later years in such translations of
relics, though less frequently than his son Louis. If Charles did
not attribute as great importance to such things as Louis did,
it was not because he objected on principle to these expressions
of popular piety, but rather because he was leading a secular
life, whereas Louis the Pious often endeavoured to live and act
like a religious. The 'rationalistic' tendencies that used to be
attributed to Charles[2] are hardly compatible with the fact that
he treasured a large collection of relics.[3] But it is conceivable
that Charles was personally intent upon restraining the proli-
fication of popular cults through legislation, especially in so far
as these cults were connected with residues of paganism. Here
we can also detect the operation of tendencies that reveal the
influence of Theodulf, of Agobard of Lyons, and of the other
'Spaniards' in the palace. These tendencies did not represent
'enlightment' or 'rationalism' but reflected a sober, rigorous
faith[4] which resisted the worship of new and uncertain saints
and which tried, among other things, to eliminate the frauds that
were being practised in places of pilgrimage.

---

[1] MGH, *Script.*, xv, pp. 6 sqq.

[2] H. Reuter, *Geschichte der religiösen Aufklärung im Mittelalter*, Berlin, 1875, p. 1.
Cf. also Hauck's statement that there was no conflict, in that age, between pious
belief and enlightenment; *Kirchengeschichte Deutschlands im Mittelalter*, Leipzig,
1900, ii, p. 706; W. Pückert, *Aniane u. Gellone*, Leipzig, 1899, p. 120, n. 14 and
others.

[3] Angilbert spoke of the relics which 'a ... domino meo maxime sunt congre-
gatae' (MGH, *Script.*, xv, p. 175). On Charles's collection of relics and on the
political significance of the worship of relics in general, see H. Fichtenau, *Zum
Reliquienwesen im früheren Mittelalter*, MIÖG, 1952, lx, pp. 60 sqq.

[4] Cf. the German edition of this book, Zürich, 1949, pp. 198 and 208.

At bottom, Charles's attitude towards relics was not opposed to that of his Frankish subjects. This is proved by his behaviour before the decisive trip to Rome in 800. Before proceeding to Rome Charles undertook a journey through the whole land of the Franks. The journey was undertaken not only for political and military reasons but also because Charles wished to pray at the tombs of the great saints.[1] Even his expeditions to Rome were in part pilgrimages : that is to say, Charles used the occasion to make numerous donations to the pope for the salvation of his soul,[2] and also to conclude both with Hadrian I and with Leo III, not only political treaties, but also a religious pact. This pact, the *pactum paternitatis.* was a form of spiritual adoption by the successors of Peter and amounted to a reception into the ' family ' of the saint. Through it Charles was admitted to the great prayer-confraternity, and the pope was obliged to pray daily in the church of St. Peter for the salvation of the souls of the king and his followers, as well as for the welfare of the empire.[3] On another occasion Alcuin sent money to England for prayers to be said for himself and for Charles.[4] After the great victory over the Avars, Alcuin wrote to the king : ' O happy king, how great will your glory be on the day of the Last Judgment. All those that were converted from idolatry to the knowledge of the true God will follow you. And you yourself will be on the side of the just. The reward for eternal bliss will be increased for all.'[5] Wars increased the size of one's retinue, and earthly glory was measured in terms of the size of one's retinue. In this letter the image is applied without hesitation to the field of religion. Most probably Alcuin did not more than voice the king's own thoughts.

Charles's greatest religious desire was to be counted among the Just. Paul the Deacon relates how he heard from the king's own mouth the story about the ring which his ancestor Arnulf had thrown into the Moselle in order to obtain forgiveness for

---

[1] *Annales Regni Francorum*, MGH, *Script.*, vi, p. 110 ; Alcuin, MGH, *Epp.*, iv, p. 266, ep. 164 ; *Chronicon Moissiacense*, MGH, *Script.*, i, p. 304 ; cf. also note 49, above. [2] Cf. the passages in AS, op. cit., p. 161.
[3] H. Löwe, *Die karolingische Reichsmission und der Südosten*, Stuttgart, 1937, p. 77.
[4] Alcuin, MGH, *Epp.*, iv, p. 33, ep. 7.
[5] Ibid., p. 157. ep. 110.

his sins. After many years one of Arnulf's cooks found the ring
in the stomach of a fish.[1] Could Charles, whose achievements
had by far surpassed those of his ancestor, not be equally certain
of such manifest grace? He had built the church of St. Mary
at Aix-la-Chapelle. He frequented the church several times every
day and sometimes again during the night. He supervised the
orderly conduct of the service and admonished the priests not
to tolerate anything unclean in the church. He procured the
sacred vessels and the vestments and purged the sacred books of
all errors. As we know, he spent the very last days of his life
occupied in this labour.[2] He supported needy Christians, even
outside the borders of the empire. He sent money to Rome and
made four pilgrimages to the papal city. Such were the religious
works of Charles as related by his biographer, Einhard.[3] The
inner life of the Christian, the regeneration of the soul and the
new religious attitude which, at the very time when Einhard was
writing, Charles's son, Louis the Pious, was labouring to acquire,
are not so much as mentioned. The reason why Einhard is silent
about such things is scarcely that he could not find the words
to describe them in his model, Suetonius. Charles organized
the salvation of his soul as he was wont to organize his Empire.
It would have been contrary to his nature, and the most difficult
task of all, for him to seek the highest levels of spiritual experience
in his own heart. His task as a ruler, as he saw it, was to act
upon the world.

We must remember, however, that the world upon which
he acted bore little resemblance to the sober and dry reality
created by modern commerce and technology. Such modern
conceptions were shaped much later, mostly under the impression
of Calvinism. They were unknown to Charles, who, for instance,
first learnt of the pope's mutilation in distant Rome through a
dream.[4] He took it to be one of his duties as a ruler to observe
the course of the stars with the greatest of attention,[5] for the

---

[1] *Gesta epp. Mettens.*, MGH., *Script*, ii, p. 264.
[2] Thegan, *Vita Ludovici imperatoris*, MGH, *Script.*, ii, p. 592, c. 7.
[3] Einhard, op. cit., c. 26.
[4] MGH, *Poet.*, i, p. 374, vv, 326 sqq. The author of a poem destined for Charles
would hardly have dared to say anything in it which the king did not believe to be
correct.   [5] Einhard, op. cit., c. 25.

approach of misfortune for his kingdom could be foretold from
the stars more accurately than from anything else. For this
reason the emperor devoted more time and labour to the study
of astronomy than to any other of the ' liberal arts '.[1] If the
observation of the stars had been a mere hobby, he would surely
have interrupted it while he was devastating the Saxon country
with his army. But it was obviously concern for the outcome of
the campaign which prompted him to send a courier to Alcuin
with the question whether the fact that Mars had accelerated
his course and had already reached the constellation of Cancer
was to be considered an omen.[2] Astronomy, however, was
needed not only for prognostication of the future but also for
the computation of the dates of movable feasts. Charles himself
acquired the *ars computandi* ;[1] for his government might suffer
misfortune if the clergy made a mistake and disturbed the harmony
of the ecclesiastical calendar through a miscalculation of the dates
of movable festivals.

Charles the Great was not one of those men who have to
fight against their times and who, misunderstood by their contemporaries, are appreciated only after their death. He embodied
all the tendencies of his own age ; he was carried forward by
them and, at the same time, moved them forward. It is impossible
to describe him except in close conjunction with his friends and
the magnates of his land. But for the picture to be complete he
must also be shown in the midst of his family. He was surrounded
by his children, his wives and the retinue of females, whose
numbers and conduct seemed so unbecoming to the puritanism
of his successor when he first entered the palace. Such conditions
were not peculiar to Charles. It was all part and parcel of
Frankish tradition. Charles lived as the head of a clan. The
servants were, at least for the purposes of everyday life, included
in the clan. As part of the family they enjoyed peace and protection and were, together with their master's blood relations,
subject to his authority. Within the framework of the old tribal
law, the master ruled his household unconditionally. His power
was so unconditional that the enactments of the church had no
power to cross the threshold of the house. This remained true

---

[1] Einhard, *op. cit.*, c. 25.   [2] MGH, *Epp.*, iv, p. 252, No. 155.

long after the upper-class Franks had recognized these enactments as binding in the sphere of public life. Marriage, like questions of inheritance, was to a Frank an affair of his house rather than an affair of church or of Christianity.

Such conceptions favoured among the Franks, side by side with matrimony sanctioned by the church, the continued existence of the older and less formal Germanic kind of matrimony, known as *Friedelehe*.[1] Charles's predecessor Pepin had admonished people and nobility in the spirit of the church to enter into public, officially recognized forms of matrimony. But it is significant that his admonition was not accompanied by any threat of sanctions.[2] The old Germanic form of matrimony was not considered scandalous. Even in the royal house of the Merovingians, so proud of their ancestors, the issue of such connections possessed the same rights of inheritance as the issue of fully valid Christian marriages.[3] Even Alcuin wrote to Charles's son, king Pepin of Italy, who was still officially unmarried : ' Enjoy the woman of your youth ; but do not allow a stranger to share your bed, so that God's blessing may issue in a large number of grandchildren.'[4] Characteristically this advice followed an admonition to chastity and to Christian virtue of the sort one might have expected from the ageing educator of princes and the abbot of several major monasteries. It shows that the church was at least trying to discourage polygamy. According to a Capitulary of the end of the eighth century, married men were supposed to separate themselves from their concubines.[5] But monogamy was more a programme than a normal condition.

Charles could hardly be reproached if his behaviour was in close conformity with that of his ancestors. There is no need to enumerate all the sons of the older Carolingians born of such *Friedelehen*. Charles the Great himself owed his existence to such a connection which had only been transformed into a complete marriage several years after his birth.[6] If Einhard says that

---

[1] H. Mayer, in : *Festschrift f. E. Heymann*, Weimar, 1940, i, pp. 1 sqq.
[2] *Concilium Vernense*, c. 15 ; MGH, *Cap.*, i, p. 36.
[3] W. Sickel, in : ZSSRg, 1903, xxiv, p. 110.
[4] MGH, *Epp.*, iv, p. 174, No. 119.   [5] MGH, *Cap.*, i, p. 202, c. 5.
[6] E. Mühlbacher's attempt to save the reputation of Charles's parents (*Deutsche Geschichte*, i, 87) has been superseded by the arguments of W. Sickel, loc. cit.

nobody had any aknowledge of his birth and of his youth,[1] it was not merely in order to apply an apt Suetonian phrase. In the eyes of the church Charles retained the blemish of illegitimate birth even after his parents, Pepin and Bertrada, had concluded a canonically valid marriage.[2] But this fact never induced anyone to question his legal title to the Frankish kingdom. It was not before the middle of the ninth century, when ecclesiastical re-formers endeavoured to harmonize the Frankish law of inheritance with the rules of canon law, that the exclusion of the ' bastards ' came to be demanded.[3]

It is very probable that Charles's marriage to Himiltrude, his first wife from a Frankish family, was a *Friedelehe*, carried out according to native custom, and not a marriage according to canonical rules.[4] The first son of this marriage was named Pepin. This implied that he was destined to succeed his father as king of the Franks ; for it was customary to name the legal heir after his grandfather. Charles the Great himself had been supposed to be a new Charles Martel.[5] Even later, when Charles had sons from a canonically valid marriage, Pepin's name continued to occupy the first place in the litany.[6]

Himiltrude became the victim of a political plot hatched by Bertrada, Charles's mother, while she was still conducting the policies of her two sons. Bertrada's plan was to reconcile the Lombards and to seal the new alliance with king Desiderius through a marriage between Charles and his daughter. Without resistance and in spite of papal protests, the young ruler fell in with this plan. He repudiated his Frankish wife as he was to repudiate soon afterwards the girl from Lombardy and send her back across the Alps when the new political situation seemed to demand it. He then promptly married a thirteen-year-old girl called Hildegard, of a noble Swabian house. Hildegard bore him a son during the first year of their marriage.

The marriage with Hildegard was blessed with a large number of children. This may account for the fact that this connection

---

[1] Einhard, op. cit., c. 4.   [2] W. Sickel, op. cit., p. 118.
[3] Ibid., p. 112.   [4] Einhard, op. cit., c. 20.
[5] M. Tangl, *Einhard, Kaiser Karls Leben*, in : *Geschichtsschreiber d. deutschen Vorzeit*, p. 30, n. 2.
[6] S. Hellmann, in : *Festgabe f. K. Th. Heigel*, München, 1903, p. 41.

lasted till the death of the queen and that we know of no concubines during this period. The situation was quite different
in the king's subsequent marriage to Fastrada, whose evil influence on Charles is emphasized by Einhard. But we may well
doubt whether Einhard's statements do not betray a certain
tendentiousness. Einhard may well have wanted to warn his
own master, Louis, against such evil influences ; for Louis stood,
at the time in which the *Vita Caroli* was written, already completely under the influence of his wife Judith.[1] One of Charles's
letters to Fastrada which has come down to us and which was
most probably dictated by Charles himself, is a sober army
bulletin about the victory over the Avars. Only in the passages
in which he speaks of the ' sweet daughters ', can any warmth
of tone be detected.[2] At that time Fastrada's influence cannot
have been very strong. She was sickly,[3] and this may have contributed to the fact that the king finally acquired a concubine
by the name of Liutgard. After Fastrada's death, Liutgard
became Charles's last legitimate wife.[4] The poets of the palace
bestowed much praise on her and mourned her deeply when
she died. After her death Charles's mistresses and concubines
seem to have become very influential. Their presence was a
thorn in the flesh of some members of the clergy. We know at
least of four such connections : there was a Saxon girl called
Gersuinda, and three others, by the names of Regina, Adallindis
and Madelgarda.[5]

When a pupil asked Alcuin what was meant by the sixty
queens and the eighty concubines in the *Song of Songs*, Alcuin
replied as follows. In the allegorical sense the concubines are
people who produce noble sons through spiritual works, for the
sake of worldly goods, but who are themselves lacking in
nobility.[6] If we apply this reasoning to worldly affairs we must
infer from it that, in the conception of the age, only non-aristo-
cratic girls could become the king's concubines. It seems therefore that Liutgard, of whose noble origin there is no doubt, was

[1] L. Halphen, *Études critiques*, Paris, 1921, pp. 101 sq.
[2] MGH, *Epp.*, iv, p. 528, No. 20.
[3] Ibid., p. 529.   [4] AS, ii, pp. 214 sqq.
[5] S. Hellmann, op. cit., p. 69 n. 4.
[6] MGH, *Epp.*, iv, p. 200, No. 133.

something out of the ordinary. During his later years the emperor was without doubt free to choose daughters of the nobility for his *Friedelehen*. It goes without saying that the sons of such connections were considered to be of noble birth. Their capacity to inherit has been discussed above, and is well established : exactly like his fully legitimate brothers, Gribo, Charles Martel's son by a *Friedelehe* and the uncle of Charles the Great, was granted the rule over a certain territory during his father's own life-time.

Charles's oldest son, Pepin, however, was bound to realize more and more that he was destined to share his mother's fate. The fact that he was a hunchback had not prevented his being designated, through the name under which he was baptized, as the future ruler. But after the birth of Hildegard's three sons, Charles, Carloman and Louis, the father's favour was bestowed on them. Carloman, still unbaptized at the age of four, was baptized by the pope, who gave him the new name of Pepin and anointed him the king of Italy. Little Louis was given the sub-kingdom of Aquitaine. These decisions were not determined by Charles's regard for canonical principles. They were based upon his authority as master of the Carolingian family. As such he was free to grant his favour, as well as to refuse it, to wives and sons as he chose.

The result was that the older Pepin entered into a conspiracy with some discontented magnates. The meetings were discovered by a member of the clergy who betrayed the conspirators. Thereupon Charles confined Pepin to a monastery. He died as a monk of Pr m in 811, in the very same year in which the eldest son of Charles's marriage with Hildegard died. The younger Pepin had died the year before. The older Pepin's death took place therefore at the very moment in which he might have become a dangerous rival to the only other surviving son, the future ruler, Louis. This coincidence has not remained unnoticed.[1] It calls to mind the complete disappearance of two of Charles's nephews, taken prisoner by Charles after the king of the Lombards, Desiderius, had decided to set them up as Frankish anti-kings in opposition to Charles.[2]

[1] M. Tangl, loc. cit.   [2] AS, i (2nd ed.), pp. 135, n. 5, 139, 152.

On the other hand, Charles the Great's favour was bestowed
unstintingly upon his daughters and granddaughters. Einhard
expressed surprise that the daughters were not allowed to marry
during the king's lifetime and that Charles prepared to tolerate
their love affairs and their illegitimate children rather than their
departure from the palace. The emperor maintained that he could
not do without the presence of his daughters at table. When he
was in one of his palaces, he never took a meal without them.[1]
Theodulf, in a description of one of these dinners, mentions first
Charles's three favourite daughters, Berta, Rotrud and Gisla,
then his wife, Liutgard, and finally the other daughters.[2] Two of
his sons, on the other hand, were sent away from the palace
when they were still children. They were to be trained from the
earliest age for independent action and for the administration
of the kingdom. They were too valuable to serve as toys and
to be used as mere objects of fatherly love. On one occasion
only was the little Louis made to appear in front of his father
on horseback, dressed up in the local costume of Gascony, in
a round coat and puffed trousers, wearing boots and spurs.[3]
The daughters, on the other hand, could never wear enough
jewelry and make-up.

It is a pity that we do not possess a description by Theodulf
or one of the other court-poets of the entry into Rome before
the coronation of 800. We only know from an incidental remark
that Charles's daughters were present.[4] We have better information, however, about the king's departure for the hunt. The
finery worn by Charles's daughters was more reminiscent of a
fashion parade than of hunting.[5] Charles himself always dressed
with the greatest simplicity. But he must have been pleased to
see Theodrada, wearing on this occasion a whole set of precious
stones : ' her feet, her hands, the seams of her dress, her temples
and her breast were gleaming and sparkling '.

After Pepin's death in 810, his five daughters were added to
the numerous legitimate and illegitimate offspring of Charles
living in the palace. The emperor was very fond of presiding

---

[1] Einhard, op. cit., c. 19.   [2] MGH, *Poet.*, i, p. 483, No. 25.
[3] Astronomus, *Vita*, c. 4 ; MGH, *Script.*, ii, p. 609.
[4] *Vita Leonis III* ; L. Duchesne ed., *Le Liber Pontificali* Paris, 1889, ii, p. 9.
[5] MGH, *Poet.*, i, p. 371 , vv, 220 sqq.

patriarchally over a large family whose members either had no political ambitions or were not allowed to display them. Administration and all matters of high politics were kept as far as possible from this large household. Neither the plan for the division of the Empire in 806 nor the testament of Charles contains any provision for the maintenance of the daughters and the illegitimate children. According to Einhard's report Charles had planned to leave them certain properties. If this was the case, the plan was not carried out, possibly because there was not enough time to elaborate a plan which was less important to him than the affairs of state.[1] His daughters had lived by his favour and were left dependent on the kindness of the man who was to succeed him in the government both of his household and of his empire. According to his last will, only one-twelfth of Charles's treasure was left to his heirs. The remainder was to be spent for the benefit of his own soul.[2]

The hunt to which we referred above ended with a banquet for king and magnates in a hunting-lodge. Male children who could not yet carry arms and Charles's daughters participated in the banquet.[3] Here, in the ' shade of the leaves ' and the enjoyment of ' wine of Falerno ', to quote the poet's description, Charles indulged even more freely than in his palaces in the kind of life which was to be so much disapproved of by the following generation. The story is probably exaggerated according to which only one of the unmarried women in Charles's circle had not succumbed to these temptations.[4] All the same, the clergy were well advised to stay away. Alcuin, who had by no means always been aloof from worldly enjoyments, advised the abbot of Corbie to forbid the palace to a certain monk who had on an earlier occasion very nearly lost his soul in the midst of such temptations.[5]

At Charles's table entertainment was provided by the recital of old epics as well as by coarse stories such as the one about the flea and the gout.[6] They were for the most part genuine minstrels'

[1] Einhard, op. cit., c. 33.   [2] Cp. pp. 184–185 below.
[3] MGH, *Poet.*, i, pp., 366 sqq.
[4] *Vita Adalhardi* ; Cp. M. Chaume, *Les origines du Duché de Bourgogne*, Dijon 1925, i, p. 143 n. 1.   [5] MGH, *Epp.*, iv, p. 364, No. 220.
[6] Paulus Diaconus, MGH, *Poet.*, i, p. 64, No. 29 ; cf. also p. 50, No. 12.

stories; and minstrels and mimes always found a grateful audience in Charles's palace. Many of his magnates shared the emperor's love for these things; for example, his unofficial son-in-law, Angilbert, the lay-abbot of Centula (St. Riquier) so much so, that Alcuin expressed grave concern in one of his letters.[1] These wayfaring people not only contributed to the entertainment but also helped to increase the splendour of the palace and the fame of its ruler which they spread through distant lands. If he caused people to say prayers for him in distant Britain,[2] why should he not also avail himself of this more direct and effective means of increasing his reputation? The minstrels were the best instrument for influencing ' public opinion '; they were, in fact, its mouthpieces. We can well understand Notker's report[3] that a minstrel's song, recited at the right moment before the emperor, caused him to change his mind and restore property and titles to a count who had been condemned to forfeit them.

In all courts and at all times poets, jugglers and fools have always enjoyed a licence to say things to the ruler which none of the courtiers would have dared to say. A very telling story has come down to us in the form of a fable about beasts which the minstrels were wont to recite.[4] It is a pity that, owing to our ignorance of the actual situation to which it referred, we are no longer in a position to interpret it. According to this particular fable, the lion, the king of the beasts, was sick. The bear persuaded the assembly which had been called on account of the king's sickness, to sentence the fox to death. The fox, however, managed to clear himself of all charges by shrewdly misrepresenting the facts. In the end, the bear was punished and sentenced to lose his fur. The story is obviously a commentary on some intrigue among the magnates, pleasantly presented and meant as food for thought for the king.

In the king's palace there was a constant going and coming. Emigrés from England and from Byzantium rubbed shoulders

---

[1] Ibid., p. 290, No. 175 and p. 381, No. 237.
[2] See above, p. 35 n. 4.
[3] MGH, *Script.*, ii, p. 736, c. 13 ; for the probable form of the minstrel's verse see AS, ii, p. 194.
[4] Paulus Diaconus, MGH, *Poet.*, i, pp. 62 sq.

with foreign ambassadors and all manner of public officials. There must have been, nevertheless, a few fixed key positions in the organization. There was little love lost among the occupants of these positions. For the most part, our sources remain silent on this matter. But now and again we catch a glimpse of the situation. The office of the chamberlain[2] was one of these key positions. It was he who received the people who had come to demand an audience. He decided whether and in what order they were to appear before the king.[3] He also received the annual ' donations ' of the magnates to the royal treasure which was in his custody. Alcuin considered himself happy to count this man among his friends and emphasized again and again how many envious people and evil counsellors were busy in other places trying to ruin the king.[4]

Alcuin wrote repeatedly that, though the king tried to enforce justice, he was surrounded by predatory men.[5] His judgment was probably no less partisan than that of his opponents who maintained that he himself was ruining the king.[6] But we have no reason to doubt that such occurrences as the following one, reported by Notker,[7] actually took place. A certain Liutfrid who had been in charge of Charles's building works had used his position to enrich himself, at the expense of poor people, in the most shameless manner. We can form our own conclusions from the fact that the great purge at the beginning of Louis's reign was not confined to the restoration of the principles of Christian morality in the palace of Aix-la-Chapelle, but was especially designed to investigate and abolish the usurpation of revenues and titles. Charles's own open and generous nature had never

---

[1] The notary Elissaeus, a eunuch, was supposed to educate young Rotrud with a view to the planned marriage with Constantine IV. Porphyrogennetos ; AS, i (2nd ed.), pp. 385 sqq. The English noble Umhringstan, from Mercia, had taken refuge at the Palace with his men ; Alcuin, MGH, *Epp.*, iv, p. 128, No. 85.

[2] Meginfried, who led an armed division against the Avars in 791, was a chamberlain. He was probably identical with the Meginfried who died in 800 in an epidemic in Benevento ; BM, i, p. 314b ; AS, ii, 221 sq. He was succeeded by the Ebehard mentioned by A. Dopsch, *Wirtschaftsentwicklung d. Karolingerzeit*, Weimar, 1921, i (2nd ed.), p. 167.

[3] Theodulf, MGH, *Poet.*, i, p. 483.

[4] Alcuin, MGH, *Epp.*, iv, p. 161, No. 111, pp. 410 sq., No. 254 ; cf. p. 335, No. 202 and n. 5.

[5] Ibid., p. 411, No. 254.   [6] MGH, *Epp.*, iv, p. 89 n. 3.

[7] Notker, op. cit., p. 745, c. 31.

been inclined to inquire too closely into the intrigues and corruptions of his trusted friends and servants.

All things considered, there is little difference between the picture we form of Charles's surroundings and the one we have of his ancestors and of other princes of the period. The only difference was that the imperial household, as in fact the empire itself, was greater, more splendid and therefore also more exposed to danger. As long as its power and splendour were increasing, the cracks in the structure remained concealed. It was the achievement of Charles's own powerful personality to have brought about this rise which, without him, might have taken generations to reach its zenith. His efforts were crowned with success because his whole personality was in tune with the progressive forces active among his people. If this had not been the case, no amount of power concentrated in the hands of the king would have sufficed to stamp his countenance upon the age. If this is remembered much of the illusion of well-nigh superhuman achievement, that has inspired both the mediaeval legend of Charlemagne and many modern narratives, is dispelled. What remains is quite enough justification for calling Charles historically great.

CHAPTER III

THE IMPERIAL TITLE

' There is only one who is enthroned in the realm of the air, the thunderer. It is proper that under him, one only be the ruler on earth, in merit an example to all men.'

These words of an Irishman at the imperial palace[1] are more than a poetical phrase. They present in a brief formula the main point which the defenders of monarchy, from the ancient orient to the times of Donoso Cortes, have again and again advanced as justification for their standpoint. The conception of the Cosmos as an orderly system and of the earth as a mirror of the heavens was the foundation of all political thinking. The cosmic harmony appeared to be divided into several spheres. According to the plan of creation the human sphere had been established parallel to the divine sphere. Although this parallelism had been destroyed by original sin, its rough outlines were still discernible. Though the multiplicity of faiths and of political constitutions showed the extent to which this parallelism had actually been destroyed, people remained quite certain that one God, ' the highest and true Emperor ',[2] was the model and source of all political power. If we wish to understand not only the outward appearance but also the foundations of Carolingian rule we must, therefore, begin with a description of the conception of God that was current in that age. We must try to understand the model to which the earthly ruler sought to conform.[3]

The people, as well as Charles's poets, who were, for the most part, also theologians, showed an ineradicable tendency to think as concretley as possible of heavenly matters. Officially nobody would have dared to doubt that God was as incorporeal and as omnipresent as the fathers of the church had taught. Never-

[1] Hibernicus exul (Dungal?), MGH, *Poet.*, i, p. 395, vv. 10 sqq.
[2] E.g. Gelasius I, quoted after E. Eichmann, *Die Kaiserkrönung im Abendland*, Würzburg, 1942, ii, p. 301.
[3] Cf. E. Eichmann, op. cit., i, pp. 109 sq. and the passages quoted there.

theless Alcuin wrote to one of his pupils that, if he were converted, God would not only go out and meet him but would also embrace him and kiss him, clothe him in beautiful garments and shoes, put a ring on his finger and lead him into the house of heavenly joys.[1] He omitted to add that all this was meant figuratively. He also never mentioned that his description of hell with its icy cold, with the gnawing tooth of the serpent and the wailing of the people who were condemned to cruel punishments, should never be taken literally.[2] Laymen as well as monks had frequent visions of the other world from which we can perceive that their conceptions of the other world were of a concrete and lively nature. The ideas of the Jews dwelling in the Frankish kingdom were no less concrete ; they imagined that God was sitting ' in the manner of an earthly king ' on a throne in a large palace.[3]

The poets in the age of Charles referred to this palace as a fortress. This comparison was in full accord with a more ancient stratum of Frankish ideas. In this fortress, however, there were to be found separate apartments for important people, such as the saints and the magnates of the empire, and its plan corresponded closely to the plan of the palace of Aix-la-Chapelle.[5] God the Father, according to an antiphon sung in the churches of Lyons, was the master of the heavenly fortress. It was He who had sent His son from the fortress to earth.[6] The whole conception of such a household conformed to Germanic ideas. But the need for a firm front against Arianism had forced the figure of Christ more and more into the foreground. At first people had merely emphasized the unity of the three Persons in the Trinity ; but in the end Christ Himself had become the lord of the Heavens and the ' thunderer '.[7]

The Visigoths had given an independent development to the doctrine of Arius. They had thought of the Trinity in terms of a divine clan.[8] Christ, for them, was the Son of the king of

---

[1] MGH, *Epp.*, iv, p. 452, No. 294.
[2] Ibid., p. 453, No. 295.   [3] Ibid., v, p. 189.
[4] For examples from Alcuin see MGH, *Epp.*, iv, p. 329, No. 198 ; p. 386, No. 240.   [5] Hrabanus Maurus, MGH, *Poet.*, ii, p. 166.
[6] MGH, *Epp.*, v, pp. 233 sq., No. 18.   [7] Godeschalk, MGH, *Poet.*, i, p. 94, No. 7.
[8] K. D. Schmidt, *Die Bekehrung der Germanen zum Christentum*, Göttingen, 1939, i, pp. 275 sqq.

Heaven. He was the executor of the paternal will among men ; but strictly subordinate to the head of the clan, the Father. The unity of the Trinity was thus sacrificed for the sake of a concrete image. In the end, however, it was the church in the Visigothic kingdom of Spain which reacted, after the King's conversion to Catholicism, most strongly against such images. The Spanish theologians almost over-emphasised the identity of Father and Son and the unity of the Trinity. Although they did not deny the humanity of Christ, they laid little emphasis on it.[1] Charles's theologians were very much under the influence of these views. Their attention was drawn to them all the more strongly as it became increasingly their lot to fight in Spain against a theology which followed in the footsteps of Arian doctrine.

Since the Franks took upon themselves the defence of orthodoxy, Christ came to be conceived by them as the creator of the universe. He had descended to earth but had never ceased to be together with the Father. He had been born but had remained at the same time as divine as the Father Himself.[2] Christ governed the world and the Heavens, and all nations and kings must be subject to Him.[3] He had descended into the underworld in order to break the iron gates of hell and to shake Tartarus. On His return to Heaven as a victorious king he had been received by the heavenly armies and the ' magnates ' of the kingdom of Heaven as an earthly ruler was wont to be received.[4] He would return on the day of the Last Judgment to light the fires and burn the wicked.[5] Obviously, the old pagan conception of the cosmic conflagration was still alive.

Christ was thus made almost the sole representative of the holy Trinity.[6] In this way people achieved a compact notion of God which was apt to influence any image of earthly rule by king or by emperor.[7] Christ's human and friendly traits were pushed into the background. It was stressed that His humility,

---

[1] J. A. Jungmann, in : *Zeitschrift f. kath. Theologie,* 1947, lxix, pp. 36 sqq.
[2] Council of Arles, 813, c. 1 ; MGH, *Conc.,* ii, 1, pp. 249 sq.
[3] Hrabanus Maurus (?), *De nativitate domini,* MGH, *Poet.,* ii, p. 353, No. 13.
[4] Ibid., p. 249, No. 8.   [5] Loc. cit.
[6] Cf. the examples given by J. A. Jungman, op. cit., pp. 74 sqq.
[7] It goes without saying that the cult of the emperor has left its traces upon the ways in which Christ was worshipped ; cf. e.g., J. Kollwitz, in : *Römische Quartalschrift,* 1936, xliv, pp. 57 sqq.

E

which was expressed in His assumption of a human body, signified no more than pity and was not a sign of weakness so unbecoming to kings.[1] The bishops of the realm were ordered by Charles to preach about the Trinity, the Incarnation, the Judgment and the Resurrection.[2] Christ's activities among peasants and fishermen were either omitted completely or mentioned only in so far as they were concerned with the healing of the sick or the resurrection of the dead.[3] The choice of subjects for pictorial representation in Carolingian art shows a similar preference. Of the Old Testament books Genesis was treated at great length. But instead of painting the stories of the Gospels, frequently only the evangelists themselves were portrayed. Pictures representing scenes from the Apocalypse were more frequent, especially pictures of the Lamb (alone or worshipped by the twenty-four elders), the Hand of God, and the Fountain of Life.[4]

People were clearly preoccupied with the creative and ruling omnipotence of God; with the written doctrine, perhaps in the form of a collection of valid laws represented by the evangelists, the *missi dominici* of Christ; with the adoration of the heavenly ruler by the magnates of the realm. Why, then, it may be asked, was the heavenly ruler represented in the by no means imperious figure of the Lamb? The answer must be that the choice of the Lamb obviated the need for a pictorial representation of the second Person of the Trinity. In the same way people preferred, in awe and respect, to indicate the first Person Himself only in the form of the commanding Hand of God. The ' Lamb of God ' was God himself, the ' omnipotent Lamb '[5] was a symbol of Majesty, not of peace.

The image of the Fountain of Life leads us into a different sphere. Any realistic pictorial representation of Christ's sacrifice on the cross, of the greatest humiliation of the heavenly ruler, was avoided. But as the central importance for all men of the fact of the sacrifice could not be denied, people substituted the effect for the cause. They represented the effect of the sacrifice,

---

[1] Agobard, MGH, *Epp.*, v, p. 211, No. 13.
[2] MGH, *Conc.*, Vol. ii, i, p. 213, c. 1 (799–800).   [3] See p. 49 n. 3.
[4] H. Janitschek, in : K. Mentzel u. P. Corssen, ed., *Die Trierer Ada-Handschrift*, Leipzig, 1889, pp. 65 sqq.
[5] Agobard of Lyons, MGH, *Epp.*, v, p. 154, No. 2.

the salvation; for Christ, physician and Fountain of Life, had saved mankind. In poems he appeared again and again as *salvator mundi*, as the world's physician. Churches dedicated to the Saviour shot up like mushrooms, and many people founded Saviour's altars. Furthermore, here again we have an example of the parallelism between earth and heaven. To the heavenly saviour there corresponded an earthly saviour, the pope, who acted through his ' medicinal power ' which he had inherited from his predecessors but which had originally been conferred by Christ. This power was not confined to the sacraments. The pope's very speech contained something of the 'saving medicine'.[1]

The most tangible and easily comprehensible aspect of authority is the effective fullness of power accompanied by its blinding splendour. This splendour was exemplified in a famous manuscript of the Gospels written entirely in golden letters on a purple background. Godeschalc, the writer of this manuscript, emphasized in a poem that the golden letters signified the splendour of heaven and of eternal life. The word of God, written with precious metal, luminously indicated the road to the illuminated halls of the eternal kingdom.[2] Paulinus, among all the Carolingian men of letters, excelled in the description of these heavenly splendours, which illuminated the earth.[3] For a concrete example one may turn to the abbey church of St. Denis. Its roof shone in gold, its walls were covered with silver ;[4] the whole building mirrored the splendour of the palace of the King of Heaven.

It accordingly became the earthly ruler to be the shining centre of his realm. Charles's name was said to radiate as far as the stars, and even the sun was said to receive a splendour from it which no clouds could ever conceal.[5] The following is Notker's description of the reception of an embassy in Aix-la-Chapelle. ' The king was standing by a bright window, radiant like the rising sun, clad in gems and gold '. And round about him stood, ' as if it were the chivalry of heaven ', his family and the magnates.

---

[1] MGH, *Epp.*, iv, p. 68, No. 27.
[2] MGH, *Poet.*, i, p. 94, No. 7.
[3] Ibid., p. 137, No. 6 ; p. 138, No. 7 ; p. 140, No. 8 ; p. 141, No. 9 ; etc.
[4] MGH, *Poet.*, i, p. 401.
[5] *Karolus Magnus et Leo papa*, MGH, *Poet.*, i, p. 336, vv, 13–18 and 25.

Overwhelmed by this impression, the envoys, speechless and lifeless, fell upon the ground.[1] Whether or not this story is to be taken literally, it shows how people thought of their ruler on such occasions. The use made of the effects of light must have corresponded to the actual practice in the palace.

Power and splendour helped to erect an immovable barrier between God and men, between ruler and ruled. Christ the mediator was pushed into the background by the image of an over-powering God, whose splendour dazzled every human eye. God was the ' wholly other ', at once fascinating and terrible. It need not surprise us that many people hardly dared to partake of the body of such a God in the shape of bread. Even monks contented themselves with bread that was blessed during the Mass but whose substance had not been transformed in the miracle of the Eucharist into the very substance of the body of Christ.[2] Already John Chrysostomos, the great Syrian doctor of the church, had spoken of the ' terrible sacrifice ', the ' awesome table ' and the ' terrifying hour '.[3] The Saxon Gottschalk held that the body of Christ as it had risen from the tomb was so full of glory that nobody would be capable of partaking of it.[4] The Greeks used the word σέβας for the terror and trembling which overcame a man when he beheld the ' wholly other ' of the deity whose countenance he could not bear. The deity of the ancients,[5] like the deified Emperor himself, was *sebastos* and *augustus*.

The wrath of the godhead was the direct expression of this character. This wrath was, though in the last analysis inscrutable, by no means arbitrary. It was merely enigmatic.[6] Syrian theologians, especially Ephraim, had emphasized this element in the Christian tradition. According to them not only men, but angels too, trembled before the judging God.'[7] The Passiontide

[1] MGH, *Script.*, ii, p. 750 (lib. 2, c. 6).
[2] For these *eulogiae* cp. MGH, *Cap.*, i, p. 347 ; H.v. Schubert, op. cit., p. 658 ; G. Schreiber, in : ZSSRk, 1943, xxxii, pp. 226 sqq.
[3] J. A. Jungmann, op. cit., p. 47.
[4] MPL, cxii, col. 1513 ; cf. G. Ladner, in : *Zeitschr. f. Kirchengeschichte*, 1942, lxi.
[5] R. Otto, *The Idea of the Holy*, London, 1946, pp. 14, 54.   [6] Ibid., p. 19.
[7] K. Strecker, in : *Zeitschr. f. deutsches Alterum*, 1909, li, pp. 238 and 240. The Cappadocian Basilius, one of the most widely read church Fathers, endeavoured ' to persuade his readers that the Saviour's divinity was beyond question and to imbue them with a mood of awesome respect and even of trembling fear towards it ' ; A. J. Jungmann, op. cit., p. 47 n. 7, after Lubatscheskyi, ibid., 1942, lxvi, pp. 20 sqq.

Preface in the Mass addresses God as follows : ' The angels praise Thy Majesty, the Dominations adore it, the Powers tremble before it.' Dominations and Powers are the names for two degrees in the hierarchy of angels. Their existence had already been hinted at in the Old Testament and Pseudo-Diony- sius had developed the conception into a gigantic system of heavenly officialdom.

Charles the Great, whose title *augustus* had long since lost its grand ancient meaning, was known as ' the terrible and pious king '.[1] From time out of mind people had expected the terror of the ruler's wrath to be directed against the enemies of his government. This was expected of the heavenly king as much as it was expected of his reflection and representative, the earthly ruler. Alcuin said to Charles : ' God's grace has impressed the terror of your power upon all nations. Those who could never be subdued by armed might approach you now in voluntary subjection.'[2] When the military power of the Frankish armies was represented symbolically by a single personality it was possible for the ruler's overpowering terror to act like a shock. Many a tribe on the frontiers may have succumbed to that shock rather than to the mere force of arms.

During the conversion of the Germans, the decisive argument had always been the creative omnipotence of the Christian God. To Angilbert, God was ' the ominpotent ruler who governed high and low ', who looked down from the highest throne and came to the assistance of His servants as a ' good king '.[3] The strength of these servants was not diminished but increased when they subjected themselves to His power : for God then allowed them to participate in His rule and thus gave them a higher authority than they could ever have attained by their own efforts. To serve God—or to serve a king—did not imply loss of status.

In the *Libri Carolini* there occurs the following passage : ' The Creator is called a creator with reference to the creatures in the same way as the master is called a master with reference to his

[1] MPL, c, col. 99 ; cf. p. 32 above.
[2] MGH, *Epp.*, iv, p. 414, No. 257.
[3] MGH, *Poet.*, i, p. 365.

servants.'[1] This ' unoriginal proposition of Augustine's ',[2] was certainly not intended to create the impression that Charles was comparable to the Creator. The gulf between the Creator and Charles was as great as that between master and servant. Not even the most devoted poets of the palace ever attempted to efface the humanity of their master and to surround him with a semi-divine splendour. Charles had too much commonsense to enjoy such exhibitions of arrogance—a fact which must be continually remembered in spite of the extravagant language sometimes used. The parallel between the rule of God over all creatures and the power of the king of the Franks and of the Christian Emperor over all his peoples was manifest. But the difference between the two kinds of power remained clear to everybody.

When the palace chapel at Aix-la-Chapelle was built, it was planned as a double church. On the ground level the servants attended divine service at the altar of Mary. The magnates assembled in the choirs of the octagon around the king's seat. From that seat one could look down upon the altar of Mary and, looking across the centre of the octagon, one could see the altar of the Saviour in the eastern choir. Masters and servants were strictly separated; so much so that even Mary, the Lord's servant, had to have her altar below that of her Son. One might even wonder whether it was more than accident that her altar was below the royal seat. We must avoid rash conclusions because, although the altar of the Saviour and the royal seat were on the same level, the one was in the east and the other in the west end of the building. In the symbolism of ecclesiastical architecture the contrast between east and west plays a decisive role, by separating the sacred east part with the space for the altar from the western part, built like a stronghold and reserved for the faithful.

Above the places reserved for the people and the king there was the sphere reserved for God. The cupola which rose above the octagon is no longer in existence and we can form an impression of what it looked like only by reconstruction. The

---

[1] MGH, *Conc.*, ii, Suppl. ; *Libri Carolini*, iii, 4b.
[2] W.v.d. Steinen, in : *Neues Archiv*, il, pp. 246, 254.

inside of the cupola was covered with golden mosaics illustrating the fourth chapter of the Apocalypse. Christ was shown enthroned among the twenty-four elders and among the four symbols of the evangelists, the lion, the ox, the man and the eagle. This was the first important representation of *maiestas* on German soil. During the Romanesque period such representations were to become the dominant themes of pictorial and plastic art.[1] The heavenly splendour of this sphere outshone the spectacle of earthly pomp offered on the middle floor by the gilded bronze railings and the polished pillars. From the ground floor the servants and the common people looked up to all this splendour, while they themselves stood among the plain pillars of ordinary stone. A modern historian of art has remarked that the whole structure ' in its well-graded economy must have been highly decorative '.[2] To Charles's contemporaries it must have been more than decorative. The palace chapel of Aix-la-Chapelle was the reflection of the great cosmic order of government.

The different spheres of the cosmic order, though clearly distinct, showed a similarity in structure. Any occurrence in one of the spheres produced an effect in all the others. If the ruler was angry there appeared threatening signs in the sky. Comets, downpours of blood or of stones, storms and floods signified *discord*, dissension and disturbance of the cosmic order.[3] The devil himself was anxious to promote such occurrences. As father of all dissension he wanted to produce confusion in nature as well as in the hearts of men by inciting servants against their masters and the masters against the ruler. On the other hand, if everybody willingly accepted their status and the undisturbed exercise of royal authority under God and over men, the result would be victory for the royal armies, calm winds, fertility of both earth and women, and the health of the whole people.[4] Such conditions meant that the world was well balanced and

---

[1] P. Clemen, *Die romanische Monumentalmalerei der Rheinlande*, Düsseldorf, 1916, pp. 21 sqq., 62 sqq.

[2] G. Dehio, *Geschichte der deutschen Kunst*, Berlin, 1930, i, p. 45.

[3] E. Bernheim, op. cit., i, pp. 84 sqq. ; cf. Astronomus, *Vita Hludovici*, c. 51, MGH, *Script.*, ii, p. 638.

[4] Alcuin, MGH, *Epp.*, iv, p. 51, No. 18, lines 29 sqq.

in a state of *pax*. The king's most important task was to achieve such peace and to maintain it.

This task had been assigned to him by Christ. The king was the vice-regent of the earthly sphere which he ruled on behalf of the King of the whole creation which included both the upper and the nether regions. An earthly king was therefore no absolute ruler. He was the lieutenant of a greater power to whom he had to render the strictest account.[1] He was supposed to appear, on the day of the Last Judgment, as a faithful servant and steward. Towards Christ he occupied the same position of service as the officials of his own realm occupied towards himself. The church, far from protesting against the idea that the heavenly King had set a special task for the earthly king, emphasized it through unction. An attack upon the ruler was an attack upon a person removed from the sphere of everyday life by a heavenly mandate and invested with a ' taboo '.[2] The person of the ruler was sacred *ex officio*. But this did not mean that the ruler as a human being was a saint, still less that he was more sacred than the saints. There are, indeed, some ninth-century texts which seem to indicate that the ruler was considered, in some special sense, the son of God ;[3] but such a view had no practical significance for Charles the Great and his contemporaries. It certainly did not correspond to his own way of thinking.

The ruler was appointed by the grace of God, by the favour of the real, heavenly Emperor, to govern his Christian subjects as his lieutenant. The right to judge and the power of the ' ban ' formed the essence and the mark of all government. This power meant the right and duty to punish evil-doers, to issue orders to the law-abiding and to summon them to military service in the Christian army in the cause of order against all devilish attempts to sow dissension. We may well ask at this point whether

[1] For example, Catwulf, MGH, *Epp.*, iv, p. 503. Cf. also E. Eichmann, op. cit., i, pp. 109 sqq.

[2] Ps. 104, 15 : ' Nolite tangere christos meos ' ; cf. MGH, *Cap.*, ii, p. 439, (Kiersy, 858) : ' Qui infideliter et contumaciter in unctum qualemcumque domini manum mittit, dominum christorum Christum contemnit.' This wast the ' social ' effect of unction ; the personal effect consisted in a strengthening (*confirmatio*, confirmation) of the anointed.

[3] Smaragdus, *Via regia*, MPL, cii, 933 ; cf. H. Löwe, *Die karol. Reichsmission*, p. 34 n.65. Later (881) also the *Ludwigslied* ; see K. Hauck, in : MIÖG, 1954, lxii, p. 135.

the earthly emperor or king had received, from the hand of the heavenly ruler, not only his administrative, judicial and military authority, but also the power of the sacred mysteries. Was the earthly ruler, in the proper sense of the words, a *rex et sacerdos*, king and priest at the same time?

People were wont to compare Charles, as well as his predecessors and his successors, with David and Solomon. But, according to the Old Testament, neither David nor Solomon were priest-kings. In the Old Testament Melchizedek was the only priest-king; and when the Byzantines wanted to justify the formula, βασιλεῦς καὶ ἱερεῦς, the formula for the priest-kingship, they cited him.[1] This formula and the conception it implied had already, during the eighth century, been decisively rejected by the church. The pope actually forbade the Byzantine emperors to use that title, and subsequent conciliar decrees laid down that it was reserved for Christ alone.[2] What applied to the Byzantines applied even more to the Carolingians. It is therefore not true hat at the Carolingian court the comparison of king Charles and King David was connected with the idea of priest-kingship.[3]

The priest's main fuction was to administer the sacraments and to mediate the sacrificial mysteries in the Mass. But he had another function as well. He was the pastor of his flock. He had to teach by his sermons and to judge good and evil according to the law. Since for the enlightened Protestantism of recent times all the emphasis lay upon this latter function of the priesthood,[4] historians have not hesitated to postulate the

[1] F. Kampers, in: *Hist. Jahrbuch*, 1925, xlv, p. 515.

[2] Ibid., p. 501 n. 28; L. Knabe, *Die gelasianische Zweigewaltenlehre*, 1936, p. 27; F. Kern, *Gottesgnadentum u. Widerstandsrecht im frühen Mittelalter*, Leipzig, 1914, p. 113 n. 202.

[3] Thus F. Kampers, op. cit., p. 501, following MGH, *Poet.*, i, p. 106, where Christ is said to have come from a line of priests and kings. In this place the (wrong!) construction was used to prove that there was a distinction between kings and priests. E. Eichmann, op. cit., i, p. 106 uses MGH, *Epp.*, iv, p. 84, No. 41, in order to prove that, according to Alcuin, David-Charles was both king and prophet. But the passage deals with ' legis . . . Dei . . . praedicator ' David, with the office of the preacher, not with charismatic functions.

[4] Since the Reformation there has been a tendency, in Protestant circles, to render the word *presbyter* as *preacher, pastor* or *parson* and not as *priest*; cf. J. and W. Grimm, *Deutsches Wörterbuch*, Leipzig, 1899, p. 2117; and for an illustration see H. v. Schubert, op. cit., p. 360, who appeals to those passages in the sources in which Charles is described as *priest*. In actual fact the word used in those passages is *praedicator*.

existence for a Carolingian priest-kingship, whenever they saw
the king mingling his concern for the preaching of the Word
of God with his secular right to control the organizations of the
church and the ecclesiastical ceremonies. Such considerations
influenced the selection and interpretation of sources produced
in support of the theory.[1] The much quoted passage about
Charles as *rex et sacerdos*, written by Paulinus probably under
Byzantine influence, was interpreted in this sense. But Paulinus's
real meaning only becomes clear when his statement is confronted
with Alcuin's statement : ' He is a king in his power, a priest in
his sermon.'[2]

Charles, we must take it, was supposed to be able to preach
like a priest. Alcuin explained this in greater detail in another
passage. Not only the clergy, but ' good lay men ' as well, and
especially the most noble—but not exclusively the king—were
supposed to live in such a way that their example was a ' sermon '
to their subjects. The king especially had to admonish his
subjects, to improve them through punishment, and to educate
them.[3] It was his task to set an example by a Christian conduct
of life, to legislate and to administer justice, and to foster education and instruction. Was he, therefore, with the fulfilment of
these tasks, a priest in the narrower sense of the word?

But, it may be argued, this is not the whole of the matter.
On the contrary, the *Libri Carolini* prove that Charles acted as
if he were an authority in matters of faith.[4] He summoned
synods and, in Frankfort in 794, he even presided over one.
In Frankfort, the assembled bishops claimed that their assembly
was an oecumenical council. He was, therefore, not only a
governor of the church,[5] but was known in later ages as the
' bishop of bishops '.[6] To these arguments the reply must be
that every royal decision amounted to a clarification of divine
law, for according to Germanic conceptions it was not possible
to distinguish the secular parts from the spiritual parts of divine

[1] Cf. F. Kampers, op. cit., pp. 498 sq. ; L. Knabe, op. cit., pp. 33 sq. and note 63,
etc.
[2] MPL, ci, col. 251 ; H. Löwe, op. cit., p. 43 ; F. Kampers, op. cit., note 2.
[3] MGH, *Epp.*, iv, pp. 208 sq., no. 136 ; cf. p. 415, No. 257.
[4] F. Kampers, op. cit., p. 498.   [5] Ibid., p. 499.
[6] Notker, op. cit., i, 25, p. 742.

law. Charles felt it to be not only his right but his duty to make such decisions, for he felt that he had been appointed by Christ to guard and to administer that law. For this reason he gave his judgments not only on matters of secular concern but also, as became the governor of Christianity, on matters of faith. This function, however, was very different from the pope's sacramental power to loose and to bind, in the exercise of which he was, in fact, never challenged. The right of the Frankish ruler to supervise the bishops was part and parcel of his duty to protect the church. The designation *episcopus episcoporum* meant ' overseer of the overseers'. It did not mean that the emperor pretended to be the supreme priest of the church of Christ.[1]

According to canon law, however, the pope was also a judge, namely the supreme judge in matters of faith. This claim was never denied ; but it is true that it was, at times, ignored. So long as the imperial authority was in the habit of taking the initiative in spiritual matters, the pope could only express either his assent, his qualified assent or his dissent, after the imperial decision had been made. In such cases the decision was discussed and attempts were made to effect a compromise between the two standpoints. When the star of the Carolingians was sinking, this relationship came to be reversed. More and more oppor-

---

[1] The reception of the ruler into the ranks of the spirituality through unction is unknown in the sources before the tenth century ; E. Eichmann, in : ZSSRk, 1912, ii. and the same author in : Festschrift *G. Hertling*, 1913, p. 269. Even if we knew of such a reception in an earlier century, it would not prove that the anointed was a priest. Even the people who were only in minor orders were of spiritual status. The similarity between the imperial coronation and the consecration of bishops, and the ecclesiastical garments worn by Louis the Pious, merely show that the ruler held the office of pastor over the *populus christianus* ; they do not show him to be the dispenser of the mysteries. There is, unfortunately, widespread confusion in the whole of the literature. When one comes across statements like the following, one might well wonder why neither Charles nor Louis ever celebrated Mass, as was not only the right, but the canonical duty of a priest : ' The unction with the holy oil made a priest of the king, for the royal unction is closely related to that of the bishop in that it confers the priestly quality ' (J. Calmette, op. cit., p. 21 sq.). It is also very unlikely that such a ' bishop ' should ever have foregone his right to ordain other priests ! The essential element in conferring priestly or episcopal power, was the laying on of hands ; and, at times, under the influence of Germanic thought, the investiture with the priestly, or (in appropriate cases) the episcopal, insignia. The anointing with chrism, which was used, after all, also for baptism, was by no means of the essence of the consecration. On the other hand, the omission of the laying on of hands signifies that the emperor is ' only externally compared to the consecrated bishop ; he never becomes a complete bishop ; ' E. Eichman, op. cit, i, p. 108 ; cf. 83.

tunities arose for expanding papal jurisdiction over secular affairs, for which the canons offered some indirect justification. Gregory IV's unsolicited crossing of the Alps in order to interfere in the quarrel between Louis the Pious and his sons, is the reverse of the picture offered by the ' council' of Frankfort, over which Charles the Great had presided without papal authorization. When Gregory IV crossed the Alps, Franks themselves had assured him that ' everybody was subject to his judicial power, so much so that nobody was entitled to judge him '.[1]

There was nothing in the sacramental sphere corresponding to the association of emperor and pope in the judicial sphere. The slogan of ' Caesaro-Papism ' has obscured the fact that none of the Carolingian rulers, although they governed ' the treasures, the clergy and the people' of the church,[2] ever considered themselves stewards of the church's spiritual treasure of grace. Even if the imperial coronation of Charles's successors resembled, in the way the unction was carried out, the consecration of bishops, the most important part of the ceremonial—the laying on of hands—was left out ; they did not in fact become bishops.[3] Charles expressed himself to the pope in the following words : ' My part it is, in accordance with the aid of divine piety, to defend on all sides the holy church of Christ from pagan incursion and infidel devastation abroad, and within to add strength to the Catholic faith by our recognition of it. Your part it is, most holy father, having raised your hands to God, like Moses, to aid our arms, in order that, by your intercession, God granting and leading us, the Christian people may everywhere be always victorious over the enemies of its holy name.'[4]

The second part of this famous statement, addressed by Charles to Leo III, is as important as the first part. People remembered that the armies of the Israelites had fallen back whenever Moses lowered his arms.[5] We have already seen how

---

[1] *Vita Walae*, ii, 16 ; MGH, *Script.*, ii, p. 562.

[2] ' Tu regis eius (sc. ecclesiae) opes clerum populumque gubernas ', Theodulf, MGH, *Poet.*, i, p. 524.

[3] E. Eichmann, op. cit., i, p. 183 ; and pp. 101sq. for a discussion of Louis the Pious's episcopal garments which can only be explained on the basis of this ceremonial.

[4] MGH, *Epp.*, iv, pp. 137 sq., No. 93. Cf. A. Brackmann, in : *Sitzungsberichte d. preussischen Akademie d. Wiss.*, phil.-hist. Kl., 1931, ix, p. 76.

[5] *Exodus*, 17, 11 : ' Cumque levaret Moyses manus, vincebat Israel : sin autem paululum remississet, superabat Amalec.'

important for the salvation of his soul the pope's prayers appeared to be to Charles. He also obliged the popes to pray daily for the welfare of his realm.[1] The passage quoted therefore does not mean that the papacy is simply pushed aside with the help of a few high-sounding phrases about assistance through prayer. On the contrary, the letter shows that in Charles's opinion there was a whole sphere of activity in which he could never replace the pope. The pope's function of praying could never be added to his own duties. Assessed in terms of political power the function thus reserved to the pope was insignificant compared to the influence resulting from the king's domination over the Frankish territorial church. The pope's claims were certainly confined by the Frankish kings to the most inward and spiritual sphere. But this sphere was his preserve, even according to Frankish opinion. In the meantime the pope could at least lay claim to the position which his successors were to secure during the Investiture Controversy : overlordship over the whole ecclesiastical hierarchy and the right to be the sole judge in matters of faith.

When all is said and done, however, it must be conceded that a weak reflection of the priestly character of the pagan Germanic rulers had persisted into Carolingian times. It was such a weak reflection that the upholders of the theory that Charles was a priest-king forgot to quote it in their support. When Charles or his successor Louis observed the course of the stars and other natural marvels with the greatest of attention, seeking in them some sign as to the fate that was to befall the realm and its ruler, they did so, not only in order to predict the future but also in the hope of being able, perhaps, to avert an impending divinely ordained disaster. The king never performed sacrifices ; but he gave alms to the poor and joined with both clergy and laity in fasting and prayer. Although Louis the Pious had been brought up in a strictly clerical environment, it was still necessary for his bishops to warn him ' that it was not the King's office to propitiate God but that such propitiation was the business of those who had the power to loose and to bind '.[2]

---

[1] See p. 55 n. 3.
[2] Synod of Paris, 829 ; cf. E. Mühlbacher, op. cit., p. 368.

The rule of a single man, put in charge by God over all men, was supposed to correspond to the rule of God over the universe. It is true that the pagans were not yet converted, but remained, as the servants of the devil, outside the pale of the Christian order. Thus the area over which the ideal monarch was to rule was confined to Christendom, although it was understood that the rest of mankind should be incorporated as soon as possible.[1]

These views were by no means new. They had been current in the Roman empire for centuries and had served as a basis for the policies of the Christian emperors. Much has been written about the ' political theology ', current in that age, which assumed that the emperor is the vicar of Christ on earth and the absolute ruler of all Christians in political as well as in religious matters. The civilized world, the οἰκουμένη, was equated with the territories in which Christianity was the recognized religion. These territories, in turn, were identified with the *orbis romanus* which was subject to the emperor's authority, to the authority of the *dominus imperator*, the *christianissimus imperator*. All this was the *imperium christianum*, one and only ; for Christ could have only one vicar. In theory the unity of the empire continued to exist as long as the authority was exercised by the members of the same family. It even continued to exist when the western part of the *populus christianus* was in fact being ruled by Germanic princes. In the west the idea of the *imperium christianum*, which had so far been both political and religious, had begun to assume a more purely religious character ; for the actual *imperium* had broken up, and only the religion had remained. Nevertheless the ancient ' political theology ' had not been entirely forgotten. People therefore had to choose between recognizing the Byzantine emperor as the true ruler of all Christians, for whom prayers were said in church, and praying for the Germanic princes who were, in fact, exercising actual political power in the west. When people implored God's protection for the *imperium christianum* it had, after all, always been a political, not merely a religous matter ; for, among other things, they had always

[1] For literature on the mission among the heathen see E. Eichmann, op. cit., i, p. 111 n. 9.

prayed that the pagan nations (*barbari nationes*) might become subject to Christian kings.

Ever since the year 754, when the papacy had made them 'protectors of the Roman church', the Carolingians had considered themselves, among kings, specially chosen by God.[1] They had, however, remained kings; even when they had extended their power over other tribes. An emperor, on the other hand, had to have power or at least some kind of hegemony over the whole world.[2] After his victory over the Lombards, his victory over the Bavarians, and especially his defeat of the pagan arch-enemy, 'the Huns' (as people were wont to call the Avars), Charles the Great had approached this ideal step by step. It was possible to speak of an actual supremacy over at least one part of Christendom, although Byzantium still remained the master of the other, smaller part.

Now that the western Christian world had a ruler who had some claim to universal dominion and who had actually displaced the different kings, of his region the notion of the *imperium christianum* could resume political meaning for the west; for 'the expansion of the Christian empire' for which people prayed had coincided with the expansion of Frankish dominion. Alcuin's letters show that the notion of *imperium Romanum* was undergoing transformation, and that in his day these words lacked an agreed and consistent meaning. His use of them is equivocal: at times they clearly have a political meaning, hinting at the empire of the future. At times, however, he used them in an essentially religious sense; and on such occasions he betrayed his deep conservatism.

Charles the Great, of course, had been nurtured in the con-

[1] *Cod. Carolinus*, p. 545; Paul I to Pepin. Cf. K. Heldmann, *Das Kaisertum Karls d. Grossen*, Weimar, 1928, p. 58 n. 5. The belief of the Franks that they had been called to a special mission in the world, has, of course, its deeper roots outside the ecclesiastical and Christian sphere. It goes back to that consciousness of strength that found expression in the prologue to the *Lex Salica*. The specific shape which this belief was to take and the missionary work in which it manifested itself, were due to Christian conceptions and were consciously promoted by the Papacy from 754 onwards.

[2] In an early medieval list of offices of Merovingian origin, (according to F. Beyerle, in: ZSSRg, 1952, lxix, pp. 1 sqq., of Ostrogothic origin) there occurs the following remark: 'Imperator, cuius regnum procellit in toto orbe, et sub eo reges aliorum regnorum'; or, according to another wording: 'Imperator, qui super totum mundum aut qui precellit in eo'.

ceptions of his own folk, whose language did not even contain a word for the imperial dignity. But Charles had always been anxious to learn from his scholarly friends and to make the culture of Christian antiquity his own. His learned friends came from the different countries of the west and were wont to emphasize the factors they had in common rather than those that separated them from each other. It seems that the word ' Europe ' which had hitherto had a purely geographical meaning, acquired, in their usage, a political sense. When they used the word ' Europe ', they came to mean the political aspirations of the Christian west in contrast to Byzantine claims to universal dominion. During the crucial years the ruler of Byzantium was a woman, and in Charles's circle it was stressed that it was impossible for a woman to exercise the highest authority in Christendom. ' The frailty of the (female) sex and the mutability of a (woman's) heart does not permit woman to place herself in supreme authority in matters of faith and rank. She is compelled . . . to submit to the authority of the male.'[1]

What Alcuin wrote on the *imperium christianum* was by no means an expression of purely personal ideas. Rather it shows the kind of thoughts Charles's friends were experimenting with during the years that preceded the imperial coronation. The letters of Charles's other friends are unfortunately lost.[2] Alcuin himself, of course, though not a politician, did not confine his attention to ' purely religious ' matters without political significance, for in those times religion and politics were not clearly distinct. Alcuin was not trying to persuade his master to erect a ' city of God ' ;[3] nor was he trying to direct his attention away from political realities to the ' visible-invisible ' kingdom of Christ,[4] which was to be an ' *imperium christianum* of peace and justice, linking this world to the next '.[5] Charles had without doubt read Augustine's *De Civitate Dei* ; but he must also have realized of how little practical use its theories were for a Christian ruler. Augustine had written about the community of the righ-

---

[1] *Libri Carolini*, iii, 13 ; MGH, *Conc.*, ii, Suppl., p. 127.
[2] This disposes of Heldmann's objection (op. cit., p. 55) that the expression *imperium christianum* ' seems to have been . . . coined and used by Alcuin alone '.
[3] W. Ohr, *Der karolingische Gottesstaat*, Leipzig, 1902, p. 5.
[4] K. Heldmann, op. cit., p. 56.   [5] Ibid., p. 58.

teous in heaven and on earth and had contrasted that community with that of the evil citizens dedicated to the earth and the devil, a community which embraced even corrupt Christians. Alcuin's thoughts were hardly concerned with such unpolitical and purely ethical notions. To him, the criterion that distinguished friend from foe was not the inner attitude of a man but the formal act of baptism by which men chose their master. For him, Christendom was the sum total of all the baptized. The pagans constituted the opposition and there was no need to mention that, in contrast to good Christians, the pagans were evil. Such a conception is almost diametrically opposed to that of Augustine.

This simple and somewhat clumsy conception shows that both Alcuin and Charles had their feet firmly planted on political ground. It would be nonsensical to maintain that Augustine's *civitas Dei* had material frontiers; but Alcuin thought it possible to speak of the frontiers of the *imperium christianum* and of their expansion through conversion to Christianity by physical violence.[1] The empire that was guarded by the counts Eric and Gerold was an empire ' of this world '. For the most part it coincided with the kingdom of the Franks in its actual extension, but it was supposed to comprise the other Christian lands as well. In this empire Charles, as the steward of the church, claimed the right, as he had explained to Pope Leo III, to watch over the purity of the faith. This conception of the duties of the ruler of Christendom explains Charles's interference in the affairs and dogma of the Byzantine and Spanish churches. In both these countries this zeal was naturally regarded with a certain amount of suspicion; for from the political point of view such interference was the beginning of the peaceful penetration which Charles planned to follow up, at least in Spain, by the establishment of direct power.

[1] It was said of the counts Eric of Friul and Gerold that ' terminos custodierunt, etiam et dilataverunt, Christiani imperii '. MGH, *Epp.*, iv, p. 310, no. 185. F. L. Ganshof belives therefore that the expression *imperium christianum* reterred to a territory inhabited by the *populus christianus* (*The Imperial Coronation of Charlemagne*, Glasgow, 1949, pp. 14–5). Cf., however, the remarks of C. J. B. Gaskoin in his review of E. Shipley Duckett, *Alcuin, Friend of Charlemagne*, New York, 1951, in: EHR, 1952, lxvii, pp. 561–3. For the whole question see H. Fichtenau, *Il concetto imperiale di Carlo Magno, Atti della Settimana di Studi Spoleto*, 1953.

F

Charles's rule over Franks, Lombards and ' Romans ' did not necessarily require the assumption of a new title. The Franks were accustomed to ruling over several countries, much as a noble could possess several manors. The idea that the acquisition of a new title would bring the various aspects of his authority under one unified concept is likely to have been suggested to him by men of letters, by his journeys through the territories of what used to be the Roman empire and, last but not least, by Byzantine policy. Although it was easy to scoff at the impotence of the emperors of the east, the fact remained that they possessed a higher civilization and that they represented everything Charles was striving to achieve. Diplomatic intercourse revealed time and time again how conscious of their superior culture the Byzantines were when confronted with the ' barbarians ' of the west. Their firm belief in the universal character of the empire tempted them repeatedly to make difficulties for Charles in the west. After the defeat of the Lombards for instance, Adalgis, the son of Desiderius, fled to Constantinople where he was given the title of *patricius*—the very same title which had been assumed by Charles as protector of Rome. He was even provided with a fleet which it was intended should take him back to Italy. This particular plan was never carried out ; but the incident proved that Charles could not afford to underestimate the power of Byzantium.

The death of the emperor Leo IV in 780 seemed to mark a turning point. Leo's wife, Irene, who controlled the government on behalf of her little son Constantine VI, was anxious to consolidate her position by establishing friendly relations with Rome and the west. Thus a pact was concluded between the two realms and Charles promised to marry his daughter Rotrud to the young emperor : an alliance which, presumably, would have made warfare between the two realms impossible and led the Byzantines to cease calling the Carolingians barbarians. Before long, however, it became clear that Irene, although she had made political concessions, was not willing to abandon the ancient claims of the Roman emperors. It had been the prerogative of the emperors to summon œcumenical councils and to preside over them. Irene, following the example of the great emperor Constantine,

who had watched over the purity of the Christian faith at the
Council of Nicea, decided to determine the question of the worship of images in a second Council of Nicea. There was talk of
' a new Constantine (the young Constantine VI) and a new
Helena ',[1] and even pope Hadrian used such flatteries and recognized the œcumenical character of the Council.

Charles refused to fall in with such plans. He broke off the
engagement of his daughter Rotrud to Constantine VI, and the
Byzantines, in turn, undertook a campaign against the supporters
of the Franks in Benevento. Charles, however, did not content
himself with a diplomatic gesture. Already at that time he must
have been making elaborate plans for undermining the spiritual
supremacy of Byzantium—plans which found expression in the
buildings which Charles was causing to be erected in Aix-la-
Chapelle.

The Byzantine campaign in Benevento had yielded few results.
In the following winter Charles resided for the first time in Aix-
la-Chapelle, which was to become, from 794 onward, his permanent place of residence except for short, enforced, periods of
absence on important political business. Why did Charles abandon the custom both of his predecessors and of the Merovingian
kings of travelling constantly through his dominions? His
decision can hardly have been caused simply by a desire for rest.
More probably it was due to his wish to imitate the habits of
the Byzanine rulers and of their ' predecessors ', the Roman
emperors. The buildings which he erected in Aix-la-Chapelle
confirm the view that Charles was imitating the customs of the
eastern empire. He planned the erection in Aix-la-Chapelle of
a *sacrum palatium*[2] because in Constantinople there was a ' sacred
palace ' which consisted of the most important part of the
numerous imperial buildings between the Hippodrome and the
Sea of Marmora.

At the centre of this ' sacred palace ' was a building which
contained the hall of the throne and which was known as the

---

[1] J. D. Mansi, ed., *Sacrorum conciliorum . . . collectio*, 1767, xiii, p. 416. H. Fichtenau,
Byzanz und die Pfalz von Aachen, MIÖG, 1951, lix, p. 34.

[2] MGH, *Conc.*, ii, pp. 131, 166 (Frankfort, 794). There is no evidence that the
popes had a *sacrum palatium* before 813. For this and the following, see H. Fichtenau,
MIÖG, lix.

chrysotriklinos.[1] It had the appearance of a church and was also used for liturgical purposes. It served the worship of God as well as the worship of His representative, the *basileus*.

The *chrysotriklinos* was a cupola upon square foundations and had been built by Justinian's successor. Two examples of this type of building, still extant, are the church of SS. Sergios and Bacchos in Constantinople and the church of San Vitale in Ravenna. The same forms are clearly visible in the *Anastasis*, the round church above the Holy Sepulchre in Jerusalem. The gradual development of this form can be traced in earlier churches and especially in baptisteries. These churches and baptisteries, however, are merely precursors. The characteristic type, with a number of clearly defined features, was not fully developed until the time of Justinian.[2]

We have fairly full evidence about the palace Chapel which Charles planned to build in Aix-la-Chapelle. The brick-work at least was completed by 798, and the plan corresponded in almost all important details to the *chrysotriklinos*. Although Charles had never seen Constantinople, he was well informed by his envoys about the churches of that city.[3] Moreover, there were Greeks in Italy, and others among his own retinue, who could provide information on such matters. Much technical knowledge must have been required in addition. There was, however, a building very similar to the *chrysotriklinos* within the king's own dominions, namely the church of San Vitale in Ravenna. Charles's architects were able to study this building and examine its structure, and so it became the immediate model for the palace chapel at Aix-la-Chapelle. This is,

---

[1] A. Vogt, *Le livre des cérémonies*, 1935, i, c. 1, p. 17 ; c. 41, p. 163 ; op. cit., 1939–40, ii, c. 15. Constantine Porphyrogennetos only wrote in the tenth century; but the *chrysotriklinos* had been completed by Justin II (565–578).

[2] There is a large literature on the subject. I would refer only to the following : J. Hubert, *L'art pré-roman*, 1939, pp. 68 sqq. ; R. Krautheimer, in : *Journal of the Warburg and Courtauld Institutes*, 1942, v, pp. 1 sqq. ; A. Grabar, *Martyrium*, 1946, 1.— A small round building had stood on the spot on which Charles had the Palace Chapel erected. It had been used for the keeping of relics ; H. Schiffers, *Karl des Grossen Relinquienschatz und die Anfänge der Aachenfahrt, Veröffentlichungen des Bischöflichen Diozesanarchivs Aachen*, 1951, x, pp. 87 sqq. This might have suggested to Charles the Great the idea of building a round Palace Chapel ; but one could not argue that the chapel which he caused to be erected was in any way similar to the original chapel in which the relics had formerly been kept.

[3] *Libri Carolini*, iv, c. 3 ; MGH, *Conc.*, ii, Suppl., p. 177.

of course, a well-known fact. But the reason why this church and no other was chosen as a model for the chapel at Aix-la-Chapelle, has not always been understood.

There are thus good reasons to maintain that Charles the Great, in the years immediately preceding his coronation, was already copying a building which contained the hall of the throne of the Byzantine rulers and which formed the centre of the vast imperial palaces. The object was not to make a replica, exact in all details, of the Byzantine model. On the contrary certain modifications were introduced, to take account of the different theological and political views which the Franks upheld. In spite of his wish for equality of status with the rulers of the east, Charles could not agree to the cult with which the emperor in Constantinople was surrounded, and therefore he could not allow it to find expression in the design of his own building. In the *chrysotriklinos* in Constantinople the ruler's throne stood in the east, in place of the altar. Charles, on the other hand, ' gave to God what was God's ' and had his throne placed in the choir of the western part of the building.

The different conception of the ruler's position which prevailed among the Franks was even more explicit in another work which owes its origin to the intellectual conflict with the east, the *Libri Carolini* or the ' Caroline books '.[1] The treatise which passes under this name was written to prepare the ground for a great synod summoned to Frankfort in 794 as a countermove to the Council of Nicea. The bishops who assembled in Frankfort regarded their meeting as an ' orthodox council ' which, under the presidency of the Frankish king, was called together to annul the decrees issued by the œcumenical council of the east under the presidency of the empress Irene, and to demonstrate that the Greek rulers had given their support to false doctrines and could therefore not claim to be considered orthodox.

The task facing the synod of Frankfort was certainly not easy. The problem of the worship of images, which the council of Nicea had attempted to solve, had for decades caused open enmity between Rome and Constantinople. But at the Council of Nicea it had been settled to the satisfaction of the pope.

---

[1] About the authors, cf. ch. II, p. 30 n. 4.

Irene, supported by the anti-iconoclastic party which had been persecuted in the east, had reintroduced the cult of images to which the western church adhered. In spite of this the *Libri Carolini* argued that the theologians of Nicea, including the papal legate, had succumbed to theological errors. The argument was based upon a faulty Latin translation of the Greek texts; but Charles's friends, although they were fully aware of the true meaning of the original text, took advantage of the faulty Latin version to prove that error had been committed.[1]

Both in Aix-la-Chapelle and in Frankfort it was well known that the formula devised at Nicea had destroyed the whole point of the controversy. In that formula distinction was made between the material image and the object represented by the image. It was permissible to worship a saint in the form of his image; but the worship of the image itself was condemned as idolatry. The supporters of the two opposing parties in the east could well be satisfied with such a compromise, and further discussion had become superfluous. Charles's theologians, on the other hand, refused to accept it, on the pretext that the distinction suggested by the formula was too subtle to be practicable. Such was the background and the theological content of the *Libri Carolini*. But in reality the theology was subordinate to political motives, and the real aim was to accuse the Greeks and their rulers of intellectual corruption. The *Libri Carolini* insisted that the priests and ' kings ' of the east, tempted by arrogance, pride and vain-glory, had sacrificed the salvation of their souls and destroyed the unity of the church.[2] The Byzantine emperors had idolized themselves and pretended ' to govern together with God ' and to be ' divine '; they even spoke of the emperor's ' divine ears '. In reality, however, they were not —as their own courtiers claimed—like the Apostles, but were mortals, chasing after transient things.

Charles seems scarcely to have realized that this thorough-going attack on the formulas of Byzantine ceremonial applied not only to his own contemporaries in the eastern empire but

---

[1] W.v.d. Steinen, *Quellen u. Forschungen aus italienischen Archiven u. Bibliotheken*, 1929, xxi, 25 ; and the same author in : *Neues Archiv*, xlix, pp. 262 sq.
[2] *Libri Carolini, praefatio*.

also to the founder of the imperial cult—to the emperor Constantine himself, the great model of the secular ruler, who had desired to be buried, after his death, as ' the thirteenth Apostle '. If, however, the exaggeration of political propaganda is discounted, it would seem that this energetic attack on the tendency at Byzantium to efface the boundaries between the human and the divine, was quite sincere. In the eyes of the Franks, not even the master of the world was more than the servant of Christ. In any other standpoint they sensed a pagan undertone.[1]

The Byzantine court passed over the Frankish charges in contemptuous silence. Scarcely any mention was made of the western ' barbarian ' king who had, after all, acknowledged the sovereignty of the true Roman emperor by the acceptance of the Byzantine title of *patricius*.[2] In the eyes of Byzantium Charles's attack on Irene was merely another revolt of a minor potentate against the central authority. Even after his coronation Charles, like other pretenders of his kind, lacked the necessary acclamation by the guardians of the constitution in the imperial capital of Constantinople. Only one Byzantine chronicler reports the events which took place at Christmas 800, and he holds them up to ridicule. Leo III, so his report runs, utterly ignorant of the proper ceremonial, anointed Charles ' from top to toe '. The ceremony, therefore, amounted to nothing more than the conferment of extreme unction![3]

Charles sought to obtain equality of rank with the rulers of the east by raising his own position and by discrediting theirs in the eyes of his contemporaries. The *Libri Carolini* attempted the latter. The Council of Frankfort and, so it would seem, the erection of the palace chapel at Aix-la-Chapelle, illustrated the positive side of this policy. There are other examples which testify to his aspirations. At the time of the synod of Frankfort, or a little later, Alcuin wrote a letter to Charles in which he not only praised him as the defender of the faith but also solemnly bestowed on him the *nomen*—i.e. not only the name, but also

[1] Ibid. ; also iii, 19, p. 142 ; iv, 5, p. 180 ; v, 20, p. 211, etc.
[2] E. Dölger, in : Th. Mayer, ed., *Der Vertrag von Verdun*, 843, 1943, p. 212 n. 14.   [3] Op. cit., pp. 213 sq.

the honour and dignity[1]—of the biblical king David.[2] Such
a title was meaningful—certainly more meaningful than the
nicknames which Alcuin was wont to bestow upon his friends
and pupils ; for in Byzantium it was customary for the people
solemly to acclaim the emperor as ' the other David '. At the
sixth Council of Constantinople[3] pope Leo II himself had conformed to this custom.

The influence of Byzantium on Frankish thought becomes
even more obvious if we add to these examples the testimony
of the poets, that Charles the Great was planning to build ' a new
Rome ' in Aix-la-Chapelle ;[4] for the designation ' new Rome '
had been applied hitherto to Constantinople alone. It is easy
to regard such words as mere poetical phrases, since it is inconceivable that Aix-la-Chapelle should have rivalled Rome or
Constantinople. But during the Middle Ages people not only
weighed the material forms of things but also their symbolic
significance. Materially, Aix-la-Chapelle was a palace like other
royal palaces. But symbolically it could be considered a new
Rome if one or the other of its buildings were constructed according to a Roman or neo-Roman model. The representation of
a gate or of some towers and a segment of a wall on a seal sufficed
to indicate that the whole town was meant.

In the field of practical politics, Charles's position was
strengthened as Irene's difficulties increased. Constantine VI
tried in vain to concentrate all power in his own hands and made
himself so unpopular that it was possible for Irene, in 797, to
have him removed. His mother caused him to be blinded in
the very room in which she had given birth to him. In the
following year, it is reported, Greek ambassadors appeared

---

[1] H. Fichtenau, *Karl d. Grosse u. das Kaisertum*, MIÖG, lxi, pp. 259 sqq.

[2] H. Fichtenau, *Byzanz u. d. Pfalz von Aachen*, MIÖG, 1951, lix, p. 29 ; cf.
MGH, *Epp.*, iv, pp. 84 sq., No. 41.

[3] MPL, xcvi, col. 409 sq. ; H. Fichtenau, op. cit., p. 30.—E. Stengel (*Kaisertitel
u. Souveränitätsidee, Deutsches Archiv f. Geschichte d. Mittelalters*, 1939, iii, pp. 3 sqq.)
attributed to Alcuin the role of a propagator of an 'Anglo-Saxon idea of empire '
to which he introduced the Frankish court. But it has been proved by R. Drögereit
by a thorough investigation of the sources that ' there was no Anglo-Saxon idea of
empire' ; ZSSRg, 1952, lxix, p. 72. Cf. H. Loyn, in : *History*, 1955, xl, pp. 111–115.

[4] *Karolus Magnus et Leo papa*, MGH, *Poet.*, i, pp. 366 sqq. ; cf. C. Erdmann,
Forschungen zur politischen Ideenwelt d. frühen Mittelalters, 1951, pp. 21 sq. H. Löwe, in :
Wattenbach-Levison, *Deutschlands Geschichtsquellen*, 1953, ii, pp. 243 sqq., does not
believe that the poem originated before Charles's coronation.

before Charles to transfer the imperial authority to him, (*ut traderent ei imperium*).[1] These ambassadors can only have been enemies of Irene, trying to gain support in the west. No doubt Charles was too shrewd to believe their promises. All the same, this embassy, if it took place, is likely to have strengthened the self-confidence of the Franks and confirmed their feeling of superiority over the east. Charles must have appeared to his followers, at that time, as the representative of the principle of order, while the rest of the Christian world was in chaos. Alcuin wrote in 799 that the emperor had been ignominiously deposed by his own subjects and that the pope had been maltreated by the Romans. Through these actions the church was sullied with crimes and had lost its bearings. The safety of the Christian church, therefore, rested on the shoulders of Charles, ' the governor of Christendom ', who was superior to both pope and emperor in the power, the wisdom and the dignity of his government.[2] The way in which the political situation of these years was described was reminiscent of the way in which an earlier situation had been described. Half a century previously it had been argued that, since the powerless Merovingians had lost their grip on the actual government and since the true governor of the Franks lacked the title to the crown which was his in fact, the Frankish *maior domus* Pepin ought to be king, in order to avoid disturbance of the divinely-appointed order.[3] Alcuin, of course, did not suggest that Charles ought to become emperor. If such plans were being fostered, they were not harboured by Alcuin but by the men who were Charles's political counsellors and who accompanied him on his journey to Rome.

The main object of Charles's journey to Rome was to re-establish the authority of pope Leo III who, after having been imprisoned in Rome by his enemies, had managed to escape and flee to Charles. Charles presided in person over the synod in Rome at which these events and many others were discussed.[4]

---

[1] H. Löwe, *Eine Kölner Notiz zum Kaisertum Karls d. Grossen, Rheinische Viertel-iahrsblätter*, 1949, xiv, pp. 7 sqq.

[2] MGH, *Epp.*, iv, pp. 288 sq., No. 174.

[3] ' Ut non conturbaretur ordo ', *Annales Regni Francorum*, p. 8.

[4] Not even the *Annales Regni Francorum*, though they are silent about the events leading up to the coronation, maintain that the re-establishment of Leo III was the only subject discussed ; ibid., p. 112.

Our source for the proceedings of the synod is the Annals of Lorsch; but scholars have cast doubt on the authority of this chronicle on the grounds that it is not contemporary. It seems, however, that the author of the Annals possessed and used the official minutes of the proceedings.[1] He was not an insignificant monk, but one of the most eminent prelates of the realm, Richbod, bishop of Trier and abbot of Lorsch.[2] His account states that the fathers of the synod, together with the reinstated pope, decided to 'nominate' Charles as emperor because, since a woman ruled in Constantinople, there was no east-Roman emperor and the imperial throne was vacant. Charles, on the other hand, they urged, was in possession of Rome and the other imperial cities in Italy, Gaul and Germany.[3] According to Richbod, 'king Charles did not wish to reject such a petition; he submitted in all humility to God, and, besought by the priests and by the whole Christian people, received the *nomen* (i.e. dignity and power) of emperor and the consecration by pope Leo'.

The famous events of December 25th, 800, had therefore a background of past history. They represented the culmination of proceedings that had been discussed and agreed upon by Charles. The idea of a papal *coup d'état* is out of the question. Einhard's well-known report that Charles later expressed his dissatisfaction at the way in which Leo III had proceeded,[4] cannot possibly refer to the fact of the consecration itself but can only refer to the particular manner in which it was carried out. Einhard had probably read in Suetonius that many of the ancient emperors had been reluctant to receive their title. Some show of reluctance was even part of Byzantine etiquette, because it was held that the man who did not seek power was the one ordained to have it.[5] Bearing such formalities in mind, Einhard recounted Charles's deprecatory remark; but it would be a mistake to interpret it as referring to the consecration itself.

[1] For the proof of this contention through an examination of the style of the *Annales Laureshamenses* see H. Fichtenau, *Karl d. Grosse und das Kaisertum*, MIÖG, 1953, lxi, pp. 317 sqq.

[2] Ibid., pp. 287 sqq.

[3] *Annales Laureshamenses*, MGH, *Script.*, i, p. 38.

[4] Einhard, op. cit., c. 28.

[5] For references and proof see H. Fichtenau, op. cit., pp. 265 sqq.

Possibly Charles disliked the fact that the chorus of acclamation, which was considered a decisive factor in the election of a king, had been intoned only by the ' Roman people ' and not by the Franks as well. During the Mass, when Charles had risen from Prayer, Leo went up to him and placed the crown on his head. The Romans, with whom the pope must have come to some understanding, thundered : ' To Charles the Augustus, crowned of God, the great and pacific Emperor, long life and victory '.[1] After the acclamation had been repeated three times, the Pope ' worshipped '[2] Charles ' after the custom of the ancient rulers ', i.e. of the Roman emperors ; in other words, following Byzantine custom, Leo III threw himself on the ground in front of the emperor. No doubt, he was anxious to take all precautions against a possible Byzantine charge that, owing to the non-observance of the customary ceremonial, the coronation was null and void.

Thus Charles was declared emperor of Christendom. From now on he considered himself a true emperor, no longer inferior to any of the earlier emperors of the east. It is significant that during his lifetime there was no further controversy about the worship of images ; for after the coronation there was no point in provoking the Byzantines through polemics. The problem now was, rather, to gain recognition of the Frankish empire from Byzantium. Such recognition was more likely to be secured through cautious friendliness than through abuse. Charles, it seems, even considered the possibility of resolving the whole conflict once and for all by the time-honoured method of a political marriage. On an earlier occasion, when a dangerous coalition between the rulers of Bavaria, Benevento and Byzantium had taken shape, the tension had been eased by the betrothal of Charles's daughter Rotrud to a son of the Empress Irene, and

---

[1] *Liber Pontificalis*, L. Duchesne ed., Paris, 1892, ii, p. 7. The *Annales Regni Francorum* omit the word ' *piissimo* ' and add the expression *Romanorum* to *imperatori*. One may well argue as to which form is the more correct. P. E. Schramm writes as follows : ' We must . . . assume that, already before the more or less turbulent events, opinions as to what actually had happened, were divided. It may well be that some were acclaiming the ' emperor ' and others the ' emperor of the Romans ' and, that, therefore, all sources are equally right.' (*Die Anerkennung Karls des Grossen als Kaiser, Historische Zeitschrift*, 1951, clxxii, p. 502.)

[2] ' Et post laudes ab Apostolico more antiquorum principum adoratus est ' (*Annales Regni Francorum*, loc cit.).

this had made possible the subjection of Tassilo of Bavaria. Now, once again, Charles decided to use similar methods, and, if we may believe the Byzantine sources,[1] attempted to consolidate his imperial title by a marriage with the by no means youthful ruler of the East. He sent envoys to Constantinople to convey the proposal to Irene, supported by messengers from the pope, who had every reason to desire the success of the plan. If the ruler who was master of Rome and Jerusalem, were to become also the master of new-Rome, the whole of Christendom would be united, and Constantinople would have to bow to the successor of Peter.

It is hardly possible to-day to size up all the perspectives and possibilities embodied in such a plan. Its success would have created a gigantic empire, capable of expanding not only in the Balkans but also on the continent of Asia. Such a body politic would have lacked homogeneity and sooner or later would have fallen to pieces. But if it had lasted for one single generation only, some of the projects so clumsily and so laboriously conceived in the kingdom of the Franks might have borne a rich harvest. Had the marriage taken place, Charles could only have won recognition in Byzantium by taking up residence in Constantinople as co-emperor with Irene. He could not, of course, have withdrawn permanently from the country upon which his whole dominion was based, but an alternation of the capital between east and west might have furthered in an extraordinarily fruitful way the exchange both of men and of ideas. Western civilization would then have taken a different course ; but if one measures its qualities not by its wealth but by the originality of its achievements, it is doubtful whether this would have been an advantage.

The empress Irene was not disinclined to become the wife of the western emperor. The resistance of the eastern magnates was, however, all the greater. In the end, Charles's envoys became the eye-witnesses of one of the many *coups d'état* which marred the history of Byzantium. Irene, instead of finding a

---

[1] Theophanes, *Chronographia*, quoted in H. Dannenbauer ed., *Quellen z. Geschichte d. Kaiserkrönung Karls d. Grossen*, Berlin, 1931, p. 25. Both K. Heldmann (op. cit., pp. 376 sqq., and F. Dölger, op. cit., p. 217) consider this report credible.

husband, lost her crown. She survived her fall and her exile to a distant convent only by a few months.

Charles's cause suffered severely from the turn which events had taken. With the succession of the logothete Nikephoros, the Byzantine throne was once again occupied by a man. Henceforward it was no longer possible to argue that the imperial title was not fitted for a woman. Nevertheless, Charles's envoys, bishop Jesse of Amiens and Count Helmgaud, did not return with altogether empty hands. They were accompanied by a Byzantine deputation sent to conduct negotiations about the recognition of the western empire. The negotiations, however, were not concluded successfully until two years before Charles's death. The compromise then concluded amounted to this : a new Byzantine embassy solemnly ' acclaimed ' Charles emperor, but not Roman emperor. Even this compromise, however, did not remove all difficulties, for Charles's successor, Louis the Pious, still had to face Byzantine claims.

As far as the eastern empire was concerned the concession of the imperial title to the king of the Franks had been necessitated by the difficult political situation of the times. In the long run, however, it remained without significance. Nominally, there was room for many emperors—as there was room later for an emperor of the Bulgarians. But, after Charles's coronation, as before it, the Greek *basileus* remained the only emperor of the Romans. At the same time, the Byzantine recognition of the Frankish imperial title entailed Charles's renunciation of all claims to extend his rule to the east. When Charles spoke of ' peace between the eastern and western empires ',[1] it was clear that things were still where they had been before and that the universal empire of all Christians remained an ideal unrelated to political realities. Just as Byzantium, whenever possible, remained proudly aloof from the Franks, so the western empire of Charles withdrew under his successors into itself and tried to forget what was going on outside its borders. In practice, therefore, this ' empire ' shrank into the ' Occident '. True, ' the Occident ' covered an immense space if one considered only its continental

[1] R. Faulhaber, *Der Reichseinheitsgedanke zur Zeit der Karolinger*, Berlin, 1931, p. 18.

extension and did not measure it with the eyes of the Mediterranean seafarer. At the price of this separation, Europe found
itself and was able to rise, a spiritual unit, from the ruins of the
Carolingian empire.

Throughout its existence the Carolingian empire was, of
course, based upon the foundations of Frankish kingship in
terms of both law and power. Unlike the citizens of the Byzantine
empire, only very few of its inhabitants considered themselves
as members of a Christian world-state rather than as Franks,
Saxons or Lombards. Nor was the position altered when in
802 Charles obliged his subjects to take a new oath of allegiance.
The promises of fealty and devotion to the king contained in
the earlier oath of 789, were replaced by promises to lead a pious
and god-fearing life in the Christian sense.[1] At that time the
power of the Frankish sword still seemed to coincide with the
demands of the Gospels. Throughout the happy years during
which the empire was built, the Franks cared little about the
inner tensions and contradictions of an edifice that had risen so
rapidly. The epoch of Charles's rule was characterized in many
spheres by the co-existence of diverging tendencies without
apparent signs of conflict. Charles's own happy nature and
powerful personality knew how to combine incompatible traits.
Everything was attuned to the working of his personality. But
when it was removed, people went their own ways. The heritage
which Charles the Great left to his successors was a bitter one.

---

[1] MGH, *Cap.*, i, p. 92 ; c. 3. Cf. R. Faulhaber, op. cit., p. 17, and G. Waitz,
Deutsche Verfassungsgeschichte, Berlin, 1883, iii (2nd ed.), p. 224.

CHAPTER IV

THE COURT 'SCHOLARS

During the first two decades of the reign of Charles the Great the Frankish nation was, according to Einhard's testimony, ' almost poor '.[1] We have other information to prove that this statement was more than a rhetorical phrase designed to emphasize, by contrast, the wealth of the later years. During a famine of the year 780 the bishops, abbots and counts of the kingdom were obliged to make a contribution for the benefit of the stricken districts. The wealthy ones were to pay one pound of silver ; and the others were to contribute even less.[2]

Nevertheless a king was expected to distribute gold among his followers. Nobody asked where he took it from. Charles was highly praised for his practice of the old German princely virtue of generosity.[3] He would not have been able to practise it without the income derived from those military expeditions which, often enough, were barely disguised wars of aggression. No doubt there were military, political and religious motives for such enterprises. But one must not forget the very simple necessity for a ruler to capture loot and to distribute it ' without setting his heart on it '.[4] The Saxon treasures found at the Irminsul in 722 went straight into the coffers of the magnates of the kingdom,[5] and this practice was maintained until their greed was satiated. The enormous booty plundered from the main Ring of the Avars in 795 was carried to Aix-la-Chapelle and thence, some of it, to Rome. It was no longer reserved for the exclusive benefit of the magnates. Some time earlier, but not later than 794,[6] Charles had introduced a new coinage of greater weight. This measure was probably designed to further foreign trade,

---

[1] Op. cit., c. 13.   [2] MGH, *Cap.*, i, 21, p. 52.
[3] Thus Notker, op. cit., i, 29 ; MGH, *Script.*, ii, p. 744.   [4] Loc. cit.
[5] AS, i (2nd ed.), p. 129.
[6] A. Dopsch, *Wirtschaftsentwicklung d. Karolingerzeit*, Weimar, 1922, ii, pp. 312 sq. and pp. 321 sq.

and showed that the military and political progress of the kingdom
had resulted in a certain degree of economic prosperity.

According to Einhard the Franks were more enriched by
the treasure of the Avars captured in 795 than by all the other
' wars waged against them '.[1] Fifteen waggons, drawn by four
oxen each, were needed to carry away the loot of gold and silver
and of precious garments.[2] This report could well be true.
Byzantium alone paid during almost a century a yearly tribute
of between 80,000 and 100,000 gold *solidi* to the Kagans of the
Avars. Once they even paid twice that sum.[3] Now the Frankish
king had suddenly come into possession of a part of those fabulous
treasures, which probably compared favourably with the sum
total at the disposal of the Byzantine rulers for diplomatic
purposes during those troubled years.[4] There seems to have
been a political reason why Charles had part of the Avar loot
sent to Rome.[5] What was left behind was obviously sufficient
not only to cover the daily needs for a long time, but also to
make available the means which facilitated the cultural progress
of the royal court and of the kingdom.

It would certainly be one-sided to see in this single event,
as the chroniclers tend to do, the cause for the development or
that prosperity which was so characteristic of the third quarter
of Charles's reign. Gold came in from all the newly-won territories. ' Treasures from various nations '[6] accumulated in Aix-
la-Chapelle in many forms, including presents from ambassadors
and tribute, such as was paid, for instance, by the Duchy of
Benevento to the tune of 7,000 gold solidi every year.[7] Theodulf,
in a poetical epistle, invited even the Caliph of Cordova to follow
the example of the Avars and to send the accumulated treasures

---

[1] Loc cit.
[2] *Annales Northumbran.*, 795 ; cf. AS, ii, p. 104 n. 2.
[3] Ibid., p. 102.
[4] According to E. Stein (*Studien zur Geschichte d. byzant. Reiches*, Stuttgart, 1919,
p. 142), it seems likely that the total Byzantine revenue was ' considerably less '
than 8 million *solidi*. The army and the navy cost between 2 and 3 million *solidi*
yearly ; it is probable that the ' diplomatic budget ' was a mere fraction of that
sum.
[5] A. Brackmann, in : *Sitzungsberichte d. preussischen Akademie*, 1931, ix, p. 75.
[6] *Chron. Moissiac.*, 796 ; MGH, *Script.*, i, p. 303.
[7] B. Simson, *Jahrbücher d. fränkischen Reiches unter Ludwig d. Frommen*, Leipzig,
1874, i, p. 28

of his capital to the Frankish king.[1] The Christians under Moorish rule felt that the king of the Franks was not so much concerned with their liberation from the heathen yoke as with gold. This is proved, among other things, by a story related by a monk in the monastery of Silos, even though the story itself may have been an invention.[2]

Not only were foreign nations compelled to hand over their wealth, but also the magnates of the kingdom were obliged to make yearly 'donations' to Charles's coffers. Many of them were the better able to pay because they held profitable positions in the royal administration. As we shall see later, not only counts but also *missi dominici* exploited their authority for financial purposes and saw in the collection of personal 'donations' the most important aspect of their activity.

All this was possible only because the political progress under Charles had brought at least a measure of prosperity to the mass of his subjects. The king's peace, the establishment of which was the ruler's paramount duty, may have had more exalted purposes—namely, the promotion of order in the universe in conformity with God's will—but it also had strictly material aspects. The country could thrive only when civil war and private feuds had been curbed. Mobilization for service on the frontiers was after all less oppressive than arson and devastation in one's home district. Only when peace had been established was it possible for trade to flourish. Such trade was, by modern standards, of small importance; nevertheless there was enough of it for one of the court poets to imitate Ovid's description of the golden age : ' The whole earth is carrying the traffic of goods ; poverty has fled from the earth to Hades. There is no scarcity in this our age and the world abounds in riches.'[3] At least this is how people at court saw it—or wanted to see it when it was a question of flattering Charles.

It seems that the treasure brought to Aix-la-Chapelle considerably reduced the cost to the royal lands of rewarding loyal

[1] MGH, *Poet.*, i, p. 484, No. 25, v. 43 sq.
[2] ' Quum Caesaraugustam (Saragossa) civitatem accessisset more Francorum auro corruptus, absque ullo sudore pro eripienda a barbarorum dominatione sancta ecclesia ad propria revertitur.' AS, i (2nd ed.), p. 300 n. 5.
[3] Naso, MGH, *Poet.*, i, p. 390.

G

followers. It had always been customary to reward the magnates for service to the king with royal land, manors or villages and at times with church property. We know of cases where people were invested with a whole abbey and its property. To mention only one example, the man who discovered Pepin's conspiracy against Charles was gratefully rewarded by the king with St. Denis, the most famous of all abbeys. Even Louis the Pious was forced, in contravention of his own edicts, to hand out imperial abbeys to secular magnates. He was even compelled to break up the ancient hereditary property of his house in order to give some kind of reward to those who had supported him against his sons.

In times of stress no ruler could afford to scrutinize too closely the worthiness or even the education of a claimant for ecclesiastical property. But during the second half of Charles's reign there was a notable change. There was now available a vast reservoir of confiscated property in the newly-subjected provinces, all available as rewards for political services. There was also the accumulated treasure of the kingdom. At least a part of church property, such as important bishoprics and abbeys, could now be distributed for non-political purposes. In fact, it was used to attract poets and scholars, theologians and teachers —or men who were all of these—from the provinces, and even from Spain and England, and to attach them permanently to the intellectual circle at Charles's court. The newly-acquired wealth made the so-called ' Carolingian Renaissance ' possible : it served not only to draw the men but also enabled Charles to commission buildings and luxurious manuscripts. These resources would not have been available if the kingdom had not flourished during the later years of Charles's reign.[1]

It may appear one-sided to stress the material aspects of culture when it is well known that its rise is not conditioned by material circumstances and that culture often flourishes spontaneously in times of economic decline. But in such cases civilization is always carried forward by its own impulses, and develops according to its own inherent laws. How different it was in the days of Charles ! Splendid manuscripts were needed in

[1] E. Patzelt, *Karolingische Renaissance*, Wien, 1924, p. 111.

order to proclaim and embody the prestige of the Frankish kingdom. They were either acquired wherever they happened to be found or copied irrespective of the quality of the original. ' Whether the originals used by this or that school of copyists as a model for their " style " were of high or low quality, must often have been determined accidentally '.[1] Nobody was troubled by the fact that the models differed ' in age, in origin, in style and in quality '.[2] The position was analagous in regard to architecture. In Aix-la-Chapelle men felt close to the spirit of King Solomon ; but at the same time they sensed an affinity with the style of Constantine the Great and of Christian antiquity in its western as well as in its eastern, or Byzantine, form. On the other hand, the Lombard Fardulf, who governed St. Denis, erected for Charles a royal palace ' in the style of our fore-fathers '—that is to say, in all probability in the style of German wooden building.[3]

There was little in this splendid, official art that grew natur-ally. Almost everything was commissioned from above. A poet has described Charles supervising the rebuilding of Aix-la-Chapelle. He stood at an elevated point and designated the place for the ' forum ', the ' senate ', the theatre and baths and the aqueduct.[4] Not even the ' Lateran ' by the church of St. Mary, the hall in which the ' councils ' were to be held, was omitted.[5] It is unlikely that any of these buildings were erected because of love for classical antiquity. They can only be explained by reference to late, Christian antiquity. The popes described Charles as a ' new Constantine '. On the frescoes of the Palace of Ingel-heim, Charles did not appear by the side of Ninus, Alexander, Romulus, Hannibal, and the other pagan rulers of the world ; but, together with his forefathers Charles Martel and Pepin, by the side of the Christian emperors, Constantine and Theodosius.[6]

[1] G. Dehio, *Geschichte d. deutschen Kunst,* Berlin, 1930, i, p. 59.
[2] W. Köhler, *Die karolingischen Miniaturen*, Berlin, 1933, i, 2, p. 306.
[3] Fardulf, *carm.*, i, v. 17 ; MGH, *Poet.*, i, p. 353. Cf. H. Naumann, in : *Karl der Grosse oder Charlemagne*, 1935, p. 31.
[4] MGH, *Poet.*, i, pp. 368 sq., v. 94 sqq.
[5] MGH, *Cap.*, i, p. 334 n. 1.
[6] MGH, *Poet.*, ii, pp. 63–66 (Ermoldus Nigellus, 4, 172). The paintings at Ingelheim were completed in 826. It is not certain whether they were begun during Charles's lifetime.

Charles the Great wanted to build a ' new Rome '[1] in order to displace the New Rome of Constantinople, which considered itself the capital of Christendom. On the other hand, Alcuin's desire to build a new Athens in the land of the Franks, was certainly destined to remain a mere literary allusion.[2] Charles himself pursued the ideals of classical antiquity only in so far as they were connected with his religious and political concepts. He never sought them for their own sake.

Although the remains of Charles's architectural activities hardly convey to us an idea of imperial greatness, we must not forget that they exhausted all the technical and economic resources available at the time. Charles's building activities not only used up any ready cash there might have been, but were also a considerable burden upon the whole country. Few dared to criticize during Charles's lifetime; but there is at least one complaint that it was hardly necessary for a king who owned flourishing lands, had inherited vast properties and enjoyed large revenues, to erect his palaces upon the tears of the poor. He should use his own income, it was argued, supplemented by the donations of the magnates, to carry out these building plans.[3] A more outspoken criticism was expressed against one of the prelates of the kingdom, the abbot of Fulda, who had been infected by the imperial passion for building. It was said that his enormous and superfluous building activities ought to be stopped. Everything ought to be done with restraint and due purpose.[4]

The models for the style of building were derived indiscriminately from a large variety of sources. Charles's scholars, who were responsible for the education of the public as well as for the culture of the court, were collected in much the same way. He never succeeded in finding the dozen men stipulated by Augustine. Nevertheless, Angilbert was his ' Homer ' and, although he had no Ovid, he had his ' Naso '. Such men were

---

[1] Cf. for instance Naso, MGH, *Poet.*, i, p. 386, esp. verse 40.

[2] MGH, *Poet.*, ii, p. 279, No. 170: 'forsan Athenae nova perficeretur in Francia, immo multo excellentior.'

[3] Smaragdus, *Via regia*, c. 27, MPL, cii, col. 966. For the date, see M. Manitius, *Geschichte d. lateinischen Literatur im Mittelalter*, München, 1911, i, p. 463.

[4] MGH, *Epp.*, iv, p. 594, No. 33 (812).

a requisite part of the court of an emperor, just as were a Forum and a Lateran. Like the buildings, they were expensive and had the task of displaying both the power and the dignity of the new empire.

It has sometimes been alleged that idealism prompted the artists and scholars of Europe to gather at the court of Charles in order to unite their efforts for the cultivation of classical beauty and wisdom. They were, after all, so the argument runs, true humanists who endeavoured to re-kindle the fire of culture and to keep it alive for coming generations. They had no interest in material gain. Alcuin, the model of this kind of humanism, repeatedly praised poverty and impressed his idealistic motives upon his readers. Notker, also, explained that the first of the ' humanists ' had not been prompted by desire for material gain when they had first approached the royal court. He wrote of two Irishmen who had landed in Gaul and had found that there was a demand only for things that could be acquired commercially. Therefore they had offered themselves for sale much as street vendors would offer their goods. They had cried : ' Ho, everyone that desires wisdom, let him draw near and take it at our hands ; for it is wisdom that we have for sale.' King Charles himself negotiated with them about the price of wisdom. It turned out that the price was low. It comprised only the barest necessities in food and clothing.[1]

It would appear, thefore, that popular imagination, so remarkably represented by Notker, equated at least these modest, early heralds of wisdom with the travelling mimes and bards. Later on, of course, when there was not one from among the pupils of the palace school who was not given ' bishoprics and splendid monasteries ,[2] such confusion was no longer possible. None of the scholars, so far as we know, ever actually refused

[1] *Gesta Karoli*, c. 1. MGH, *Script.*, ii, p. 731. L. Halphen (*Études critiques sur l'histoire de Charlemagne*, Paris, 1921, p. 129 sq.) in view of the fact that the two Irishmen bear the names of historical persons from the reign of Louis the Pious, has dismissed the anecdote as worthless. I do not mean to defend the anecdote ; but I may be permitted to draw attention to the fact that already in 772 a *Clemens peregrinus* wrote a letter to Tassilo and the Bavarian nobility (MGH, *Epp.*, iv, pp. 496 sq.). There is therefore no reason why we should assume that Notker was writing about the Clement in the reign of Louis the Pious.

[2] Notker, op. cit., i, c. 8 ; MGH, *Script.*, ii, p. 734.

preferment in order to continue to live as a true philosopher in poverty and independence. Alcuin himself certainly did not do so. He was full of praise for Charles because the latter had generously honoured every one of the promises made at their first meeting. This was no exaggeration. Alcuin had obtained the monasteries of Ferrières, of St. Loup near Troyes, of Flavigny, of St. Jossé-sur-Mer, of Berg, and, above all, of St. Martin of Tours. The last was the famous abbey of which it was said that its abbot could travel from one end of the empire to the other without ever being compelled to spend a night in a house other than his own.[1] Alcuin had crossed the English Channel with a single companion. In the end he was the lord of 20,000 human beings.[2]

Einhard became no less wealthy, although he did not reach the peak of his prosperity until the reign of Louis the Pious. Probably only the fact that they were not ordained prevented both him and Alcuin from becoming archbishops, like so many of the lesser spirits of their circle. These included Beornrad of Sens, Richulf of Mayence, Richbod of Trier, not to mention such bishops as Arno of Salzburg, a special friend of Alcuin and, as abbot of St. Amand, his former neighbour.

Alcuin, when he grew old, was oppressed by the thought of eternity and began to fear for the salvation of his soul. His barge, he wrote, had been driven by the gales of the ' world ' into the vortex of wealth.[3] He added that he was making haste to send much money to England for prayers for his soul.[4] On the whole, however, there were no complaints that Charles rewarded the faithful scholars, who had lent him their pens and their knowledge, as generously as he rewarded his warriors and administrators. The scholars, in turn, showed their gratitude by bestowing on him the degree of a doctor of grammar, by praising him as a teacher of rhetoric and as the finest dialectician in the world, and by acknowledging him as the superior of Cato, Cicero and Homer.[5] Again and again they compared him with King David, the master of song and the Biblical type of Christ.

[1] C. Gaskoin, *Alcuin*, 1904, p. 95.
[2] MGH, *Epp.*, iv, p. 302, No. 182 ; p. 332, No. 200.
[3] Ibid., p. 97, No. 53.　　　　　　　　　　[4] Ibid., p. 33, No. 7.
[5] MGH, *Poet.*, i, pp. 367 sq., vv. 67 sqq. ; cf. vv. 79 sq.

It was taken for granted that Charles, like David, would find a place in the heavenly kingdom by the side of the saints.

Far be it from us to convey the impression that such a description of the relations between Charles and his scholars goes to the root of the phenomenon which is called the ' Carolingian Renaissance '. It was neither the gold nor the dignities conferred by Charles which had led an Alcuin to the problems of education or a Theodulf to theology. The latter would have espoused the anti-Arian cause without the *Libri Carolini* and without the quarrel with Byzantium. And it lay in Alcuin's blood to become the teacher and propagator of *sophia*. But the fact that such men gathered at the palace is most certainly not to be explained by idealistic motives alone. Precisely this was the real achievement of Charles the Great. He organized and centralized the cultural activities which otherwise would have remained scattered among a large number of different local schools. He created a broad material basis for the intellectual work of his scholars and their pupils by putting at their disposal the rich resources of his realm. He encouraged the best of the sons of his nobility to follow intellectual pursuits on the ground that a good education was the beginning of a career which would lead more certainly and more quickly to the highest posts in the realm than a purely worldly and military training.

As far as Charles himself was concerned, he believed that his own preoccupations with the arts and the sciences was not only permissible but the very duty of a ruler. ' We are concerned ', runs one of the Capitularies, ' to restore with diligent zeal the workshops of knowledge which, through the negligence of our ancestors, have been well-nigh deserted. We invite others, by our own example, as much as lies in our power, to learn to practise the liberal arts.'[1] He seems to be referring to his own ancestors in a sense wide enough to include the Merovingian kings, when in the Capitulary he emphasizes the contrast between his attitude and theirs. The justification of this attitude lay, for him, in the fact that it is ' our duty to ensure the progress of our churches '.[2] He was convinced that a decay of the church of

[1] Ibid., p. 301, No. 83 (Alcuin).
[2] *Epistola generalis*, MGH, *Cap.*, i, p. 80.

Christ through a ruler's negligence meant a disturbance of the universal order, a deviation from law and unity in favour of diabolical arbitrariness and confusion.

The good old order, however, was disturbed equally by the material decay of churches and by neglect of divine service. Thus there was need both for the building and repair of churches and for the restoration of a unified liturgy, purged of all accidental corruptions. The search for the latter necessitated accurate textual interpretation of the church-books as well as a reform of the chant which had deviated from the ' Gregorian ' norm. To restore the old order it was equally necessary to celebrate the movable feasts of the church on the correct day. Hence the renewed interest in astronomical studies. But liturgy, preaching, building of churches, and the calculation of the right dates of the feasts, required a mastery of nearly all of the seven ' liberal arts '.

People thought of order in the sense of legal order. Charles always thought of himself as a judge and acted like one. He took his task as a law-finder equally seriously in all matters connected with religion. Misunderstandings and additions, he thought, had corrupted the ecclesiastical law which had been written down, with the help of the Holy Spirit, by the venerable fathers of the church. It was therefore necessary to obtain a pure text which corresponded to the will of God. Charles turned to pope Hadrian —for where was he to procure such a text, if not from the successor of St. Peter? In this way he obtained a copy of the collection of canons and decretals of Dionysius Exiguus. This version of ecclesiastical law was made universally binding by a resolution of the synod of Aix-la-Chapelle in 802. The precious original itself was retained in Charles's library. All copies carried a certificate to the effect that they were copies from the ' authentic ' original.[1]

A similar course was pursued in order to obtain a correct and authoritative liturgical manual. On this occasion, however, Hadrian was embarrassed. He was not able to meet the demand for the pure sacramentary of Gregory the Great, ' as it had been

[1] L. Traube, in : *Abh. d. bayr. Akademie d. Wissenschaften, Phil.-Hist Kl.*, 1895, xxi, p. 675.

edited by its author '.[1] Nevertheless, the version sent from Rome was accepted at the court of the Frankish ruler as the authentic work.[2] It was laid down that henceforth all copies were to be made from that work. Fifteen such copies are still extant and they all carry the prescribed certificate. Thus it was believed that unity and purity had at last triumphed over the negligence of past generations. People were content because they were once more in tune with the old, divinely-established order. These achievements were not less important for the *renovatio* of the Christian empire than the imperial coronation itself.

There is a story that Romans and Franks once quarelled in front of Charles about the genuineness of the collection of the antiphonies of the ecclesiastical chant. Charles is said to have composed the quarrel by asking whether the spring or the brook was likely to have the purer water.[3] Whenever it was impossible for the original spring of such texts to be found in Rome, it was necessary for the scholars of the palace or perhaps for Charles himself to search for a pure brook. Thus Alcuin was given the task of preparing a correct text of the Bible, but in his last days the emperor together with his philological ' counsellors ', Syrian and Greek, was still labouring at this task.[4] Even where there was no question of divinely inspired books sanctioned by the church, we hear the slogan : back to the sources! A standard edition was prepared of the works of Gregory the Great,[5] and also an edition of the rule of St. Benedict,[6] as well as a collection of grammatical rules which was considered authentic because it had been brought from Rome.[7] Collections of sermons, the writings of the church fathers, apocryphal collections of letters, and even Vitruvius's treatise on architecture,[8] which was to be

---

[1] Alcuin's prologue to the *Sacramentarium Gregorianum* ; quoted by Th. Klauser, *Historisches Jahrbuch*, 1933, liii, 178 n. 30.

[2] Cf. Th. Klauser, op. cit., p. 181.

[3] L. Traube, op. cit., p. 674, after Johannes Diaconus, *Vita Gregorii*, MGH, *Script.*, ii, pp. 1, 9. [4] Thegan, MGH, *Script.*, ii, p. 592.

[5] M. Manitius, op. cit., i, p. 248.

[6] L. Traube, op. cit., pp. 600 sqq. [7] Ibid., p. 676.

[8] Ibid., p. 673. How anxious people were to imitate ancient models is shown by the fact that Einhard, in a letter which has come down to us, ordered the bricks for his church in Seligenstadt according to specifications that corresponded exactly to those of Roman buildings. In Seligenstadt as well as in the building of the Palace Chapel at Aix-la-Chapelle, the Roman foot was used as the unit of measurement. M. Buchner, *Einhards Künstler-u. Gelehrtenleben*, 1922, pp. 144, 220.

used as a guide for the building of churches, were all held in similar esteem. As far as classical authors are concerned, we can speak of a ' renaissance ' only in so far as they were caught up in the movement for the restoration of Christian texts which was promoted so energetically by Charles. His scholars saw him as the warlike hero who took the field against literary error.[1] All this was done in the service of the heavenly King—never for the sake of antiquarian interests. Similarly the art of writing,[2] liturgical chanting, and many other things, were reformed purely because of their religious implications.

It can hardly be maintained that Charles the Great in this way accomplished something new and original. He merely made himself responsible for a work which had commenced sporadically long before his time, largely without the backing of royal authority. St. Boniface himself had been not only the apostle of Germany but also the author of a grammar and of a manual for versification. Exactly as Alcuin did later, he had corrected the poetical works of his pupils.[3] The school of Utrecht had flourished under Pepin. It had been the centre of Frisia but had also been visited by Franks, Saxons, Angles and even by Bavarians and Suabians.[4] The reason why this school was never supported by Charles and was not even allowed to play a part in the conversion of the Saxons, although it was still flourishing at the end of the eighth century, was purely personal. It was because its head, Gregory, was a scion of the Merovingian house. He was politically so suspect to the descendant of the mayors of the palace that Charles did not even grant him a bishopric.[5] Apart from such considerations, however, Charles was more interested in organizing a cultural centre according to his own plans than in taking over a well-established school with all its personal as well as its institutional traditions. Gregory's work was connected with his city, Utrecht; but the school of the palace had to travel with the ruler. Only during the last years of Charles's reign did Aix-la-Chapelle itself become noteworthy as

---

[1] MGH. *Poet.*, i, p. 89.
[2] H. Fichtenau, *Mensch u. Schrift im Mittelalter*, Wien, 1946, pp. 150 sqq.
[3] R. Stachnik, *Die Bildung des Weltklerus in Frankreich*, Paderborn, 1926, p. 15.
[4] Liudger, *Vita Gregorii*, c. 11 ; MGH, *Script.*, xv, pp. 75 sq.
[5] AS, i (2nd ed.), p. 115.

the residence of scholars and their pupils.[1] This was probably due to practical considerations and was connected with Charles's plans for a permanent capital.

In Charles's eyes the circle of teachers and pupils he gathered together did not exist for the sake of knowledge and its propagation. A regular course in the seven liberal arts, the Trivium and the Quadrivium, was probably never given. The main purpose of the institution was to train the sons of noblemen and probably also many a commoner's son for the tasks of the secular as well as the ecclesiastical administration of the realm. The teachers themselves were by no means exclusively devoted to the contemplative life. Their advice on political matters was often required. Alcuin complained of the small degree of interest in such a theoretical discipline as astronomy. The students rejected it[2] because, unlike the king, they could not hope to derive any practical benefit from such knowledge.

The institution which contemporary sources described as the school of the palace, *schola palatina*, continued in a tradition which had begun under Constantine the Great and had been imitated under the Merovingians. It had been customary to maintain at court a school for young men to train them not only in letters but also in the use of arms and in aristocratic discipline and manners.[3] We must think of the palace school in this wider sense. It was more than a secondary school with headmaster and his staff. The young pupils had a personal tie to their master and that personal tie was an efficient substitute for a formally regulated institution. It would be wrong to see in Alcuin, and later in Einhard, the heads of an educational establishment.

It is a pity that we know hardly anything about the routine of the palace school. We can only surmise that there was a definite contrast between disciplined elementary instruction and a more informal kind of teaching for the more advanced pupils. We know of one instance where Charles himself meted out punishment during the course of elementary instruction.[4] Even

---

[1] Cf. H. Janitschek, in: K. Mentzel u. P. Corssen, ed., *Die Trierer Ada-Handschrift*, Leipzig, 1889, p. 64.
[2] MGH, *Epp.*, iv, p. 239, No. 148.
[3] E. Weniger, in: *Hist. Vierteljahrsschrift*, 1935, xxx, pp. 482 sq.
[4] See p. 32 above.

at meal-time education was not neglected. There is friendly irony in the description given by ' father Alcuin ' of how he himself, while giving pious instruction, did not fail to lubricate his throat with beer and wine so as ' to be able to teach and sing the better.'[1] Many a letter by the master himself proves that there was a fair amount of jovial drinking. On one occasion, when a journey to his English homeland had deprived him of his customary wine, he sent an urgent request for the two barrels which had been promised to him by Charles's own physician. He addressed a veritable dirge to one of the pupils and urged him to drink in the meantime in his stead, since he, Alcuin, was forced to lead a sad life far from the customary fountains of joy.[2]

Such letters are composed in conscious imitation of the spirit of classical antiquity. They have nevertheless also a Germanic root. We still possess hymns for holy days from the second half of the ninth century, each one of which concludes with an invitation to drink the health of the saint.[3] In spite of its pre-Christian origins, the custom of communal religious drinking survived well into the later Middle Ages.[4] In this field, the pupils' ability to learn seems to have surpassed by far their ability to learn astronomy. One of them, nicknamed ' the cuckoo ', must have gone especially far, for he was admonished by Arno of Salzburg ;[5] and Alcuin himself, aware of his own responsibility, wrote : ' Woe to me, if Bacchus should drown the cuckoo in his floods ! '[6]

The massive fleshiness which characterizes the human figure in the illuminated manuscripts of the palace school,[7] corresponds well to the tenor of life at court. This is true both for the scholars and for their pupils. Their boisterousness was no doubt toned down by the clerical garb worn by most of these men and youths.

---

[1] MGH, *Poet.*, i, p. 488, vv. 191 sqq. I do not believe that Dr. E. Shipley Duckett's translation of these lines (*Alcuin, Friend of Charlemagne*, New York, 1951, p. 106) is correct.

[2] MGH, *Epp.*, iv, p. 33, No. 8 ; cf. p. 318, No. 192, addressed to Theodulf, with an almost blasphemous use of Biblical quotations. Not even the idolising *Vita Alcuini* could pass over the delight he took in drinking wine : MGH, *Script.*, xv, p. 195, c. 23.

[3] MGH, *Poet.*, iv, pp. 350 sqq.

[4] S. Singer, *Germanisch-romanisches Mittelalter*, Zürich, 1935, p. 117.

[5] MGH, *Epp.*, iv, pp. 109 sq., No. 66.

[6] MGH, *Poet.*, i, p. 269.   [7] W. Köhler, op. cit., i, 2, p. 308.

But only a few of them were actually priests. Even Alcuin was only a deacon. Theodulf, the bishop of Orléans, had a daughter Gisla who participated, at least indirectly, by the side of her father in the artistic and liturgical activities of the court circle.[1] Angilbert and Einhard remained laymen even as abbots. Their whole tenor of life belonged to that plane on which the secular and the spiritual were united without much conflict. With some, such as Alcuin and Einhard, this continued unchanged until they reached extreme old age. Only the later reforms of Benedict of Aniane effected that separation of spheres which made this fusion of divergent ideals impossible.

Alcuin never tired of exhorting his pupils to shun the dangers of fame, wealth and sensuousness, for in the palace it was easy to fall a victim to all these vices.[2] It would appear from his own statements at the end of his life that he himself had by no means always been a shining example of virtue in this respect. All the same, he did try to snatch his pupils from the all too worldly round of court-life. Perhaps it was as a means to this end that he adopted the custom of bestowing honorary names which had been practised in his home country, at the cathedral school of York. Just as the monk was supposed to become a new man through the adoption of a new name, so the aspirant to wisdom was supposed to live up to higher ideals when ' father Alcuin ' judged him worthy of a classical or a Biblical name. This practice was undoubtedly popular because it was attractive to wear the insignia of scholarship. But in many cases its educational purpose is too obvious to be overlooked.

The members of this group must have been conscious of a sense of fellowship, for they were a group of educated people among a crowd of the uneducated. Such a sense of fellowship may well have been heightened by the custom of bestowing new names that were known only to the initiated, a custom which introduced a semi-esoterical note into this learned circle. From time to time we can discern also an erotic trait although it would certainly be wrong to exaggerate its importance. Alcuin, for instance, longed for the time when he could clasp his friend

[1] MGH, *Poet.*, i, p. 541, No. 43.
[2] Cf. e.g., MGH, *Epp.*, iv, Nos. 65, 131, 251.

round the neck ' with the fingers of his desires. Alas, if only it were granted to me, as it was to Habbakuk, to be transported to you, how would I sink into your embraces . . ., how would I cover, with tightly pressed lips, not only your eyes, ears and mouth but also your every finger and your toes : not once, but many a time.'[1] There are several such passages ; but we must remember that they had not only specific literary sources,[2] but also reflected an old Frankish tradition that stretched back right into Merovingian days. People would not have written such letters had they not been aware that such effusions were literarily quite respectable ; or at least, they would have been purged from later collections. The age which did not know love lyrics eagerly sought poetical friendships between men, without however passing, on the whole, beyond the limits of decency. Nevertheless, several kinds of perversion were not unknown.[3]

Every member of the circle, pupil or poet, who left the palace to take up a position as bishop or abbot in another part of the kingdom, maintained his connection with his friends by letters and was able to use his newly-acquired influence on their behalf. Whenever one of his pupils undertook a journey, Alcuin furnished him with letters of introduction ' to all friends '. These letters made them welcome everywhere. In fact, they often seem to have availed themselves all too liberally of such hospitality, especially of their master's hospitality. Once he was forced to confess that the resources of certain of his abbey's manors were quite exhausted because during the past year his friends had eaten up everything.[4] These friends can certainly not have been popular with the clergy of the stricken abbey. They were especially unpopular when they were not Franks but Englishmen or even Irishmen, for people showed little friendliness to these nations.[5] In the *Vita Alcuini* there is a characteristic description of how the monks of St Martin of Tours growled when their abbot was once again expecting a visit from his countrymen. Here is another Briton or Irishman come to visit that other

---

[1] Ibid., p. 36, No. 10. [2] S. Singer, op. cit., p. 118.
[3] E.g. MGH, *Epp.*, iv, p. 451, No. 294 ; cf. MGH, *Cap.*, ii, p. 44, c. 54.
[4] E. Lesne, *Histoire de la propriété ecclésiastique en France*, Lille-Paris, 1922, ii, p. 129.
[5] Cf. the statements of the Irishman Dungal, MGH, *Epp.*, iv, p. 433, No. 49.

Briton in there! O God, free our monastery from these Britons! Just as bees return from everywhere to their queen, so these people are in the habit of returning to that fellow'.[1] The prayer does not seem to have been granted: the Anglo-Saxon Fridugis became Alcuin's successor as abbot of St. Martin.

To understand the mind of the scholars of Charles's palace, it is best to begin with the description of one definite personality, and the choice is easy. It is Alcuin and only Alcuin whom we can meet face to face, so to speak, in his letters. He was, furthermore, the model for a whole generation of pupils who imitated him in their attitudes, so much so that, at times, they grotesquely exaggerated certain features which we cannot but criticize to-day. Alcuin was, after all, in every respect a collector. He amassed huge quantities of information on all manner of subjects. He collected riches; he collected friends; and, especially during the last years of his life, he collected intercessors in all countries to pray for the salvation of his soul. He was glad to pass on knowledge, money and protection, for he lived with his students and identified himself with them. But in the last resort all these things were a means to insure himself in this world against the hostile blasts of fate. Such an attitude was thoroughly unheroic and rather bourgeois. Alcuin confessed as much in his reply to Charles who had invited him to join him in the military encampments in Saxony. 'What business,' he wrote, 'has the small hare among the boars, the lamb among the lions?'[2] It was the reply of a born civilian. When there was unrest in England, he was even loath to undertake a journey to his home country.

It was not given to Alcuin to be creative in any field. For that very reason he needed his fullness of knowledge, and immersed himself in educational work and in literary and theological activities. He was much of an extrovert and deeply immersed in everyday life. His curiosity was attracted by everything that was unusual. He asked Angilbert to buy things for him in Rome[3] and his joy was complete when his pupil, Richulf, the archbishop of Mayence, sent him a camel, ' a marvellous animal

---

[1] MPL, c, col. 102. [2] MGH, Epp., iv, p. 234, No. 145.
[3] Ibid. p. 141, No. 97.

with two heads and sixty teeth '.[1] His letters were full of requests to be kept informed of everything that was going on.[2]

His method is best illustrated by his ability to produce apt information and quotations. There was no situation and no person for which there was not a heading in his enormous ' card index '. There was consolation for the sick, moral exhortations for the king and his magnates, unctuous edification for a patriarch. 'Advise everybody to obey the will of God; advise the king gently, the bishops with dignity, and the princes with confidence '.[3] As this quotations shows, he clearly had a formula for every rank. It was used repeatedly in his letters.

At the same time we must not underestimate Alcuin's achievements. He gave to his age that which it demanded, and what it could scarcely have obtained so fully without him. He transmitted to his age the knowledge and the doctrine of the past. It is very unlikely that anybody ever asked for his, Alcuin's, own opinion. His great memory offered answers with the precision of a dictionary. There was nothing which his pupils, not even Charles, could appreciate more. Alcuin was quite aware that he was in this respect a unique phenomenon among his contemporaries. With dignity he wrote to the patriarch of Jerusalem : ' The eminent men and sons of the holy church of God call me Albinus. We would like you to know that we are not oblivious of your name when celebrating holy Mass '.[4]

Together with such egotism we find in the ageing scholar— we first know him through his letters at the age of sixty—an unmistakable tendency towards sentimentality. This sentimentality is apparent not only in his constant lamentations about the absence of friends, but also in the well-known song about the idyllic situation of his cell,[5] and in the epitaph which he wrote for himself. He composed ever new variations upon the theme of the vanity of the world. In his last years these variations were no longer mere copies of an elegiac spirit but were full of an

---

[1] Ibid., p. 67, No. 26 ; cf. also p. 67 n. 3, and also MGH, *Script.*, iv, p. 197, c. 28.

[2] Cf., e.g., MGH, *Epp.*, iv, p. 31, No. 6.

[3] Ibid., p. 125, No. 82. For these formulas cf., e.g., Nos. 14–16, 28 etc. Already Gregory the Great in the *Regula pastoralis* had been of the opinion that this type of pastoral care was advisable.

[4] MGH, *Epp.*, iv, p. 350, No. 210.   [5] MGH, *Poet.*, i, p. 243.

original, emotional religiosity. At this period of his life he wept over all his earlier sins, over the wounds which greed had inflicted on him,[1] and over the ' pigs of uncleanliness ' which he had tended in the fields of Gaul.[2] He also cried about the whole world and the dirt in which he had been accustomed to wallow.[3]

All this went far beyond the conventional style of the clergy. It was certainly customary to confess one's sins. But Alcuin's confessions betray a transformation which is clearly visible in the letters written between 793 and 796. In this latter year he even wrote to the pope and asked him to pray for the forgiveness of his, Alcuin's sins. He added that Angilbert, in Rome, would give an oral explanation of the reasons for Alcuin's need.[4] Alcuin was able to take Angilbert, the lay abbot of Centula-St. Riquier, into his confidence, for he knew him to be guilty of the very same sins.[5] At this juncture in his life we perceive a last-minute change of heart, a turning towards inwardness.[6] During the earlier periods of his life such inwardness had rarely been mentioned and then only in a conventional manner. This newly-found inwardness sprang from the terrifying thought of the Last Judgment, the fear of which made him tremble more and more.[7] Thus we are given for the first time, in the man who was the very model of a Carolingian humanist, an inkling of that transformation which was to influence the spirit of later generations, or at least of some of their representatives, so profoundly.

This fear of the Last Judgment, transforming and determining his individual way of life, must not be confused with the general feeling which people had, that they were living at the end of all time. Nevertheless it would be incomprehensible without that feeling, which was so widespread during the earlier Middle Ages that the period has been described as an age of

[1] MGH, *Epp.*, iv, p. 312, No. 186, etc.
[2] Ibid., p. 130, No. 86.
[3] Ibid., p. 275, No. 167.   [4] Ibid., p. 139, No. 94.
[5] Ibid., p. 141, No. 97 : ' Nam nos ambos, ut recognosco, quaedam necessitatis catena constringit et libero cursu voluntatis castra intrare non permittit.'
[6] Ibid., p. 254, No. 156, to Arno.
[7] Ibid., p. 360, No. 216 : 'Adhuc restat maximus timor de iudicio Dei, quod nullus effugere valet ' ; p. 384, No. 239 : ' Huius vero iudicii terrore totus contremesco ; ' etc.

H

senectus.[1] From a theological point of view the covenant of the New Testament and the extension of the church's province almost to the very borders of the then known world, had well nigh completed all historical development.   Moreover, the Fathers of the church, whose thoughts were considered to contain the sum of wisdom, had expressed the deep concern felt by all educated people at the fall of the Roman Empire.   They thought a new flowering of culture quite impossible.   The Carolingian scholars willingly followed this train of thought. Their work was concerned with the preservation of the past ; for the culture of Christian antiquity seemed to them an inseparable part of Christianity itself, which must not be allowed to be crushed by Antichrist and his precursors.

Thus all creative effort was replaced by the wish to pass on a tradition and to hold fast to the authority of earlier Christian authors. ' We are *homunculi* at the end of all time ', wrote Alcuin ; ' there is nothing better for us than to follow the teaching of the Apostles and the Gospels. We must follow these precepts instead of inventing new ones or propounding new doctrine or vainly seeking to increase our own fame by the discovery of newfangled ideas '.[2] The quality of a theological treatise depended on the degree to which it was based upon the teaching of the Fathers. This principle was justified on the ground that physicians, too, were wont to prepare their medicines from herbs and other ready-found materials. They never pretended to create or produce the ingredients themselves, but acted instead as the collectors and preparers of the healing powers which the ingredients contained.[3] Theologians ought to follow the same course. Alcuin had in fact adopted the method of composing his works by linking quotation to quotation, without attempting to express his own views or to reconcile inconsistent quotations. The method had been used by Bede, the great Anglo-Saxon, who had compiled his writings, like a jig-saw puzzle, from innumerable quotations from the Bible and the Fathers. The method suited the great collector Alcuin and was used by his

---

[1] J. Bühler, *Die Kultur des Mittelalters*, Stuttgart, 1943, pp. 81 sqq.
[2] MGH, *Epp.*, iv, p. 61, No. 23. E. Shipley Duckett, op. cit., has stressed that Alcuin's importance does not lie in his originality but in his role as a transmittor.
[3] MGH, *Epp.*, iv, p. 356, No. 213.

contemporaries and pupils, particularly by Hrabanus Maurus and Frechulph of Lisieux.

As a matter of fact, Hrabanus was once criticized for not producing any original ideas of his own.[1] In reply, he appealed to the humility that was prescribed for Christians and contrasted it with the pride of those that have no concern other than their own fame.[2] One of Hrabanus' contemporaries, the Presbyter Amalar, found himself in a very awkward situation at a synod. His opponents had proved that his doctrines were not in conformity with the Bible and the Fathers. When he was forced to admit that the thoughts he had expressed were his own, his career as a theologian was ended.[3]

Such conservatism reigned supreme not only where questions of faith were concerned but in all spheres of knowledge. Even in poetry, which was considered a science, the knowledge of which could be acquired by teaching, we find a similar conservatism. Similarly, the illuminators of the sumptuous Carolingian manuscripts had a fixed number of colours and designs, which they assembled, especially during the earlier period, without any clear articulation. Their productions are characterized by a haphazard assembly of classical oriental and Germanic elements, and we can only assume that they made use of manuals in which each single motive and the different types of figures were listed.[4] The school of Tours, where Alcuin resided during the last years of his life, developed this type of work to a high point, just as in theology it piled quotation upon quotation.

The laws and administrative regulations collected by Charles the Great in the capitularies, were put together in much the same way. Regulations governing the currency stood side by side with prescriptions about public morality, and rules on ecclesiastical matters side by side with orders governing the military levy. It is, indeed, possible to discern in almost every single sphere of life disintegration of large-scale, systematic organization into independent elements. People, it seems, had lost the sense of how things fitted together. This is apparent even in agri-

[1] J. Hablitzel, in: *Biblische Studien*, 1906, xi, No. 3, p. 96 n. 1.
[2] MPL, cx, col. 498.
[3] MGH, *Conc.*, ii, pp. 779 sq. (838).
[4] W. Köhler, op. cit., i, 2, pp. 281 sq.

culture. Contrasted with the large highly-organized estates of the later Roman empire,[1] the Carolingian units of cultivation were small and well separated from each other. A similar state of things is apparent in Carolingian feudalism, where the vassals do not yet form a distinct group or social class.[2] For the time being it was felt that the dominant personal position of the monarch—of the heavenly ruler as well as of the earthly king— sufficed to hold these single, disparate elements together. But nobody really endeavoured to replace the older forms, which had developed organically, by new ones which would reflect and do justice to the altered circumstances.

For the very same reason the spirituality of the theologians often strikes us as superficial. Only rarely did it avail itself of the forces which the early Christian church had released, after the collapse of ancient civilization, through the regeneration of human nature. The purpose of the Carolingian sermon was not to lead people to the inner experience of divine grace and love. It merely served to cast the 'light of knowledge' on grace and love.[3] People sought 'wisdom'—wisdom defined in the manner of the ancient philosophers as 'knowledge of things divine and human'.[4] Wisdom was thus equated with philosophy. It was not contrasted with theology but was a substitute for it. Such philosophy provided fame for the mighty, ornaments for the living and glory for the dead. Charlemagne always loved it and preached it. He invited people to study it and made his invitations attractive by presents and preferments. He summoned its devotees from every corner of the world to his court,[5] and even Alcuin described himself, in his epitaph, as a lover of wisdom.[6]

This Christian philosophy therefore was, in the first place, a matter of the intellect. Its greatest enemy was ignorance. Its terminology was partly reminiscent of the 'Enlightenment' of the eighteenth century: for example, in the statement that Charles, 'with the help of God, rendered his kingdom which, when

---

[1] H. Sée, *Les classes rurales et le régime domanial en France au Moyen Age*, Paris, 1901, p. 63.
[2] This has been stressed by H. Mitteis, *Lehnrecht und Staatsgewalt*, Weimar, 1933, pp. 34 sq.
[3] MGH, *Epp.*, iv, p. 89, No. 43.
[4] Ibid., p. 466, No. 307.
[5] Ibid., p. 373, No. 229.
[6] MGH, *Poet.*, i, p. 351.

God committed it to him, was dark and almost wholly blind, radiant with the blaze of fresh learning '.[1] But we must not allow ourselves to be misled by such statements, any more than by many of the criticisms of the worship of images and of the popular cult of relics.[2] Charles's own piety was the massive piety of the common people. As a whole it would have appeared to the *philosophes* of the Enlightenment as a form of superstition. In some of Charles's councillors it was disguised under a thin cloak of Christian rationalism. But such rationalism lacked any clear conceptual framework : it was such a loosely-worn cover that it never led to any real conflicts with the inner piety of that generation. As in so many other fields, such opposites as reason and superstition managed to live peacefully side by side.

According to Alcuin beatitude was to be obtained through the rational insight of faith, acquired by study, and the assistance of the love of God and one's neighbour.[3] But what was this love? It seems clear that people's ideas were very superficial, and that all manner of different things were referred to by the same word. Love of God, love of one's neighbour, and profane love between friends were all utterly confused. Similarly the covenant with God was placed on the same level as a pact of friendship. In heaven we will learn to distinguish true friends from mere flatterers, for many are called—to God, as well as to friendship—but few are chosen.[4] Statements such as ' Charles loves God ' and ' Charles loves poets ' are mentioned quite naturally in one breath.[5] Alcuin based his own friendships upon the Lord's command ' love one another ',[6] and believed that it was the ' virtue of love ' which made him long for Arno, his distant friend.[7] If one must love one's enemy, how much more must one love one's friend![8]

This naive identification of heavenly and earthly love was

---

[1] Walahfrid, prologue to Einhard's *Vita Karoli*, MGH, *Ger.*, xxv, p. xxviii.

[2] *Libri Carolini*, i, 2 ; MGH, *Conc.*, ii, Suppl., p. 14. Cf. p. 35 above. I have not had access to the dissertation of H. Frederichs, *Die Gelehrten um Karl den Grossen*, Berlin, 1931, in which the concept of *ratio* in Alcuin and his pupils is examined.

[3] A. Hauck, *Kirchengeschichte Deutschlands*, ii (2nd ed.), p. 139, after Alcuin, *De Trinitate*, 1.

[4] MGH, *Epp.*, iv p. 408, No. 252.

[5] MGH, *Poet.*, i, pp. 362 sqq. ; (Angilbert).

[6] Ibid., p. 116, No. 74.

[7] Ibid., p. 362. No. 218.

[8] Ibid., p. 53, No. 19.

possible because nobody sought a distinction of concepts. It followed popular linguistic usage, and the popular mind had no use for such distinctions. Even in Middle High German, for example, the word *minna* was used for *amor*, worldly love, as well as for *caritas*, spiritual love. And this usage was accepted in spite of the fact that it would have been possible to render *amor* as *liubi* and *caritas* as *minna*.[1] In this instance, as in so many others, it is evident how close to popular thought was the ' wisdom ' of the court scholars. Both were equally undeveloped.

When all this is considered, we must conclude that the Franks were far removed from a true ' renaissance ' of classical antiquity. True, Carolingian scholars saved much of the precious inheritance of antiquity and transmitted it to later generations. We are certainly justified in considering this to have been among their most important achievements. But such work was not done for its own sake. It was done in the spirit of Origen and of all those who followed him in his belief that wordly knowledge was a useful servant of theology. The first of Charles's Capitularies, expressly sanctioning the pursuit of profane knowledge and its propagation throughout his dominions, did so with these words : ' Therefore we exhort you . . . to pursue the study of letters . . . in order that you may be able more easily and more correctly to penetrate the mysteries of the divine Scriptures.'[2]

And yet, if we are to believe his own words, Alcuin, who was responsible for the drafting of this statement, by no means despised profane knowledge. Following ancient custom he wished to see it used as the foundation of education during the first years of schooling. He hoped that the pupils would be able to use it as a ladder and reach evangelical perfection with its help.[3]

Even the apostle Paul had made use of rhetorical devices. He had found, according to Alcuin, the gold of wisdom in the mud of poetry.[4] This was ample justification for the study of pagan poetry. But in another place Alcuin wrote that wisdom could not be found in the lies of Virgil but only in the Gospels.[5]

---

[1] P. Wahmann, *Gnade*, Berlin, 1934, iv, p. 166.
[2] *Epistola de litteris colendis* (probably 787), MGH, *Cap.*, i, p. 79.
[3] MGH, *Epp.*, iv, p. 437, No. 280.
[4] Ibid., p. 345, No. 207.   [5] Ibid., p. 475, No. 309.

Perhaps we can detect in this harsh judgment a note of jealousy, for Alcuin once blamed the archbishop of Trier for loving Virgil as he used to love him, Alcuin, himself.[1] This remark throws a special light on Alcuin's edifying advice to study the Gospels instead. All the same, none of the court-scholars went so far as the monks of Fulda, according to whom Virgil, together with Jove, was placed in hell itself.[2]

The Carolingian humanists moved therefore in a Christian atmosphere. But Christianity was not offered in its fullness but only, as it were, in an abridged edition. Nobody realized, and nobody could realize, how far away they were from the living fountain of Christian faith, as distinct from its purely philological sources. This was true even when they stood in terror of the Last Judgment. Alcuin's wisdom could make people more learned ; but it could not really help them. Ignorant of the internal and the external needs of mankind, these scholars were under the illusion that they were missionaries when they were no more than propagandists. This is all the more striking when one remembers, as we shall do presently, how great men's needs were, on all fronts, during the very period of greatest 'progress '. Indeed, it may even be questionable whether this small group of intellectuals was not simply content to enjoy the spiritual and material benefits they were able to reap from the rich soil of Charles's palace.

It must be said again, however, that this criticism, however justifiable, does not detract from the real significance of these imperial ' paladins ' ; for their achievement as the preservers and transmitters of a cultural inheritance was quite extraordinary. To-day, after more than a millennium, we owe a debt of gratitude to them ; and yet it must be admitted that none of these men can be counted among the great in the realm of the intellect or among the saints. Neither past nor recent eulogies can modify this verdict.

[1] Ibid., p. 39, No. 13.   [2] Johannes of Fulda, MGH, *Poet.*, i, p. 392.

Chapter V

NOBLES AND OFFICIALS

God was looked upon as the true governor of the whole creation. He had, however, delegated one part of His power over human affairs to an earthly ruler. In the same manner the earthly ruler did not always exercise personally the powers thus granted to him. He too was able to delegate powers and appoint 'faithful servants' and administrators to take charge of part of his office. Originally, the term *imperium* simply meant the king's power of 'ban'. It signified his right to command and to prohibit under pain and punishment. In time of war the power of 'ban' was manifest in the *hari bannus*, in the king's right to levy and lead the host; in times of peace, it was seen as the power to administer justice which, like the *hari bannus*, was a means for re-establishing and preserving the peace. If one considers the vast extension of the Frankish dominions, it must be clear that the king could not carry out either his military or his judicial duties without delegating them to a large number of men trained in the use of arms and in the administration of the law. Such men were supposed to carry out their duties in the spirit of the ruler and of his divine Lord. The count's power of *bannus* was derived from that of the king. The count was the king's lieutenant in administrative districts, small enough to be supervised by one single man.

It is likely that the word *greve*—in modern German, 'Graf', or count—itself denoted the bearer of the royal power to command.[1] The power delegated to the count was, however, only a part of the royal power, and the king was always entitled to interfere directly in the sphere of the count's authority. God too had not forgone His right to supervise kings, even though He had appointed them to be His lieutenants. When they were

[1] H. Brunner and C. v. Schwerin, *Deutsche Rechtsgeschichte*, München-Leipzig, 1928, ii, p. 219.

negligent in carrying out their duties (they had to reckon with His wrath.) God never allowed a king to rule in an arbitrary manner but had laid down that he should merely administer the divinely ordained, unchangeable law. In the same sense no count had arbitrary power to punish, but was supposed to administer justice according to the divine as well as the royal law. He was, for instance, not entitled to exercise mercy towards criminals without royal consent. The king's ban was higher than the count's ban, even when it was only a question of assessing a monetary fine for the expiation of a crime. In order to allow the count to act, in special cases, with the full weight of royal authority, it was necessary to grant him a special mandate. Whenever the Frankish ruler appeared in person in the county, his will, not the count's, prevailed. But even at a distance he could, at any time, curtail the count's powers or deprive him, in the event of unsatisfactory service, of his office.

The king, therefore, not only had power to govern but was also entitled to appoint agents to carry out some of his duties. The same was true of the counts themselves. They were entitled to appoint lesser officers in their counties without asking for the king's persmission. These were their servants (*ministri*), as they themselves were the king's servants. In such cases, however, the king had the right to interfere in person, to annul such appointments and to appoint his own men instead. Charles the Great, however, rarely availed himself of this power. The counts, too, were hardly ever changed during his reign; the same man might remain in charge in the same area for fifteen, twenty or even thirty years.[1] For any interference that was not strictly necessary was considered an arbitrary act, and arbitrary acts were unworthy of a Christian ruler who was bent upon the quiet maintenance of the legal order. The local sphere in which the court's subordinates exercised their authority, was practically removed from royal control.) For in the sphere of local government, at least so far as the eastern parts of the realm were concerned, remnants of the old non-royal local organization still survived, from the time before the extension of royal power,

[1] Ibid., p. 229; L. Halphen, *Charlemagne et l'empire carolingien*, Paris, 1947, pp. 147 sq.

when the kingdom had been built up of small, more or less self-governing bands or tribes.

It was therefore not always easy for the counts to exercise free choice in appointing their subordinates. In many parts *centenarii* or 'hundredmen' had continued to exercise their offices according to age-old custom. Familiar with local conditions, they were often enough the most respected and wealthiest members of the village community. Even such a powerful king as Charles often encountered great difficulties when he tried to plant men whom he trusted in provinces in which they were strangers. In a province in which they could not fall back upon their own property and their clan and had no backing save the royal command, they faced grave difficulties. When royal authority was at its peak, the magnates of a county were sometimes forced to bow to a new arrival even if he were of inferior social status, for example, a royal freedman. But their stubborn and tacit opposition continued. It was certainly easier to choose a count from one of the great families of the district. Things had changed since the time of the Merovingian, Chlothar II, who had been forced to promise his magnates never to appoint an officer from a different province[1]; yet Charles often retained the services of local men in newly-conquered territories. In such districts he used as counts Saxons, Suabians and Lombards, as well as Franks.

Following upon the occupation of a country by Frankish troops, some native leaders would probably profess themselves unconditional followers of the king and accept countships from his hands. The mere fact that they had thus sided with the conqueror might well estrange them from their own people. But the further the pacification of the newly-acquired territory progressed, the more strongly the older ties were bound to reappear. It was difficult to be an imparital judge when the interests of cousins and brothers were involved. It must have been equally difficult for a count to keep estates and rights which he possessed *ex officio* permanently separate from his own private property. Slowly in each country the royal domain became the count's domain, and the counts showed an obvious desire to hand it on, together with their family properties, to their sons. During the

[1] H. Brunner and C. v. Schwerin, op. cit., p. 228.

last years of Charles's reign, when the king's control relaxed considerably, it would appear that the expectation of the count's son to succeed to both the office and the property of his father was no longer unusual.[1]

At the Frankish court people were well aware of the dangers inherent in these tendencies. Even if they could not be abolished, it was realized that steps should at least be taken to counteract an excessive accumulation of power in the hands of a single magnate. According to Notker, Charles never, except in the frontier districts of the kingdom, assigned more than one county to a single magnate.[2] Although in general this principle was followed there were exceptions,[3] for often political necessity was stronger than fundamental principles.

The office of count, in many ways, worked badly from the king's point of view. Already the first Carolingians had tried by different but fairly effective methods to keep it under control. It was the ruler's duty to supervise all office-holders in the exercise of their functions. The larger the kingdom became the more difficult it was to do this effectively. Thus it became necessary to introduce a new delegation of royal authority. It was decided that special envoys sent out by the king, *missi dominici*, who were equipped with the full weight of royal authority, were to act as royal agents in the provinces of the Frankish kingdom.[4] In the case of military expeditions which the ruler was unable to lead in person, and also of embassies and a few other political undertakings, the transfer of primary royal powers, where necessary, had long been usual. Now, however, the employment of *missi dominici* was no longer confined to such special tasks. For these 'extraordinary' delegations might still be used as of old; but Charles now added as a routine procedure of ordinary internal administration the regular appointment of 'ordinary' *missi*, invested with full royal powers. He dispatched them year after year throughout his dominions. They were under strict orders to fill all the gaps in the network of administration left by local office-holders. The latter were even obliged to support

---

[1] Ibid., p. 229 n. 79 ; L. Halphen, op. cit., pp. 147 sq.
[2] Notker, op. cit., i, 13.
[3] G. Waitz, *Deutsche Verfassungsgeschichte*, iii, p. 382.
[4] On the *missi dominici* see esp. V. Krause, in : MIÖG, 1890, xi, pp. 193 sqq.

the *missi dominici* and their entourage at their own expense until such time as all complaints had been received and all abuses remedied.

The object of this measure was to use the trusted servants of the king and his tried vassals, secular as well as spiritual, to ensure that justice triumphed over the self-interest of aristocratic local officials and their clans. These royal envoys, it was thought, would be most likely to administer justice impartially in regions where they were strangers.) For this reason the *missi dominici* acted almost exclusively outside the districts in which they themselves held office as archbishops, bishops or counts. Only a few, of whose integrity Charles had no doubt whatever, were entrusted with plenary authority in the district in which they otherwise held an office. Such were, for example, archbishop Arno of Salzburg and abbot Fardulf of St. Denis. The latter was a Lombard who was estranged from the magnates of his province, the more so because he had betrayed to the king the nobles who had participated in Pepin's conspiracy.

Even in its most highly-developed form under Charles the Great, however, the office of *missus dominicus* remained always a makeshift device. They appeared but once a year ; but how much injustice could be perpetrated in the course of a whole year, before the opportunity arose to lodge a complaint ! Moreover, the *missi dominici* could not hold their yearly sessions everywhere. Especially in the eastern parts of the kingdom, one court a year was rarely sufficient to counteract the particularist tendencies of the local magnates and of the local officials chosen from them. Consequently we find again and again, side by side with the 'ordinary' *missi*, 'extraordinary' *missi* appointed with special duties. They were used especially when troops had to be levied and a major military expedition carried out.

The need for the grouping of several counties and for more permanent supervision of the counts, led also to the establishment of permanent provincial governors, set over the counts.) It was only in the old core of the Frankish kingdom, which could be supervised and governed without difficulty, that provincial governors of this type are missing. Elsewhere they appear under the titles of prefect, duke or margrave. These were the titles borne in the eastern and southern parts of the realm by those officials who, in addition to their own counties, had the task of supervising a wider territory.[1] Their position was different from that of the ancient tribal dukes, even when the district under their jurisdiction was partly co-extensive with a tribal territory. The essential difference lay in the fact that they were royal officers and held office, like the counts, at the king's pleasure. Even when such positions were conferred on members of the Carolingian family, with the title of king, their holders were still not supposed to be anything but functionaries of the supreme power in the kingdom.

Royal governors, usually with the title of margrave, acted also in the newly acquired frontier-territories or ' marches ', in which the county organization was still fluid. There was much experiment in such districts and the forms of administrative organization changed rapidly. On the frontiers *missi dominici* could effect but little. The firm hand of a magnate, who was not a member of the native nobility, was needed to keep down an unfriendly population of Slavs, Bretons, Goths or Arabs. Like the prefects, dukes and margraves in the core of the kingdom, the lieutenants on the frontiers also were in charge of a county for the administration of which they were immediately responsible.

The result, at a later date, was that they developed local interests, struck root in their provinces, and finally escaped from the control of the central government. To begin with, however, the central government was still powerful enough to appoint and depose such governors, as they did the counts in the marches. It was only later that the ' governors ' used the influence they had acquired in their provinces to establish an independent position for themselves.

When necessary, the king could use his own vassals as a counterweight to the counts in the counties. These vassals, the *vassi dominici*, were closely tied to the king because he had granted them ' benefices ' from royal or ecclesiastical property. Under Charles the Great it would seem that they were permitted to levy troops themselves, and take their own contingent to the royal army.[2] Thus the king had a number of men at his beck and call

---

[1] For the following see E. Klebel, in : *Deutsches Archiv.*, 1938, ii, pp. 1 sqq.
[2] L. Halphen, op. cit., pp. 204 sq.

in the counties, who were not subject, at any rate in time of war, to the count's command. When the monarchy was strong, the institution of *vassi dominici* was an effective instrument. But during the period of decline many of the royal vassals must have pursued courses opposed not only to the interests of the counts but also to those of the king himself.

The transfer of nobles, as holders of offices and benefices, from one part of the kingdom to another effected a profound change in the structure of many of the aristocratic families. Such a policy of transfer had already begun under the Carolingian mayors of the palace. Eventually it resulted in the transformation of a purely provincial aristocracy, tied to its inherited estates, into a European aristocracy. The members of this European aristocracy often chose their wives from among families in distant parts of the kingdom. They formed a supra-national aristocracy interested in all matters of high policy and connected through manifold interests with the royal government. Under Pepin, Franks had held the chief offices of Aquitaine ; and under Charles the Great, Franks not only became counts and abbots in this territory, but also were established there as minor royal vassals.[1] A veritable stream of noblemen poured out from Austrasia, the core of Carolingian power, into the other parts of the Frankish west. These newcomers fused with the local families into a new aristocracy ; and this in its turn, moved into Bavaria and Italy and into all the other newly-conquered territories. There they appeared as a ' Frankish ' aristocracy and formed an upper class, above the indigenous nobility. By this time it was hardly possible to distinguish between members of ancient, well-nigh princely families, which had always enjoyed a certain supra-national status, and Carolingian officials who had originally been members of the provincial nobility and who had achieved the same supra-national status through the king's favour. In our sources most of these families appear only at the peak of their careers and prosperity, and then it is hardly possible to determine what their origins were.

[1] Astronomus, *Vita Hludovici imperatoris*, c. 3 ; MGH, *Script.*, ii, p. 602. For the following, see R. Poupardin, *Le royaume de Provence*, 1901, pp. 373 sqq. ; M. Chaume, *Les origines du Duché de Bourgogne*, 1925, i, pp. 528 sqq. ; F. L. Ganshof, *Feudalism*, London, 1952, p. 24.

Among the ancient aristocratic families we may certainly count the Otakars, who had possessions in the vicinity of Paris as well as in central Germany, in the Bavarian Chiemgau, and in the Austrian district of St. Poelten.[1] Another ancient family, which originated from a female branch of the royal Burgundian house, and which had supplied the Merovingians with officials and bishops, seem to have been identical with the later family of the counts of the Thurgau. This family also supplied a ' duke ' of Provence, a ' duke ' of Raetia and several west-Frankish counts.[2] Family connections with the Carolingians consolidated the position of such families without necessarily determining their attitude. Supported by their far-flung, hereditary possessions and by their relatives, they were able to pursue an independent policy in times of crisis. At the very beginning of Charles's reign, for instance, a member of the Otakar family supported Charles's most dangerous enemies. The same situation was to recur during the later years of Louis the Pious.

The families which had been neighbours or even relatives of the Carolingians before the latter had risen to be mayors of the palace and kings, were of more lowly origin. They owed practically everything to the ruling dynasty, even if their rise to power and prosperity was not always quite as fabulous as that of the Widones, or Guidones. This family hailed from the region of the Moselle and its members rose, in a single century, to be margraves of Brittany and dukes of Spoleto, and in the end succeeded to the legacy of the Carolingians in Italy and to the imperial title.[3] By the time of Charles the Great such families had long ago erased all traces of their provincial origins, and probably looked down with contempt on newcomers who owed their position to Charles's favour.

Among these newcomers there were not only men of lowly origin, but also the ancient princely families of Germanic tribes which the Franks had conquered. Although it was apparently official policy not to bestow offices upon foreigners, the human

---

[1] E. Zöllner, in : *Neues Jahrbuch d. heraldisch-genealog. Gesellschaft 'Adler'*, Wien, 1945–6, pp. 7 sqq.

[2] M. Chaume, op. cit., i, pp. 530 sq.

[3] G. Tellenbach, *Königtum u. Stämme in der Werdezeit d. deutschen Reiches*, Weimar, 1939, pp. 43 sq.

resources of the Franks themselves were not sufficient to fill all
vacancies. Once the stubborn spirit of resistance of a tribe was
broken, it often furnished, in the second or third generation
after the conquest, the king's most faithful vassals. This was
certainly the case in Saxony. It had also been true, much earlier,
of the Alamans—once their dukes had been removed and the
last defenders of their independence had perished on the bloody
field of Cannstatt (746). Gerold, a descendant of the Alamannian
dukes, was made a count in the Anglachgau. Charles the Great
himself took Gerold's daughter Hildegard, to be his wife. His
son became a governor of Bavaria, and his grandson was count
of Metz. His great-grandsons, finally, obtained the counties of
Orléans, Blois, Angoulême, and Auvergne. The county of the
Anglachgau itself seems to have remained in the possession of
the family.[1]

Thus the young body politic, because if offered undreamed of
opportunities for successful careers, became a melting-pot for
the older tribal and social groups.   Among the Franks themselves the aristocracy, in the sense of a well-defined caste, separated from freemen by the prohibition of intermarriage, had disappeared long ago. In Charles's time, a man was valued because
he had power and prestige, rather than because he was of noble
blood. The ruling class consisted of the powerful, the *potentes* ;
and all others, however noble their ancestry, were forced to
submit.[2] Power was measured either by the possession of 'much
wealth '[3] or by an office which permitted its holder to acquire it.
Once the old order of rank and status had been destroyed, however, the race for money and property became the guiding
motive of many public officials. They no longer served an
impersonal ideal of justice, but were intent upon grasping for
their families whatever there was to be grasped.

The families that furnished the high-ranking officials were
internationalized. The non-Frankish nobility was mixed with the

[1] M. Chaume, op. cit., p. 551.
[2] A. Dopsch, *Wirtschaftsentwicklung d. Karolingerzeit*, Weimar, 1922, ii (2nd ed.),
p. 67.
[3] ' Potens : qui multas divitias habet '. M. Conrat, *Ein Traktat über romanisch-
fränkisches Ämterwesen*, ZSSRg, 1908, xxix, pp. 249 and 254. For the question of
origins see above, Ch. III, p. 63, n. 2.

Frankish nobility. People of lowly origins made their way, by the king's favour, into the ranks of the 'powerful'. Such developments produced a colourful mixture and a fusion of elements that had been separate and distinct in an earlier age. The class which thus assumed the leadership of society was held together by little more than the personal energy of the great ruler who forced his will upon it and made it follow his command, the royal 'ban'. As soon as the strength of the royal will was impaired, however, and as soon as the great boom which the rise of the empire brought with it, began to decline, the lack of homogeneity in the ruling class of officials and in the aristocracy was bound to become apparent.

But if many members of this class became uprooted and demoralized, there is also a positive side to the picture. These people were educated to have a broad outlook and to replace a narrow-minded provincialism by the realization that they were Europeans. In those days this European spirit could only be a Christian spirit. We know, for example, of a certain Isanbert, whose family had come originally from a district which later was to form part of Austria. He himself had been born in Gascony and grown up in Francia, probably in its eastern parts. He had entered the monastery of Fulda and his famous contemporary, Hrabanus Maurus, composed his epitaph.[1]

Anything which touched all aspects of life as closely as did the Carolingian state, forced every individual to decide whether he was to submit or to resist its impact. In earlier times the subjection of the duchies to the central power had been little more than nominal; but now their independent institutions were no longer an effective protection. Tribal levies were still summoned in time of war, and sometimes in times of peace the different tribes had to send representatives to the general assembly of the empire. But in both cases leadership was in the hands of trusted royal officials. Both in peace and in war the ruler demanded continuous service from the tribal nobility. For service over and above what was owed he was prepared to give generous reward. But he was equally prepared to punish those who tried to evade their obligations. Thus it was natural that the circle of nobles

[1] MGH, *Poet.*, ii, pp. 241 sq., No. 92.

I

who adopted an attitude of reserve towards the king should become smaller and smaller as time went by. From the days of the Carolingian mayors of the palace onward, more and more members of the independent nobility joined the ranks of the ruler's following. They realized that the king was accustomed not only to invest his faithful followers with briefs and benefices and to appoint them as judges, but also to choose many of the counts from among their number.[1]

On the other hand, the repeated attempts made by the Carolingian rulers, including Charles himself, to turn all free-men and all nobles into *vassi dominici*, firmly bound by ties of vassalage to the royal house, were destined to remain a mere aspiration. The method was simple enough. All that was required was a compulsory oath of fealty, to be and to remain faithful to the king.[2] But it was impossible to enforce vassalage and fealty merely through an oath. There were always nobles who secretly or openly opposed Charles's centralizing rule. Einhard tells us of a conspiracy of Thuringian and east-Frankish counts and nobles who, in 786, wanted to depose Charles.[3]

The public oath, imposed probably as a result of this conspiracy, was not confined to the nobility but was to be taken by the middle ranks of society as well. All who fled to another county in order to avoid taking the oath were threatened with punishment.[4] Again and again, obviously without much effect, capitularies were issued, prohibiting the nobility from raising private armies.[5] It is doubtful whether such armies were ever a real danger, for Charles was so powerful that no opposition could hope to develop into a permanent political threat. Open resistance was possible only for a few nobles who were lucky enough to find refuge with the enemies of the Frankish

---

[1] Cf. D. v. Gladiss, in : ZSSRg, 1937, lvii, pp. 442 sqq.

[2] ' Fidelis sum et ero ' ; a similar formula was used already by Chlothair II ; see D. v. Gladiss, op. cit., pp. 448 sqq.

[3] AS, i (2nd ed.), p. 523.

[4] MGH, *Cap.*, i, p. 67, c. 4.

[5] ' De truste facienda nemo praesumat '. Similar formulas are frequent ; see e.g., *Breviarium Missorum Aquitanicum*, c. 15 ; MGH, *Cap.*, i, p. 66. See H. Mittels, *Lehnrecht und Staatsgewalt*, Weimar, 1933, p. 181. My translation of *trustis* as ' private army ' has been criticised by W. v. d. Steinen in his review of the German edition of this book (*Zeitschrift f. schweizerische Geschichte*, 1950, xxx, p. 107). But I would point out that this translation was first introduced by Mitteis.

king. One of these men, a member of a renowned Lombard house, was captured among the Avars in 796, by Charles's son, Pepin.[1]

The real problem of Carolingian government was therefore not so much the struggle against enemies of the state as the formation of a broad class of faithful followers, who were not merely indifferent, and who would seek office for reasons other than the desire for profit. The problem was to find men with enough of the public spirit that was implied in the concept of fealty. It cannot be denied that Charles the Great failed to solve this problem.

He could hardly be expected to solve it in an age in which the old concept of the common weal and the Roman notion of *res publica* had been lost. Furthermore, the age was still lacking in a new Christian basis for such concepts, which might have kept the interests of individuals and of single families in check. In Germanic tradition fealty meant first and foremost loyalty in battle, and it is most unlikely that any of Charles's officials would have been guilty of breach of fealty at such a moment. But to be a faithful administrator in times of peace was quite a different matter. It required a subtle conscience to find the right path on the many occasions when individual interests and the duties of office came into collision. It is true that Charles had men of such calibre at his disposal. But their numbers did not keep pace with the rapid growth of his dominions.

We must therefore not be surprised by the frequent evidence of the corruptibility of public officials. Nor is it surprising that such evidence concerns not only minor local officials but also counts and even *missi dominici*. Theodulf of Orléans has described in detail how, after he had been appointed a *missus*, both magnates and lowly people, as was their custom on such occasions, approached him with a veritable flood of presents. These bribes ranged from rare objects of art, fit to delight the eye of a connoisseur, to modest offerings such as linen cloth, a beret or a pair of shoes, which peasants could afford.[2]

Theodulf castigated such practices with indignation in his poem *Against Judges*. There is no doubt that he endeavoured to

[1] AS, ii, pp. 124 sq.   [2] MGH, *Poet.*, i, pp. 498 sq.

abolish them. Alcuin's attitude was the same. When Arno of
Salzburg was appointed a *missus dominicus*, he wrote to him :
' You must not accept presents from anybody in matters of
justice. . . . This vice is extraordinarily widespread among
Christians. The very people who are supposed to think little of
their own interests, are in the habit of seizing unjustly other
people's property.'[1] What is surprising is less the fact than
Alcuin's belief that even a man like Arno, a pillar of the administration, stood in need of such advice.

The greed in high officials which caused many complaints
among the scholars of the royal palace,[2] made an even stronger
impression upon the poorer classes who had no rights and who
could not demand redress. After the death of Bego, the most
powerful man in Aquitaine and a son-in-law of Charles the Great,[3]
an old woman had a vision. Hellish demons were pouring liquid
gold into the mouth of Bego, saying : ' all your life you have
been thirsting for such gold without ever being able to quench
your thirst ; quench it now.'[4]

In the struggle for power and wealth, family connections
with the royal house and with highly placed members of the
nobility not only created opportunities for appointment to office
but also served as a protection against the accusations of the
oppressed. Conscious of this security, many magnates could
say : ' If I am ever charged in the palace with a crime I shall
have my advocates there. I shall find there a large number of
relatives and friends who will see to it that the king's wrath will
not fall upon me.'[5] We may surmise that much protection was
available not only when the charge was one of corruption but
also when it was of a more serious nature, such as private revenge
or even plain murder.

A man of the rank of a judge in Italy had been supposed to
administer the property of a widow. He had broken his trust and

---

[1] MGH, *Poet.*, I, pp. 498, sq.

[2] Thus, e.g., Cathwulf, MGH, *Epp.*, iv, p. 503, No. 7 (about 757).

[3] According to M. Chaume, op. cit., p. 126 n. 10, Flodoard was wrong in making
Bego the son-in-law of Louis the Pious ; Bego was married to a daughter of Himil-
trud and Charles.

[4] *Visio pauperculae mulieris*, in : W. Wattenbach ed., *Deutschlands Geschichtsquellen
im Mittelalter*, Berlin, 1893, i, p. 227.

[5] MGH, *Epp.*, v, p. 202, No. 10.

had taken possession of the property. A complaint lodged with the emperor led to an inquiry, which, however, owing to the combined efforts of secular and ecclesiastical dignitaries to shield the culprit, was allowed to fizzle out. Thereupon the widow herself journeyed to Aix-la-Chapelle. She crossed the Alps in winter, hoping to find justice at court. Wala, a cousin of Charles the Great, was put in charge of the case. But before judgment was given, the accused had the widow removed by paid assassins; and in order to make doubly sure he also had two of the assassins murdered by the third. Wala tried to get to the bottom of the crime, but ' the whole of Italy and its dignitaries, corrupted by bribes, was busily intriguing to make sure that he who was known to all as a rapacious murderer, should not be found guilty. . . . In fact, all the most influential persons in the royal palace endeavoured to produce witnesses and all manner of subterfuges in order to obtain the acquittal of the guilty man.'[1]

This case, in the end, was brought to a just conclusion. But this was probably due primarily to the fact that too much dirt had been raked up for the scandal to be passed over quietly. The complainant must have been of high rank and her property considerable. But how often must small men, whose resources did not permit them to take their case to the king's court, have bled to death in the claws of officials of ' judicial rank '. These persons were certainly not always satisfied with a pair of shoes or a beret, such as had been offered to Theodulf. And yet, if such was the behaviour of the representatives of the emperor himself, how much greater was the opportunity of the nobles and advocates to enrich themselves at the expense of their own immediate dependents. For this purpose they made great use of their right to raise aids and taxes. Wherever the traditional contributions proved insufficient they displayed great inventiveness in prescribing new ones. For example, a contribution could be demanded for a pious pilgrimage to Rome or to Tours; but the pilgrimage was, in fact, never undertaken.[2] Such was the Christian piety of the ruling class, or at least of some of its members. The basic principle of the *imperium christianum*,

---

[1] *Vita Walae*, c. 26; MGH, *Script.*, ii, pp. 543 sq.
[2] MGH, *Conc.*, vol. ii, i, p. 282, c. 45 (813).

the rule of eternal, divinely ordained law, was more honoured in theory than in the actual behaviour of its most prominent upholders.

It would be unfair to emphasize corruption and crime without inquiring also into the conditions which at least partly explained them. Even in the Merovingian period the lack of firm roots among the Frankish nobility had been the cause of political corruption. This lack of roots was itself a result of the total change of environment caused by the migrations, probably accelerated by certain internal tendencies which speeded up the decay of ancient ties.[1] It was hardly to be expected that the newly-converted aristocratic families of Merovingian times should have led blameless Christian lives. Although there must have been some improvement in this respect since the Merovingian era, the adoption of Christianity had still not succeeded in bringing about a complete change in outlook among the laity or even among the majority of the clergy. This is no cause for surprise, for among the Franks themselves there is little sign of the sort of missionary activity at home which might have resulted in the instruction of the nobility in a Christian way of life. There was no articulated ethical system for the laity, to replace the crude worldly ethics of the primitive Germanic tribes. Moreover, there were not enough priests sufficiently educated to undertake moral regeneration. The monks were not supposed to preach. The bishops themselves looked upon the business of administration as their proper task and preached only perfunctorily and then only because they were obliged to do so by royal order. The parish clergy, on the other hand, were only too often considered the servants of their noble lord, if not his living chattels, and for this reason were in no position to influence his conduct and way of life.

Only rarely do we obtain a glimpse of the religious needs of the laity. In one of his letters, for example, Alcuin wrote of a count who wanted to see him in order to obtain instruction. The meeting could not take place. Alcuin therefore gave him some pastoral advice in writing, in the form of a collection of

[1] See H. Fichtenau, *Askese und Laster in der Anschauung des Mittelalters*, Wien, 1948, pp. 104 sqq.

those commonplaces which he had ready for every occasion.[1]
One wonders whether they had much effect. Alcuin does not
seem to have been of much greater service to his royal master.
When Charles asked him for a book of prayer for the laity, Alcuin
compiled a collection which, although it has been preserved
only in fragments, clearly missed the opportunity which Charles's
request offered.[2]

At the royal court at least there was always an opportunity
for laymen of high rank to obtain information on theological
and moral problems. But even these men were only too often
of the comfortable opinion that knowledge of the Gospels was
the business of the clergy only.[3] The synod of Aix-la-Chapelle
in 1816, discussed the common argument of laymen, when
reproached for their conduct, that the commands of Holy
Scripture applied only to monks.[4] Except for a thin layer of
Christianity on the surface, aristocratic ideals still hardly differed
from those of the ancient Teutons. Their main tenets were
well brought out in the funeral lament which Paulinus preached
for the Margrave Eric of Friuli : liberality and open-handedness,
especially towards the church ; protection for all dependents
who cannot bear arms ; generosity and friendship for all men of
his own rank, especially for ecclesiastics of noble family ; martial
valour ; and, finally, a fine or subtle disposition or nature
(*ingenium*), which signified in general great flexibility of spirit,
but in the special sphere of politics indicated something like
' slyness '.[5]

All these qualities were reconcilable with the practical
requirements of an aristocratic life. When Alcuin wrote to
Charles's treasurer, to whom he was under many an obligation,
to wish him a blessed life with Christ in heaven, he prefixed to
it a wish for health and prosperity on earth.[6] There was no
mention of Paul's insistence upon a revaluation and a regeneration of the whole man as a way to beatitude.

---

[1] MGH, *Epp.*, iv, p. 74, No. 33.
[2] Ibid., p. 462, No. 304 ; cf. also p. 463, No. 304a.
[3] Ibid., p. 205, No. 136.   [4] MGH, *Conc.*, ii, i ; pp. 394, 396.
[5] The word is still used in all romance languages in this sense. Cp. W. Meyer
Lübke, *Romanisches etymologisches Wörterbuch*, Heidelberg, 1911, p. 321, No. 4419;
and cf. also the medieval Latin usage *ingannare* = to cheat.
[6] MGH, *Epp.*, iv, p. 159, No. 111.

Alcuin and the higher clergy of the Frankish kingdom were quite content that the essential precepts of Christianity, which it was so difficult to fulfil, should be mentioned in passing in sermons. There was no point in insisting on their practical application. This attitude was due not only to the desire to please the secular magnates. For the clergy themselves were deeply committed to the same ideals and outlook as the aristocracy. They opposed, from time to time, its extreme manifestations, but never the ideal itself. Spiritual and secular magnates, after all, often belonged to the same families. They had enjoyed a similar upbringing and, whether they happened to be bishops or counts, they were fulfilling the duties of their offices in much the same spirit. Later, during the reign of Louis the Pious, when the reforms of Benedict of Aniane began to make themselves felt, the uniformity of this attitude of the ruling classes was partially destroyed, and the ranks of the clergy were strengthened by recruits educated in a new spirit. Benedict's radical application of Christian ideals and of a Christian way of life came, however, too late to transform the imperial edifice. It only served to shake its already weak foundations and to question their validity. During the reign of Charles the Great these underlying conflicts were as yet hardly noticeable. They were being prepared quietly in the monasteries while both the spiritual and the secular magnates remained untouched.

When Alcuin reminded a bishop of the duties of his episcopal office,[1] he spoke, first, of the need to care for the liturgy and of the church's prayers for the bishop himself and for his ' friends ' —a word that applied, in medieval parlance, first and foremost to the bishop's relatives. In the second place, he required him to behave honourably : ' God has ennobled you through the grant of a dignity. Therefore you must act in a noble manner.' This is much the same formula as Alcuin always held in readiness for kings : ' You, who are sitting on the throne of a king, must not behave like a peasant '.[2] ' Look at the aristocratic origin of your parents. . . . Since you come from so illustrious a family, do not lead the life of a profligate.'[3] In his list of episcopal duties Alcuin

[1] Ibid., p. 83, No. 40.   [2] Ibid., p. 71, No. 30, to King Aethelred.
[3] Ibid., p. 104, No. 61.

mentions in the third place the need for ' moderation ' in dress. Ostentation was to be discouraged, but he does not demand that it should be given up altogether. If, as Notker tells us—no doubt with a little exaggeration—the secular magnates went riding in silk and purple gowns, decorated with ermine and the feathers of exotic birds,[1] one could hardly expect their ecclesiastical cousins to go about in sackcloth and ashes. As late as 817, at the meeting of the great council at Aix-la-Chapelle, bishops were wearing splendid garments with golden baldrics from which hung daggers decorated with precious stones, while their spurs were clinking at their heels.[2]

Alcuin's fourth admonition concerned episcopal banquets. He insisted that there ought to be neither debauchery nor drunkenness, and that banquets were only to be held at specified times, and only for a limited body of guests. If we remember that Alcuin himself thought of heaven as a huge banquet,[3] we need not be surprised that he saw no reason for banning such forms of entertainment on earth. Theodulf of Orléans, to whom we owe many an incisive criticism of the manners of the age, once remarked, not without reason : 'A bishop who himself is stuffed with food should not try to stop others from being gluttons ; he should not prohibit wine for others when he is pouring it down his own gullet ; and he should not preach sobriety when he himself is drunk.'[4] To understand these habits, if not to condone them, we must of course remember that these communal drinking bouts were the relics of old sacral Germanic rites, incorporated in a somewhat attenuated form into the celebration of the numerous saints' days and holy days which figured so largely in the Christian calendar.

The fifth place in Alcuin's list is taken by an exhortation to fear God, to practise humility, to be truthful and to be compassionate and generous towards the poor as well as obliging to one's friends. There was no need to mention vassals, because generosity and good will towards them was an accepted duty. Further, Alcuin added a reminder that it was a bishop's duty

---

[1] *Gesta Karoli*, MGH, *Script.*, ii, p. 760.
[2] Astronomus, op. cit., c. 28 ; MGH, *Script.*, ii, p. 622.
[3] MGH, *Epp.*, iv, p. 131, No. 86.   [4] MGH, *Poet.*, i, p. 454.

to be a scrupulous administrator. This reminder was aimed partly at that corruptibility ' which had its beginnings among the secular judges but was also to be found among the highest ranks of the spiritual dignitaries.'[1] But there were also plenty of bishops who undertook the visitation of their parishes not in order to save souls but ' in order to rob their fellow-men and scandalize their brothers.'[2] The harshness with which the tithe was collected had, again and again, had disastrous consequences ; in Saxony, in particular, it had rendered the work of the missionaries well-nigh abortive.[3]

Alcuin concluded his letter with the exhortation to set an example to all, and with a further insistence upon the importance of truly aristocratic conduct. The points made in this letter were not casual observations designed for a single case. On the contrary, another letter addressed to an archbishop proves that they were meant to be general guiding principles, the observance of which was expected from all members of the higher clergy. In this second letter Alcuin recommends generosity towards the poor, preaching, sobriety at banquets, the reading of the Gospels, the following of the example set by the saints and by the archbishop's predecessors.[4] In a similar way an abbot was expected to take pains to preach and conduct divine service, to look after widows and orphans, to listen sympathetically to just complaints, to decide them according to the law and—this is for once a genuine and exclusively Christian requirement—to forgive those who trespassed against him.[5]

For an abbot, it would seem to follow, it was unbecoming to avenge himself upon his enemies. Alcuin did not demand such self-denial from the secular clergy. The bishops could in fact not be prevented, even by royal prohibitions, from marching out at the head of their vassals and friends, to conduct feuds against all those who interfered with their rights. No doubt, the strengthening of the central authority tended to reduce the frequency of such private wars. During the reign of Charles we know of no case in which a member of the clergy practised the old Germanic

[1] MGH, *Epp.*, iv, p. 416, No. 258.
[2] MGH, *Conc.*, ii, i, p. 276, c. 14 (813).
[3] MGH, *Epp.*, iv, p. 154, No. 107 ; p. 158, No. 110 ; cf. p. 162, No. 112.
[4] Ibid., p. 29, No. 4.   [5] Ibid., pp. 116 sq., No. 74.

custom of blood feud, as bishop Gewilib of Mayence had done as late as 744.[1] But Theodulf of Orléans, whom we know as a poet, as a connoisseur of art and as a theologian, conducted such a feud in the year following Charles's imperial coronation, against the abbot of Tours, who happened to be none other than Alcuin himself. Alcuin's defence, however, was confined to heart-rending descriptions of the acts of violence that had been perpetrated.[2]

Among the Franks the high ecclesiastical dignitary, like all secular functionaries, received his office from the hands of the king. It was his duty, like that of the secular official, to co-operate in the administration of the divinely ordained law. In confession he was the judge of sinful acts for each of which a definite measure of penitence was prescribed. In preaching it was his duty to communicate the laws of the heavenly king to the people. His voice was to be ' God's trumpet '.[3] He had to make it his business to look after instruction, the administration of the episcopal estates, the building of churches, and a host of other, purely secular tasks. The king could demand his co-operation in every sphere. Thus there was little time left over to probe the depths of the Christian faith and above all, to be, a priest and, as such, a mediator of spiritual grace and an example to the whole diocese.

If there should be time for leisure, the bishops did not willingly renounce the old aristocratic privilege of seeking relaxation from the intellectual strain of official duties, in hunting and jousting. The fact that bishops, abbots and abbesses were prohibited from keeping hounds, falcons and fools, made little difference.[4] 'The clergy of the whole of Aquitaine were more adroit in riding, armed exercises and archery than in celebrating the Christian ritual.'[5] And as for the keeping of fools and mimes, Pope Leo III once complained to Charles about the spectacle and the songs performed before the imperial ambassadors in 808 on the occasion of a breakfast on Palm Sunday. The questionable

---

[1] W. Sieber, *Das frühgermanische Christentum*, Innsbruck-Leipzig, 1936, p. 108 n. 8.   [2] MGH, *Epp.*, iv, pp. 393 sqq., Nos. 245 sqq.
[3] Ibid., p. 45, No. 17, line 22.
[4] MGH, *Cap.*, i, p. 64, c. 31 (789).
[5] Astronomus, op. cit., c. 19 ; MGH, *Script.*, ii, p. 616 .

performance had been organized by the archbishop of Ravenna,[1] and there is no indication that the two ambassadors, counts Helmgaud and Hunfried, had been shocked. Nor does it appear that Charles himself took any action in this matter.

To the mind of the Frankish clergy, it was possible to combine an aristocratic style of life harmoniously with the duties of a spiritual office. As a consequence their preoccupation with the ultimate problems of life lacked that heart-stirring quality which was to become so prominent and powerful a factor in the minds of the following generation. Mostly they were concerned with finding ways in which they could 'organize' the salvation of their souls. This was a matter of collecting the largest possible number of people to intercede with the heavenly judge and, through the sheer weight of their intercessions, to put the outcome of the heavenly judgment beyond doubt. The lower clergy had to pray during Mass for the salvation of their superiors. In Le Mans, and probably in other places too, the bishop's whole family and all his relatives by marriage were included in such prayers.[2] In his monastery of Centula-St. Riquier, Angilbert employed three hundred monks and one hundred clerks who were to provide 'by continuous prayer for the salvation of my glorious Augustus Charles and the long duration of his reign.'[3] The expression 'continuous prayer' was meant literally. They were to pray in shifts, day and night, and only one-third were allowed off in any one shift. Angilbert, proudly compiled statistics of the numbers of men and the materials employed in the battle for the salvation of Charles's soul and the well-being of the nation : 30 altars, 15 'very good' bells, 12 bishops to consecrate the church, and the relics of 56 martyrs, 34 confessors, 14 virgins and 14 other saints as well as those of many unknown people, were all assembled for the purpose.[4]

On the model of the old Germanic sworn associations 'confraternities for the dead' were founded. We find an early example of such a confraternity at the synod of Attigny in 762. Later, there was the vow taken at Tassilo's synod in Dingolfing. This vow constituted a 'confraternity formed by

[1] Quoted in AS, ii, p. 393.
[2] MGH, *Conc.*, ii, ii, pp. 785 sq.
[3] MGH, *Script.*, xv, p. 178.
[4] Ibid., pp. 175 sqq.

bishops and abbots in Bavaria for the benefit of dead brothers. Upon the death of any member, each surviving member was to have 100 Masses or Psalters sung for him. Moreover, each was to say an additional 30 Masses himself or, since this requirement was not very cheerfully fulfilled, cause them to be said by the clergy under his jurisdiction.[1] Such prayer-confraternities soon formed a net which covered the whole Frankish kingdom and even stretched into Spain and England. Just as the system of the military levy served to protect the Franks in this world, so in these confraternities they created an emergency service for the protection of their souls against all manner of unpleasant surprises in the next.

So far we have spoken of the aristocratic habits of the higher Frankish clergy. That does not mean that their ranks were filled entirely with members of the nobility. As on the secular side so also among the clergy, there were many holders of high ecclesiastical office who had been raised to their position by the king's favour without belonging to an old and renowned family. In one case, even a royal serf whom Charles had freed, rose to be archbishop of Rheims. During the whole of his tenure of office Ebo of Rheims had to contend with the indignant opposition of the nobility, and no doubt he was reminded more than once that his ancestors had been goatherds and not councillors of kings.[2] When the abbot Waldo, a relative of the Carolingians, was engaged in a feud with the bishop of Constance, he swore an oath: 'I will not acknowledge a superior of lower birth than I am, so long as I have three fingers left on my right hand.'[3] Every time the appointment of a candidate from outside the ranks of the nobility was under consideration, there seem to have been contests between powerful factions at court, and people even went so far as to enlist the support of the queen herself against her husband.[4]

When, in spite of all difficulties, such men of lesser origin succeeded in rising to the top, their style of life did not deviate

---

[1] MGH, *Leg.*, iii, p. 461.
[2] Thegan, *Vita Ludovici Imperatoris*, c. 44 ; MGH, *Script.*, ii, p. 600.
[3] Quoted in K. Beyerle, ed., *Die Kultur der Abtei Reichenau*, München, 1925, i, p. 64.
[4] Notker, op. cit., c. 4, p. 732.

from the accepted conventions. Often, indeed, they tended to imitate aristocratic habits to the point of grotesqueness.[1] Even more than the old nobility, they were anxious for their relatives to acquire a position of respect, and especially for them to be emancipated and to marry into one of the country's great aristocratic families. Some went so far as to threaten violence if these objects could not be achieved peacefully.[1] Similarly, they did not always pursue the aggrandizement of their landed property by legal methods. It is possible that these criticisms, which we owe to Thegan, a partisan of the higher aristocracy, are exaggerated. Charles's preference for men other than nobles, was probably, on the whole, well justified. But as far as we can see, the newcomers adjusted themselves to the conventional standards of conduct, and altered them as little as did the *nouveau riches* in other centuries.

An ecclesiastical dignitary who was family conscious, naturally endeavoured to let his relatives take part in the administration of the episcopal properties or even to turn them over to their direct use. By the time of his death family property and official property had frequently been so confused that it was difficult to disentangle them. Synod after synod issued decrees against such misconduct.[2] But the frequency of such decrees itself proves how ineffective they were. As a matter of fact prohibitions against alienating ecclesiastical property seem to have been one of the chief reasons for the discontent of the higher clergy. As yet, this discontent was not open ; it found expression only in letters to foreigners. Lul of Mayence, for instance, wrote to the archbishop of York, that the rulers of his day were wont to introduce new customs and laws according to their arbitrary wishes, while the church herself was being maltreated and oppressed.[3]

We can well understand how anxious Charles was to fill the episcopal sees, at least in the eastern parts of his dominions, with men who had been brought up in the palace and who owed

---

[1] Thegan, op. cit., c. 20, p. 595.
[2] MGH, *Conc.*, ii, i, p. 170, c. 41 (Frankfort, 794) ; p. 211, c. 37 (800) ; cf. *Capitulare Ecclesiasticum*, 818, c. 29, MGH, *Cap.*, i, p. 279 ; *Capitulare Wormatiense*, 829, c. 2, MGH, *Cap.*, ii, p. 12 ; *Concilium Par.*, 829, c. 16, MGH, *Conc.*, ii, i, p. 623.   [3] Quoted in AS, i (2nd ed,), p. 210 n. 3.

their position to his favour. The older generation of the pupils of St. Boniface had been accustomed to a fair amount of independence. The last representatives of this type, men such as Lul of Mayence whom we have just mentioned, Megingoz of Würzburg, Witto of Büraburg and Willibald of Eichstädt, had all died round about the year 786. Their places were taken mostly by scholars such as Richulf of Mayence, known in court circles as Flavius Damoeta. These men also were almost all of noble birth, but at the same time they were *fideles* of the king in the narrower meaning of the word. In the next generation it was to become apparent how important a role they were to play in the eastern half of the empire. The clergy of western Francia, prompted by aristocratic pride, were to dictate their ecclesiastical demands to Louis the Pious. The clergy of eastern Francia, on the other hand, sided far more strongly with the emperor, or at least they tried to minimize, by learned arguments, the conflict that had been opened by new conceptions of the dignity of the church. Jonas of Orleans, the leader of the reformed party, and Hrabanus Maurus, the scholarly encyclopaedist, were the representatives of the two types of men whose activities contributed so much to the coming separation between the western and eastern parts of the Carolingian empire.[1]

Archbishops like Ebo of Rheims and Arno of Salzburg could never forget, not even at the height of their careers, that they were the king's servants. They had issued from his household and continued, according to the king's conception, to belong to it. Every church and every church property was required in the Frankish view, to have a proprietor. Every ecclesiastic, therefore, stood in need of a ' guardian ' and a protector, since he himself had renounced the use of arms and had left the secular community. The king and the nobility shared in this guardianship over the church and the clergy. The Carolingians themselves had succeeded in obtaining all the key positions : with very few exceptions, they controlled the episcopal sees and the major abbeys. The royal house had thus acquired a proprietary right over these sees and abbeys. But such a right did not imply an arbitrary power. It is true that there was as yet no distinction

[1] H. Mitteis, in Th. Mayer, ed., *Der Vertrag von Verdun*, 843, 1943, p. 97.

between ' family property ' and ' public property '; but it was taken for granted that the ruler would be even more conscious than otherwise of his religious responsibilities when he was disposing of ecclesiastical property. After all, most church property had originated as a direct donation to a saint and had thus been placed under the protection of one of the ' magnates ' of the heavenly kingdom. The church appealed again and again to this fact, and later based its claim for the immunity of such donations from the secular power upon the saint's proprietary rights.

At the same time, so far as the higher clergy were concerned, the church's need for protection and its lack of military resources were theoretical rather than actual. The higher clergy were only too happy to ignore the synodal decrees forbidding the clergy not only to take part in actual fighting but even to carry arms or participate in military expeditions.[1] Charles himself, in the emergency of the Saxon wars, entrusted the abbot Sturmi with the command of the Eresburg and repeatedly exacted military service from his prelates.[2] This made, of course, no difference to the legal condition of their lands, which belonged to the royal house[3] and were the king's property.[4] Men invested with such lands entered into a relationship with the king which was stricter than the older ties entered into by the free nobles when they attached themselves to the Frankish rulers at the time of the distribution of the conquered lands or even earlier. After all, the people who belonged to the king's households were his ' servants '. Although it did not necessarily follow that everyone, who served the king in this manner would lose his freedom, he nevertheless remained permanently subject to the will of the lord, often in a very harsh way.

Most of the Frankish higher clergy lived, of course, not in the royal palaces, but on the church lands belonging to the

---

[1] *Concilium Germanicum*, 742, repeated in the oldest of Charles's capitularies, 769. Cf. K. Voigt, *Die karolingische Klosterpolitik des westfränkischen Königtums*, Stuttgart, 1917, pp. 56, 77.

[2] Cf. the list in E. Lesne, *Histoire de la propriété ecclésiastique en France*, Lille-Paris, 1922, ii, 2, pp. 456 sq.

[3] The bishop was supposed to quit a royal monastery as soon as he had fulfilled his official duties, ' sicut de reliqua regis domo '. E. Lesne, op. cit., p. 7 n. 4, after Coll. Flavin, 44.   [4] Ibid., p. 11.

diocese to which the king had appointed them. As in the case
of the secular ' vassals ', however, it made no legal difference
whether the king fulfilled his obligation to maintain his vassals
and servants by providing them with a place in his household
and at his table or by granting them landed property. Charles
nominated bishops and archbishops for certain dioceses according
to his own will. He took the pope's approval for granted and
often requested it after the event, merely as a matter of form.
But at the same time he kept two bishops in his household. Both
Angilram of Metz and Hildebold of Cologne had to travel with
the ruler and leave their dioceses unattended. They were given
the title ' archbishop and arch-chaplain ' and served as councillors in ecclesiastical matters regardless of their proper spiritual
duties.[1] At the synod of 813 the most prominent place was
occupied by Hildebold, ' the archbishop of the sacred palace '.[2]

Notker's story of how Charles ordered a prelate, who had
been appointed bishop and was about to depart for his diocese,
to dismount from his horse, and then retained him for further
service at court, may have been invented.[3] But there can be no
doubt that the king governed the church in an autocratic manner.
Charles damaged the spiritual welfare of his subjects when he
left not merely abbeys and bishoprics but even archbishoprics
vacant, and diverted their revenues into his own coffers. Rheims,
for instance, was vacant for nine and Metz for twenty-seven
years.[4] Charles made no distinction between episcopal office or
episcopal property and those secular ' benefices ' which were the
king's to give or to retain in his own hands.[5] The prospect of
obtaining such a spiritual ' benefice ' was the magnet which drew
clergy from the whole kingdom to the royal palace. One source
asserts that they served the king for that reason and for that
reason alone.[6]

This state of affairs was hardly consonant with the provisions

---

[1] *Synodus Franconofurtensis*, c. 55 ; MGH, *Cap.*, i, p. 78. E. Lesne, op. cit., p. 132.
[2] L. Halphen, *Charlemagne*, Paris, 1947, pp. 158 sq.
[3] *Gesta Karoli*, i, 6, MGH, *Script.*, ii, pp. 733 sq. ; cf. ibid., i, 5.
[4] Hincmar, *De villa Noviliaco*, quoted in AS, ii, p. 309 n. 2 (about Rheims) ; E.
Lesne, op. cit., ii, 2, p. 103 (about Metz).
[5] E. Lesne, op. cit., pp. 76, 79.
[6] *Vita Walae*, ii, 5 ; MGH, *Script.*, ii, p. 550. Cf. E. Lesne, op. cit., p. 77 and
n. 4.

K

of canon law which required the free election of bishops. Charles never objected to free election on principle. On several occasions he himself granted charters to particular bishops and their dioceses conceding them the right of free election. But this was always a matter of royal favour. The king was always strong enough to assure the election of his own candidate in spite of such concessions. Royal appointment to church offices fitted in with current Frankish conceptions, and the pope was always too embroiled in his own difficulties to open up a question which would have been bound to lead to a life-and-death struggle with the Frankish monarchy. It probably cost pope Hadrian quite an effort to ordain a bishop by Charles's order, and then to add: ' Full of good will, we have carried out your orders as we are accustomed to do.'[1] But resistance would have made things worse.

Charles's absolute power of disposing of bishoprics and of disregarding canonical provisions is also proved by the fact that he allowed one bishop to hold more than one bishopric, provided the incumbent was a loyal man who could be trusted not to misuse this accumulation of power for selfish ends. Waldo, the abbot of Reichenau, through whose efforts the monastery was raised to a flourishing state, was forced against his will to administer the dioceses of Bâle and Pavia as well.[2] On the other hand, Charles was opposed to the establishment of an hierarchical organization of metropolitan churches, as envisaged by Rome. His opposition was not direct, but he seems to have been quite indifferent to such plans.[3] It is true that, by the end of his reign, there were 21 metropolitan sees in the empire. But no metropolitan had any real function and his office signified little more than a mere title.

Thus the position of the higher clergy in the Frankish king-

---

[1] MGH, *Epp.*, iii, p. 600, No. 70; cf. O. Meyer, in: ZSSRk, 1935, xxiv, pp. 335 sq.

[2] E. Munding, *Abt-Bischof Waldo*, Beuron-Leipzig, 1924. It is possible that this accumulation of offices was meant to consolidate the position of Charles's ' excellent collaborator ' and the teacher of Pepin. Cf. also K. Beyerle, ed., *Die Kultur der Abtei Reichenau*, München, 1925, i, p. 64.

[3] Thus also A. Hauck, *Kirchengeschichte Deutschlands*, ii (2nd ed.), p. 209. F. L. Ganshof in his review of the German edition of this book (*Moyen Age*, 1950, lvi, p. 378) does not agree with this judgment.

dom was, in principle, not different from that of the king's other faithful servants and vassals. Bishops were included among the king's vassals and were expected to carry out a large variety of duties appropriate to a vassal.[1] They were expected to be present at court whenever the king commanded and were not allowed to leave without special permission. Like the secular magnates, they were obliged to make yearly ' donations '. They had to serve as officials of the court and on diplomatic missions.[2] They were used especially as *missi*. Arno of Salzburg once complained bitterly to his friend Alcuin about this. Alcuin, in turn, deplored that ' the people who ought to be free to serve God are compelled to travel far and wide, and God's soldiers must fight for worldly things while the sword of the divine word remains unused in the scabbard of their mouth '.[3] But secular princes, he added, were after all entitled to ' oppress ' the church of Christ through their demands for service—to prove which he enumerated a whole series of biblical quotations commending submission to secular authority.[4]

'As long as I was forced to pay for my keep with work and money, I had leisure to study the holy Scriptures. Since I have been a bishop, the amount of business has grown and has given rise to more and more worries. There is no leisure for my favourite studies during the winter, when I am travelling to and from the palace. In the middle of spring I take my parchments and my arms and go down to the coast to fight Saracens and Moors. At night I hold my sword; during the day I use my books and my pen. Thus I seek fulfilment of my dreams.'[5] This was written by the bishop of Turin a few years after Charles's death. But it is very probable that similar conditions obtained earlier. In those earlier days, however, such complaints must have been occasioned less by independent activities than by constant service at court and in war in obedience to the imperial command.

Such was the fate of a member of the clergy who sought the spiritual life whenever the pressure of business allowed. If we are to believe a complaint by Paulinus, the bishops of the arch-

[1] H. Mitteis, *Lehnrecht und Staatsgewalt*, Weimar, 1933, p. 73.
[2] Cf. the enumeration of services in E. Lesne, op. cit., ii, 2, pp. 433 sqq.
[3] MGH, *Epp.*, iv, p. 409, No. 253.
[4] Ibid., p. 423, No. 265. [5] Ibid., p. 601, No. 6.

diocese of Aquileia were of a different mettle. They never went near their towns. ' They were rapacious and aggressive. They encouraged and goaded on all bloodthirsty criminals.' They robbed the church by using her property for war and worldly vanities.[1] But these ecclesiastical princes were not merely prompted by the desire for glory and by vanity. They must also have been tempted to use their episcopal power to help their families, their relatives and their friends in worldly feuds. The admonition that nobody should be tempted by his relatives to desire wordly wealth was most opportune.[2] Frankish synods were forced again and again to protest against the practice of ' many bishops who, prompted by the love of of their relatives, bought property and serfs either in their own name or in the name of their friends and then amalgamated such acquisitions with the property of these relatives '.[3]

Such transactions usually remained unchallenged so long as the holder of an ecclesiastical office was alive. But as soon as he was dead they were put to the test, for it was always questionable whether the family of the deceased could defend these acquisitions against his successor. No matter how difficult it was for a newcomer to hold his own against the family of his predecessor, he could always rely upon the support of those people who had made pious donations to the church and who had watched with wrath how their donations had found their way into secular hands.[4] The constant repetition, throughout the whole Carolingian epoch,[5] of synodal decrees against such malpractices is ample proof of the fact that they could never be entirely eradicated.

The ruler himself often handed over to laymen property which had been donated to the church. This was, on the whole, in the public interest, especially when it was a question of making royal service attractive or of rewarding such service with princely generosity. The wishes of the abbot or the bishop, who was

[1] Ibid., p. 526, No. 18 b.
[2] Ibid., pp. 347 sq., No. 209.
[3] *Concilium Paris.*, 829, c. 16 ; MGH, *Conc.*, ii, p. 623.
[4] MGH, *Conc.*, ii, i, pp. 211 sq., c. 37 ; ' ut a cetera plebe vel his qui res suas ibidem offerunt, murmur vel detractio auferatur '.
[5] For example, *Capitulare Ecclesiasticum*, 818, c. 29 ; MGH, *Cap.*, i, p. 279. *Capitulare Wormatiense*, 829, c. 2 ; MGH, *Cap.*, ii, p. 12. *Concilium Mogunt.*, 852, c. 5 ; MGH, *Cap.*, ii, p. 186. *Cap. Tribur.*, 895, c. 32 ; MGH, *Cap.*, ii, p. 232.

charged with the control of such property, were often ignored or overruled.[1] On the death of an abbot, the whole abbey could be given to a layman. Bishoprics were, at least officially, protected from a similar fate by the fact that although it was possible to have a lay-abbot, it was not possible to have a lay-bishop. Nevertheless many a noble was ordained in undignified haste in order to become a bishop. Furthermore, most bishoprics were inferior in the wealth of their landed property to the large abbeys[2] and were, therefore, less desirable benefices. Many a bishop had to become an abbot as a sideline in order to finance the administration of his diocese with monastic wealth. As a rule, it was taken for granted that a bishop was entitled to lay claim to, and to dispose of, the possessions of churches and monasteries subject to him, even when the latter had heads of their own. In particular, the bishops often passed on military demands to their inferiors,[3] who had to serve the bishop as he himself was bound to serve his royal master.

Such obligations to the bishop, however, tended to be neglected if a monastery had a lay-abbot who, as a royal vassal, himself owed immediate service to the king.[4] In many places, moreover, the king had transformed his general protection over all churches and their property into a special protection. In this way he created a very close tie between himself and the churches in question, thus considerably reducing the diocesan's official rights. Grants of royal protection were also extended at times to monasteries owned by nobles. Resistance was impossible. ' Special' royal protection became a means of extending even further the network of royal control over ecclesiastical property.[5] It also served to create new positions and sources of revenue which were, in turn, handed out to faithful followers and vassals as a reward for their services. In principle, however, the proprietary rights of the nobility over their own churches and monasteries continued to exist. In fact, the Council of Frankfort, in 794, expressly confirmed the right of all free-born

[1] On *praecaria verbo regis* see E. Lesne, op. cit., ii, 2, p. 205.
[2] A. Hauck, op. cit., p. 216.
[3] A. Pöschl, *Bischofsgut und mensa episcopalis*, Bonn, 1909, ii, p. 204.
[4] On the position of lay abbots see K. Voigt, op. cit.
[5] E. Lesne, op. cit., pp. 40 sqq., 56 sqq.

owners of proprietary churches to give them away or to sell them. This concession was popular and thus strengthened Charles's position at home in his conflict with Byzantium.[1]

This measure shows once again that in the reign of Charles the Great people were not yet willing to translate their principles into practice. They preferred to accept existing conditions, modifying them here and there in order to bring them into greater harmony with their theories. The above-mentioned decree of the synod of Frankfort is a case in point. It contained a rider that no alienation of a proprietary church must damage the church itself or make the holding of divine service impossible. Thus a compromise was found between conflicting tendencies. The conflict itself, however, was not solved, but only postponed.

We shall have occasion later to return to the question of proprietary churches owned by ecclesiastical and secular magnates and to the lower clergy who were in charge of them. In the meantime, while we are endeavouring to draw a picture of the ruling classes of the Frankish kingdom, it is time to turn to the lesser nobility from whose ranks the ruling classes were replenished and upon whose services their power was based. Our sources are sparing enough in their information about the higher aristocracy. They fail us almost completely in regard to the lesser nobility. Yet knowledge of their position is extremely important if we are to understand the structure of Frankish society. This lack of information is, of course, not surprising when we remember that the men of that time, unless they were members of the clergy or occupied high public positions, were illiterate. Furthermore, even in the royal capitularies which contained the king's commands and enactments, the lesser nobility were usually mentioned only indirectly. Injunctions concerning them were given mostly to their lords and protectors, the ' powerful ' and ' prominent ' magnates. We are therefore, in general, dependent upon indirect evidence and our picture of the people half way between the magnates and the lowly remains shadowy.

Even for Franks from the highest ranks of the nobility it had become almost impossible to live without close ties and obligations

[1] MGH, *Conc.*, ii, i, p. 171, c. 54.

to the monarchy. For a free-man of the middle classes it was even more difficult to preserve his independence on a relatively small property and to resist the magnetic attraction of the great powers in the kingdom, either the monarchy itself or one of the secular or ecclesiastical magnates of the upper class.

Even those who succeeded in preserving their independence were, of course, not free from the obligation to pay taxes and render service. In their case, however, these obligations were due not to a noble lord but to the king himself, because the king was the protector of all those who had not entered into a special relationship with anyone else. In addition there was military service for the king. The independent free-man was obliged to find his food and his equipment for such service from his own resources. Furthermore, there was the duty to journey three times a year to the place where a court of law was held and, from time to time, the duty to pursue a criminal or to participate in an operation for clearing the forests of dangerous vagabonds. Then there were the forced labour services for the building of palaces and churches for the king,[1] and the duty to act as a messenger and to give hospitality to royal officers. Finally there were the dues rendered to the church. The most important of these was the tithe, the payment of which was prescribed by the law of the realm and could be legally enforced by the count. The duty to pay tithes was even enjoined in the oath of fealty of 802.[2]

Besides these obligations the free-man faced economic hardships in times of failing harvest or of a cattle epidemic, and the gentle (and sometimes not so gentle) pressure of neighbouring magnates—pressure which was irresistible in view of the fact that it was practically impossible to defend a legal claim against aristocratic officials. All these factors must have combined to force the small landowner into the arms of one lord or another who would protect him against his neighbours, appear on his behalf in a court of law, and ease his burden of military service. Such a lord might even give him a post in the administration of his domain, an office which was likely to be more profitable

---

[1] Cf. the comprehensive account of forced labour services for building by G. Weise, in: *Vierteljahrsschrift für Sozial- und Wirtschaftsgeschichte*, 1921, xv, esp. pp. 357, 377 sq.

[2] MGH, *Cap.*, i, p. 93, c. 8.

than the income derived from his own small property. (During
the unquiet years when the kingdom was expanding, the duty
to render military service caused many free-men to surrender
their allodial property to a lord.[1] The lord could grant the land
back to the original owner as a *precarium* for life.[2] The ' man '
was then obliged to beg (*precari*) for what used to be his own
property. He no longer had a legal claim to it. His position was
indeed ' precarious '. He himself remained, legally, a free-man ;
at least so long as he did not commend his own person into the
hands of a lord, which was more infrequent than the commendation of land.[3] The obligation to perform military service, of
course, continued ; but it was now economically less burden-
some. Similarly a lord was able to ease the burden of the labour
services expected of his ' man ' for the king's building activities,
and might even buy his release.

(The people who became the ' men ' or ' vassals ' of a magnate
in this manner retained their freedom together with the control
of, and the revenue from, their old property. But the obligation
into which they had thus entered could not be renounced without
good cause. Nevertheless, during the reign of Charles the Great
the position of the vassals improved to the extent that the ' man '
was absolved from his oath of fealty to his lord when the latter
tried to kill him, tried to reduce him to the status of an unfree
serf, denied him the promised protection or seduced his wife.[4]
These were, of course, exceptional cases which always required
trial before a court of law where, often enough, the testimony
of the *potentes* weighed more heavily than considerations of
justice. On the other hand, the lord protected his vassal against
the encroachments of superior royal officials whenever the latter
demanded, for their private profit, more services and more
payments than were actually due to the king. He also gave

[1] Cf. *Polyptichon Irminonis*, quoted in H. Sée, *Les classes rurales et le régime domanial
en France au Moyen Age*, Paris, 1901, p. 49 n. 2. Delbrück's thesis that free peasants
were able to get relief from military service has been criticised by W. Erben in :
Historische Zeitschrift, 1908, cl, p. 333.
[2] H. Sée, op. cit., p. 22 ; F. L. Ganshof, *Feudalism*, London, 1952, pp. 11, 18.
[3] F. Lütge, *Die Agrarverfassung des frühen Mittelalters im mitteldeutschen Raum*, Jena,
1937, pp. 97 sqq. ; also for earlier literature on the subject.
[4] H. Mitteis, *Lehnrecht und Staatsgewalt*, Weimar, 1933, pp. 88 sq. ; cf. pp. 45 sq.

protection if these officials were guilty of blackmail or simply requisitioned whatever they happened to need in order to ingratiate themselves with the officers of the royal palace or with other magnates.[1] It was also possible for the poor and powerless to find redress of their grievances through their lord if, on the day on which a court of law was to be held, the counts preferred to go hunting or to attend a banquet rather than the *mallus* ;[2] or when—like 'friends of Satan', as they were once called— they devoured the population of their province instead of protecting them.[3]

In return, the 'man' had to obey his lord who demanded a variety of services from him. He now belonged to his lord's household and was one of his servants. He could not take offence if he were put in charge of the lord's stables or asked to count the chickens, pigs and cheeses delivered by the peasants. Similarly, he could be detailed to guard the wife and children of his lord during the latter's absence on public service.[4]

The vassals of the nobility were still obliged in principle to render public service, but they were no longer summoned as individuals to the fyrd. Instead they took part in military expeditions in the retinue of their lord. It was not, however, in the lord's interest to deplete his domain of all able-bodied men and to expose all of them to the dangers of a military expedition. Many of Charles's capitularies were directed against the various pretexts under which magnates arbitrarily excused their vassals from military service.[5] On the other hand, many a count tried to excuse his friends and relatives from the general levy.[6]

The efficiency of the royal army must have been greatly impaired by the prevalence of such practices, and the manpower thus withheld from the army was often enough diverted to private feuds and local wars. The *potentes* were always willing to let the struggle for power and prestige in their provinces degenerate into an open feud. During Charles's reign they were

---

[1] Thus Duke John of Istria, 805 ; quoted after AS, ii, pp. 340 sq.
[2] MGH, *Cap.*, i, p. 63, c. 17 (789).
[3] *Visio Wettini* ; Fr. v. Bezold, *Historische Zeitschrift*, 1924, vol. cxxx, p. 382.
[4] H. Mitteis, op. cit., p. 39 ; see also the following note.
[5] *Capitulare Missorum*, 819, c. 27 ; MGH. *Cap.*, i, p. 291.
[6] MGH, *Cap.*, i, p. 93, c. 7, 9 (802). Cf. also MGH, *Cap.*, i, p. 124, c. 9.

afraid of his wrath and of the authority of a strong, central power. But as soon as the central government had lost its overpowering authority, these forces threatened to lead to a war of all against all and to a complete anarchy among the aristocratic factions.

It was in vain that orders were given for all who refused to abandon private feuds and to settle their quarrels in a court of law to be sent to the king's palace, where they might expect to be punished by banishment to another part of the kingdom.[1] Not even the general oath of fealty imposed by Charles contained a general prohibition of feuds. Instead the government contented itself with prohibiting the carrying of arms ' within the fatherland ', and with setting up courts of arbitration with the possibility of appeal to the tribunal of the palace.[2] But as far as the prohibition of carrying arms was concerned, not even the clergy were inclined to obey it. The lesser vassals who were themselves hardly in a position to conduct a feud, could always induce their lords to interfere in their quarrels by invoking their right to protection. There was enough inflammable material everywhere to cause a conflagration, and to involve lords and vassals in private warfare on the slightest provocation. The institution of the *missi* was primarily designed for the settlement of such disputes. But not even the most primitive form of private warfare, the blood feud, actually died out. On the contrary, it appears to have flourished especially among the lesser nobility and the stewards of large domains.[3]

The vassals were too weak and too dependent on their lord to resist him individually. As yet there was no such thing as an ' association of vassals ' which could act on behalf of its members and call the lord to account when he violated the oath of fealty. A single vassal was powerless ; only all the vassals together would have been strong enough to demand redress. But there were associations of a different kind, formed by the members of the minor nobility and sometimes also by members of the lower classes, which must have played a very definite role in the political life of the times. Here again the sources are far

[1] MGH, *Cap.*, i, p. 51, c. 22.   [2] MGH, *Cap.*, i, p. 123, c. 5.
[3] Cf. e.g., MGH, *Cap.*, i, p. 97, c. 32 (802).

from explicit and yield little more than occasional details. Nevertheless we have some information ; for example, the decree issued by Louis the Pious and Lothar, which enacts that ' assemblies (*collectae*) for the performance of evil actions are prohibited. . . . We are to be informed if such associations have been formed through the count's negligence, or if their formation has remained unpunished. The leading spirit, if he is a provost, an *advocatus*, a *hundredman*, or any other free-man holding office, is to be brought before us. The others, whether they be serfs or free-men, are to suffer the punishment prescribed by law '.[1]

Provosts—that is, superior officers in the widest sense of the term—were, like the *advocati*, administrative officers on the domains of secular and ecclesiastical magnates. The hundredman, however, was first and foremost a judicial officer, the successor of those popular officials who had enforced customary law in the days before tribal custom was submerged by the institutions of the Frankish kingdom. All these functionaries, typical of that middle group in the Frankish society we are dealing with, would therefore seem to have collected around them a following of their own. Their intention was not to compete with the higher nobility. What, then, was their purpose? What else, but the desire to revenge in justice where the ordinary courts had failed, could have induced them to ' do evil ' or ' cause damage '? All the participants must have been aware of the grave consequences joining in such an association might have for them. Nevertheless collective self-help was the only means of restraining the *potentes* : process of law, as available to lesser men, was useless.

Among the ancient Germans the formation of fellowships and associations had been an ingrained custom. The habit of forming guilds seems, indeed, to have been taken over from the age of paganism. Originally such guilds had been cult-associations, centring round the communal drinking for sacrificial purposes.[2] It is unlikely that their character underwent much change when Christian saints and, later, members of the ruling

---

[1] MGH, *Leg.*, i, p. 352, c. 10.
[2] E. Coornaert, *Les ghildes médiévales, Revue Historique*, 1948, cxcix, pp. 22 sqq.

family[1] were made their patrons, or when the practical purpose of mutual help in emergencies such as poverty, damage through fire, or, in the coastal provinces, shipwreck, came to the fore.[2] Such associations always remained suspect to the ruling classes against whom they could so easily be directed; and although they could hardly be considered a danger to the kingdom, Charles was prevailed upon to prohibit them, and the magnates were charged with the enforcement of the prohibition.[3] It has been observed, not without justification, that such 'oath-guilds' were to be found especially in regions where the *potentes* had become all-powerful, the opportunities of the middle and lower orders were more and more curtailed, and in which, contrary to the law, free-men were being forced into servitude.[4] In such districts the guilds could easily become downright conspiracies, leading to open rebellion with 'robbery and arson', the marks of a true feud.

The lesser men seem to have fared better as officials and vassals of the church than under the secular magnates. This was certainly not always due to the fact that Christianity forbade the oppression of one's neighbour, although in this respect, the higher clergy doubtless exercised greater restraint than the secular nobility. But in the church the social and economic opportunities were much greater than on the estates of secular magnates. The clergy themselves were not allowed to appear in court where, often enough, ordeal by battle was still enforced. They needed an *advocatus* who could take an oath or do battle in court, who would arrest the criminals among the serfs on the church estates and hand them over to the public judges, or who, in petty cases, would mete out punishment himself. At the same time, these *advocati*—ecclesiastical landholders were supposed to have at least one in every county where their estates lay—carried out the same functions as the officials of secular landholders. They were the lords' servants and could be appointed and

---

[1] MGH, *Leg.*, i, p. 64; E. Coornaert, op. cit., p. 33.
[2] MGH, *Cap.*, i, p. 51, c. 16 (779).
[3] Loc. cit., and frequently later.
[4] A. Dopsch, *Die Wirtschaftsentwicklung der Karolingerzeit*, Weimar, 1921, ii (2nd ed.), p. 30. On the way in which feuds were conducted in the later middle ages see O. Brunner, *Land und Herrschaft*, Wien, 1943.

removed at will. There was nothing, as yet, to foreshadow the predominant position which the aristocratic *advocati* of a later age were to occupy in relation to their charges.

In many cases it would appear that members of noble families who became ecclesiastical dignitaries simply took over the vassals of their house. Such vassals retained their old place in the retinue of their lord. ' We are very surprised ', wrote Charles the Great, ' that a man who maintains that he has left the world and who will not tolerate being called a secular person, is anxious to keep armed followers and private possessions. Such things are suitable for people who have not left the world. In what way they pertain to spiritual persons, we do not know, unless those who themselves have no doubt that it is proper for them to usurp such things, will explain it to us '.[1] The king's displeasure, however, was not directed against the institution of vassalage as such but only against its excesses. For in the same year it was laid down that spiritual lords were to hand over arms only to their own vassals and to nobody else. All superfluous swords and chain mail stored in churches were to be reported to the king.[2] This order sanctioned the existence of vassals of cathedral churches and monasteries, for the military levy would have suffered considerably from their suppression. The higher clergy were certainly more punctilious in the fulfilment of their duties towards the king than were many of the less dependent secular magnates.

In many monasteries the amount of land granted to vassals reached considerable proportions. It has been estimated that, on the average, about one half of a monastery's property was thus granted away.[3] But this was by no means sufficient to free the numerous middle order of small men of its worries and its need for money. As the lord's rights usually weighed heavier with him than his obligations, he was always able, in the economic field, to increase the vassals' services until they were left with little more than the bare necessities. The vassals in turn sought to compensate themselves at the expense of their serfs, either on their own allodial estates, or those subject to them as office-

---

[1] *Capitula de causis cum episcopis et abbatibus tractandis*, c. 8 ; MGH, *Cap.*, i, p. 163.
[2] MGH, *Cap.*, i, p. 167, c. 10.
[3] E. Lesne, op. cit., ii, 2, p. 482.

holders, or on fiefs with which they had been invested. The
position of the serfs towards these lords was no better than the
position of the lords themselves towards their superiors. The
economic pressure was simply passed on, either legally or by
threats and blackmail, to the lowest orders. The 'poorer vassals'
were not allowed to become *missi* because they were known to be
open to bribery.[1] Among the officers of the large estates there
were 'evil, cruel, rapacious, perjured and false' men.[2] If a
capitulary laid down that only men with property of their own
in the county concerned could be made *advocati*,[3] this was only
partly due to the fact that, for such an office, men of standing
were needed. Often enough, it seems, the property served as a
security, in case the advocate was guilty of a transgression and
had to be called to account.

The institution of the *advocatus* afforded the Frankish clergy,
who had officially relinquished their worldly ties, an opportunity
of behaving like noble magnates and of fulfilling their obligations
to the king. The ban—that is, the secular power to command—
was transferred to an official who, in those days, was still a
pliable tool in the hand of his ecclesiastical lord. In this way the
ecclesiastical dignitary enjoyed the worldly income and prestige
of a secular magnate and was simultaneously a servant of the
church ; he was secure in both stations. But this type of small,
subordinate advocate could only cope with his task so long as
the ruler was able to control the secular nobility through the
force of his personality. Later on, the more the imperial administration lost its grip, the more difficult it became to keep the
church's estates intact. In the west, as the Empire declined,
some of the bishops and abbots managed to maintain their power.
They used the weapon of excommunication and no longer
hesitated to wield their swords, with the result that they sometimes managed to provide a haven of peace in a time of troubles.
But other ecclesiastical dignitaries were forced to choose their
advocates from the ranks of the higher nobility. The latter thus
obtained in a legal manner what they had been coveting for a

[1] *Annales Laureshamenses*, MGH, *Script.*, i, p. 38.
[2] *Conc. Mogunt.*, 813, c. 50 ; MGH, *Conc.*, ii, i, p. 272. See F. Senn, *L'institution des avoueries eccl. en France*, Thèse, Paris, 1903, p. 13.
[3] Quoted ibid., pp. 33 sqq.

long tine by means of open feuds : hereditary dominion over ecclesiastical property. And ultimately even members of the lesser nobility succeeded in acquiring such powers in a bishopric or a county.

The old class structure, already undermined, had given way to an unstable balance of power which, during the few decades when the Frankish empire was flourishing, could easily be mistaken for contentment and peace. When civil wars exhausted the material resources, the struggle for existence was to become more bitter and the methods by which it was pursued more brutal. Charles the Great's administration had succeeded in compelling people to pay lip-service to Christianity. During the later years of the Empire it was to become apparent how little Christianity had entered into the hearts either of rulers or of ruled. The failure to convert society to true Christianity meant, however, that peace—the famous peace of the Christian Empire —became little more than a word to describe a momentary lull in an armed combat.

CHAPTER VI

THE POOR

To be a Frank meant to be free. This is indicated by the very meaning of the word. The position of the serf was the very opposite of freedom, for he was not judged according to tribal custom but was subject to the arbitrary authority of his master. The *potentes*, on the other hand, the new as well as the old ones, were free. And even those ranks of society that had been forced into some kind of vassalage remained free in a legal sense. Of these it was said about the end of Charles's reign : 'For a variety of reasons the properties of the poor have, in many places, been much reduced ; that is to say, the properties of those who are known as free-men but who live under the authority of powerful magnates. If our most gracious lord instituted an inquiry into their legal condition and into litigation concerning them, it would be revealed that many, through various causes, have been reduced to extreme poverty.'[1] It is difficult to reconcile the idealized picture of the Germanic peasant, living on his hide of land and obliged to serve the king but otherwise independent, with the foregoing description. The old order of personal liberty, to which people had tenaciously clung for centuries, no longer corresponded to existing social conditions. Within the class of free-men there were inumerable forms of social differentiation : it extended from the king's lieutenant to the poor cottager clearing the forest in the service of his lord.

As is well known, in the Frankish state there was no nobility in the sense of a well-defined social order. Often nobility was simply equated with wealth ; whereas to be a peasant was synonymous with suffering and need.[2] It is true that many people had managed to preserve their economic freedom. But, in general,

[1] *Conc. Turonense*, MGH, *Conc.*, ii, i, p. 292.
[2] Paulus Diaconus to Charles : 'Coniunx est fratris rebus exclusa paternis, iamque sumus servis rusticitatae pares. Nobilitas periit miseris, accessit aegestas.' MGH, *Poet.*, i, p. 48, No. 10.

this had been possible only where none of the great lords had found their property attractive. Such had been the case especially in inclement mountainous regions such as Switzerland, upper Bavaria and parts of Franconia. In the plains, on the other hand, the domains of ecclesiastical and secular magnates had spread and absorbed the smaller properties.[1]

The minor free-men, who surrendered their hereditary property to a magnate and who were granted a tenement in exchange, often found that they had jumped out of the frying pan into the fire. It was not only that their new holding had often to be cleared of forest, which could only be achieved by hard labour; in addition, they had to perform labour-services on the estate of their lord. In St. Germain-des-Prés, for example, five weeks of labour in the year were due for ' free ' tenures, and three days a week for ' servile ' tenures; and, at times, even free-men were forced to accept an ' unfree ' tenure with its heavier burden of service.[2] The lord's rights, sanctioned by imprisonment and corporal punishment,[3] were supreme in the economic as well as in the political sphere.

In many cases the surrender of allodial property was due to threats and pressure from the *potentes*. Charles the Great laid down that royal officials at least, should refrain from exploiting the hardships of the poor and from using chicanery and subterfuge to acquire their property.[4] All sales of land were to be transacted publicly in the presence of count, judges, and nobility, or of the bishop.[5] In 802, when all free-men had been compelled to promise under oath to pay their monetary dues to the king and to the church, it had also been necessary to take measures to prevent the enforced alienation of the properties of free-men, ' lest their relatives be illegally disinherited, the king's service diminished, and heirs compelled by want to become beggars and robbers '.[6] Little did it avail these disinherited people that they were free in status! Unless they could find a place in the service of a lord, they had no choice save to accept bondage or flee into

[1] A. Dopsch, op. cit., i (2nd ed.), pp. 308 sq.
[2] H. Sée, op. cit., p. 55, after the *Polyptichon Irminonis*.
[3] H. Mitteis, op. cit., p. 35.
[4] *Conc. Arelatense*, 813, c. 23; MGH, *Conc.*, ii, i, p. 253.
[5] See G. Waitz, op. cit., iv, p. 337 n. 2.   [6] MGH, *Cap.*, i, p. 125, c. 16.

L

a monastery. But even flight into a monastery was blocked by a royal Capitulary. ' Regarding free-men who desire to devote themselves to the service of God,' it was laid down : ' they must not do so without royal permission. This is because we understand that some are prompted not so much by piety as by the desire to avoid military or other forms of royal service. Of others it is said that they have fallen victim to the greed of men who covet their property.'[1]

Evidently many of those whose descent in the social scale was not rapid enough for their neighbours' convenience, were pushed into the status of bondmen. A formulary in use under Louis the Pious includes a charter restoring freedom to those who had been forced into servitude by royal officials.[2] This fits in well with Thegan's statement that, after the death of Charles, Louis's *missi* had found ' innumerable people who had been oppressed by being deprived of their hereditary lands or of their freedom '.[3] Thegan, no doubt, was attempting to shed a rosy light upon the reign of Louis the Pious by a lurid portrayal of earlier conditions. But we have less reason to doubt that such things happened during the reign of Charles than we have to believe that they were abolished by Louis's good intentions.

It would leave a false impression to picture the decline of one section of the free population without also presenting the opposite side—namely, the emergence from obscurity of many serfs and sons of serfs, and their rise to high official positions. Just as a man who was legally free could be in economic servitude, so a serf might own land like a free-man. If on one side power was accumulating in the hands of the lords of great seignorial estates, on the other hand other estates were breaking up for political and economic reasons. Some lordships were rigorously centralized ; in others the single farms were leased at a fixed rent. The tenants of such farms had greater freedom and mobility than the average peasant who lived on the lord's land.[4] One result of this looser organization was that the serfs

---

[1] Ibid., c. 15.
[2] MGH, *For.*, pp. 291, 293 (*formulae imperiales*, Nos. 5, 9). There is nothing like this in the *formulae Marculfi* in the age of Charles.
[3] *Vita Hludovici Imperatoris*, c. 13 ; MGH, *Script.*, ii, p. 593.
[4] A. Dopsch, *Herrschaft und Bauer in der deutschen Kaiserzeit*, Jena, 1939, p. 61.

themselves might live almost like lords.[1] It was also possible
for a lord to free a serf at will. He might do so for religious
reaons[2]—for example, to enable him to take orders[3]—or when
a serf married the daughter of a free-man, or in order to increase
the number of his estate officials. Administrative positions on
seignorial estates were often deliberately filled by people devoted
to the lord and dependent on him because their economic status
did not differ from that of the other peasants.[4]

Anyone who had to direct reclamation, ploughing, or the
cultivation of vineyards required a practical knowledge of agricul-
ture.[5] The steward of a manor had also to know some arithmetic
and was probably often required to give an account in writing.
Serfs or free peasants who desired a career as administrators,
cellarers, foresters, huntsmen, builders, etc. needed both intelligence and an elementary education. These *ministeriales*, the lord's
servants and agents, shared in his position and in his political
and social prestige. Their ranks extended from the peasant
employed in clearing the forests, who was little more than a
foreman, to the official who rode on horseback through the
estates of one of the powerful abbeys or bishoprics and who
could eventually become a councillor or minister at the court
of his master. The Carolingians themselves had begun their
political career as stewards, or mayors of the household, of the
Merovingian kings.

Here, in the royal palace, there were still the greatest opportunities. The sons of poor men went to school there together
with nobles, and, according to Notker, Charles the Great made
flattering remarks about the intelligence and industry of the
former in contrast to the aristocratic ignorance of the latter.[6]
It is true that Notker, who reported that the young scholars
stemming from the middle and the lower classes were unex-

[1] One should compare A. Déléage, *La vie rurale en Bourgogne*, Macon, 1941, to
which I have not had access and of which I know only through the review in *Specu-
lum*, 1947, xxii, pp. 635 sqq.
[2] See *Formulae Sal. Lindenbrogianae*, No. 11 ; H. Sée, op. cit., p. 57 n. 2
[3] A. Dopsch, op. cit., p. 39.
[4] H. Sée, op. cit., p. 125.
[5] See the quotations, ibid., p. 126 n. 4.
[6] *Gesta Karoli*, c. 3 ; MGH, *Script.*, ii, p. 732.

pectedly intelligent,[1] was their advocate. But this judgment was confirmed by Thegan, the protagonist of the nobility and the enemy of all low-born public officials.[2] The commoners in the royal palace had, of course, been selected for their special ability. But the poorer people were also spurred on by the memory of hardships unknown to the sons of magnates. Walahfrid Strabo was a typical example of the forced precocity of such youths. The son of a free-man,[3] he had spent his youth in poverty and had been compelled to beg a cloak from the abbot of Reichenau. At the age of sixteen, or perhaps even earlier, he composed a life of a Greek martyr in verse. Soon one work followed another until he was, at the age of twenty, recommended to the court and promoted to be the teacher of Louis the Pious's favourite son.[4]

Ebo, the archbishop of Rheims, who aroused the ire of Thegan and his fellow nobles, was the son of a royal serf. ' The emperor has granted you freedom, but not nobility, for that is impossible '.[5] Thus Thegan addressed him personally ; but he cannot have been quite serious when he added that serfs were trying to ' oppress ' nobles. No doubt, such upstarts were competitors of the nobility ; but this is more true for the times of Louis than of his father. During the reign of Charles the Great the granting of offices to emancipated serfs always remained an exception ;[6] in fact, only one deed of manumission has survived from his reign.[7]

For the serfs of secular magnates the chance of rising to higher spheres seems, on the whole, to have been very small. Now and again, there was a lucky one, but the mass of serfs remained excluded. On ecclesastical estates, however, the position was different. Here manumissions must have taken place in large numbers. In St. Germain-des-Prés, for instance,

---

[1] Loc. cit. : ' Mediocres igitur et infimi praeter spem omnibus sapientiae condimentis dulcoratos obtulerunt ; nobiles vero omni fatuitate tepentes praesentarunt '.

[2] Thegan, op. cit., c. 20, p. 595 : ' Et licet aliquid sint periti, tamen superat eorum doctrinam criminum multitudo '.

[3] A. Schulte, *Der Adel und die deutsche Kirche im Mittelalter*, Stuttgart, 1910, pp. 129 sq. ; Fr. v. Bezold, in : *Historische Zeitschrift*, cxxx, p. 383 n. 2, agrees.

[4] M. Manitius, op. cit., p. 302.

[5] Thegan, op. cit., c. 44, p. 599.

[6] Ibid., c. 50, p. 601.   [7] MGH, *Dip.*, i, No. 115.

for every servile household there were twenty-three belonging to free-men and manumitted serfs.[1] Nevertheless manumission, although it was pleasing to God, made little difference to the social status of the person concerned. When people were described as *homines ecclesiastici* or as *fiscalini* no notice was taken of the distinction between free-men and serfs. When it was laid down that all owners of oxen must plough their lord's field for one or two days every week, and that those without must perform manual labour for their lord from dawn to dusk three times a week, the regulation applied to both classes alike. These regulations, it should be noted, which were issued by the government, did not always signify an increase in labour dues. In many cases, on the contrary, they meant an easing of the burden. For on many estates the tenants had been compelled to perform labour services the whole week through.[2]

The services demanded by ecclesiastical lords were not, in principle, any less heavy than those demanded by secular lords. But in fact it is probable that the prelates were better masters than most nobles. There were, of course, exceptions. We know of bishops and abbots who were utterly unscrupulous in their efforts to increase their income and who tricked men out of their property.[3] Referring to the bishops, Theodulf once paraphrased the passage in the Bible about those who, instead of searching for the lost sheep, are only capable of ruling with harshness and violence.[4] It was also possible for an ecclesiastical tenant to be given, in addition to his ecclesiastical lord, a secular master. This happened if ecclesiastical property was granted as a benefice to a noble, either voluntarily or by royal order. In such cases the tithe would be doubled; in other words, the church concerned was indemnified at the expense of the peasant for the loss of its property. In some places not even royal sanctions could enforce the payment of taxes on this scale, and some of the prelates, acting without the approval of higher authority, had recourse to spiritual penalties to secure the payment of the tithe.[5]

[1] A. Dopsch, *Wirtschaftsentwicklung*, ii (2nd ed.), p. 37.
[2] MGH, *Cap.*, i, p. 81 (800).   [3] MGH, *Cap.*, i, p. 163, c. 5.
[4] MGH, *Poet.*, i, p. 456.
[5] A. Dopsch, op. cit., p. 25.

Where the economic margin was so narrow, it was scarcely possible to build up reserves for years of want, and every failure of the harvest was bound to have the most serious consequences. Already the famine in 791 had led to cannibalism, and some people had eaten members of their own families.[1] In the year in which the imperial coronation took place, Alcuin admitted that the people were in distress, that the times were fraught with danger, and that one plague was followed by another.[2] The clouds which were to darken the whole sky in the reign of Louis, were already gathering towards the end of Charles's reign. The economic exhaustion of large masses of the people sharpened the struggle of the *potentes* for their share in the shrinking resources, which were no longer sufficient for all. The same exhaustion tempted a large number of ecclesiastical as well as secular magnates to go to extremes, and finally undermined the whole structure of the empire.

As in all times of scarcity there was much speculation and usury, although the taking of interest was prohibited. It was the church's duty to punish with fasting on bread and water for three years, all those who lent money and demanded back more than they had lent, contrary to the commands of the Old Testament and the decrees of the popes.[3] But ecclesiastical legislation could not prevent people from using the opportunity to enrich themselves through the distress of their fellow men. Nor could it prevent speculation in grain. From 794 onwards capitulary after capitulary inveighed against such speculation. At harvest-time rich people bought as much as they could from the smaller peasants and landowners in order to re-sell it at two or three times the original price in years of bad harvest. The main profit of such transactions went not to professional merchants but to the proprietors of large domains, for whom such dealings were also a lever to bring the small free and half-free peasants under their control.[4] For this reason the prohibition of usury was especially urgent in those districts where the power of the

---

[1] *Annales Mosellani*; *Annales Laureshamenses*; *Annales Moissiac.*; quoted in MGH, *Cap.*, i, p. 76 n. 31.

[2] MGH, *Epp.*, iv, p. 320, No. 193.

[3] For the following remarks see F. Schaub, *Der Kampf gegen den Zinswucher*, etc., Freiburg i. B., 1905.   [4] Ibid., p. 47.

nobility was flourishing most—that is, in the west Frankish lands and in Italy.

It has been observed that Charles's capitularies, although they denounced such practices, never laid down any sanctions against the taking of interest and usury. There was good reason for this. Since ' the usurers of these days were normally identical with the owners of the large estates, that is, with the great feudatories,'[1] it was inconceivable that any diet or great council would have assented to such a law. Moral condemnation was sufficient to satisfy Christian and ecclesiastical requirements, and the struggle to make it effective was left to the clergy who were not, in fact, always willing to enforce canon law in this sphere. The problem was shelved without being solved. Only in the stormy year 829 was the enforcement of the prohibition included among the demands of those who set out to protect the poor against ' the innumerable varieties of usury practised by the great '.[2]

The references in the sources to the exploitation of the poor cannot be dismissed as mere ' examples of conventional sermonizing '.[3] Otherwise there would not have been so many free-men and serfs who ran away from their masters. Such cases were so numerous that in an astrological calendar the days favourable for escaping were specially marked.[4] Unless such escapes had been frequent, Charles would not have made a vow not to shelter runaway royal serfs part of the oath which he required as emperor from all inhabitants of his dominions.[5] It appears that conditions on the royal demesne were no better than on many of the noble estates. Again and again we find references to the harshness and corruption of Charles's own officials. A story which Notker relates about the construction of the imperial buildings at Aix-la-Chapelle is typical.[6] An abbot had been appointed as organizer and supervisor of the building-work. In the emperor's absence he had, for a money payment, released

[1] Ibid., p. 36.
[2] *Concilium Parisiense*, c. 53 ; MGH, *Conc.*, ii, ii, p. 645 ; also for the dialogue between the poor man and the usurer.
[3] A. Dopsch, op. cit., p. 14.
[4] L. Thorndike, *A History of Magic and Experimental Science*, New York, 1929, i, p. 68 n. 1.
[5] MGH, *Cap.*, i, p. 92, c. 4.
[6] MGH, *Script.*, ii, p. 744, c. 28. See Weise, in : *Vierteljahrsschrift f. Sozial- und Wirtschaftsgeschichte*, 1921, xv, p. 370.

the wealthier of those who had been called upon to do forced labour, and to make up the deficit, the remainder had been exploited to the utmost of their capacity. Charles was (in Notker's words) too ' occupied with public business ' to busy himself with the case ; but just retribution was brought about by divine intervention. The abbot's house, in which the amassed treasures had been stored, burnt down and the abbot himself was killed by the flames in an attempt to salvage his property.

The scholars of the royal palace, so keen on the propagation of Christian doctrine, never thought it necessary to plead with their master to improve the fate of his humbler servants. In one of his poems Alcuin alluded to certain tumults which had occurred in St. Amand, the abbey of his friend Arno, because of the exaction of forced labour for building purposes. He recommended that the rioters should be punished by flogging.[1] He himself complained that his personal servant who was supposed to cook, bake and wash for him, would not return if he sent him on an errand : ' they all run away, contemplating escape at every hour.' Alcuin's servants may have been caught by slave-traders : but it may be that they were simply driven away by hunger—for in the same poem written in the year of want, 797, Alcuin himself says he was so hungry and thirsty that he used everything there was to eat and drink for himself.[2]

Of peasant conspiracies, which were probably followed by the threatened corporal punishment, we hear only incidentally. Such punishment could effect little because it could not alter the economic conditions.[3] Most of the serfs who had, owing to hardship, escaped from their masters, turned into unattached vagabonds and drifted about as beggars until they could find a new master who they were reasonably sure would not hand them back to their former lords. The capitularies mention ' the poor on the squares and at street-corners '[4] as if they were a common occurrence. In vain it was laid down that every master was to supervise his own poor, to make them work and to prevent them from migrating elsewhere.[5] Many, especially those who

---

[1] MGH, *Poet.*, i, p. 334, No. 108.
[2] Ibid., p. 228, No. 8.　　　　　　　　　　　　[3] See p. 139 above.
[4] MGH, *Cap.*, i, p. 64, c. 32 (789).　　　[5] MGH, *Cap.*, i, p. 132, c. 9 (806).

were in search of justice against their oppressors, drifted towards the royal palaces. In Aix-la-Chapelle, special bailiffs were put in charge of the beggars.[1] If the emperor could not help them, they turned to a saint. When Einhard acquired the relics of martyrs for his church at Steinbach, both the healthy and the sick gathered round the church. Among them was a beggar from distant Aquitaine.[2]

The army of wayfaring people, mentioned by Einhard in connection with the miracles performed by his relics, reveals the colourful composition of the class of the disinherited. Side by side with hardship and sickness as a cause of distress, there was crime—crime which, in turn, may have been committed on account of want. This, for instance, was the case with the two poachers who took refuge with Einhard. There were murderers[3] who felt themselves safer in a consecrated place than on the open road. Such pilgrims, however, are not to be confused with those whom Charles, according to his biographer, ' loved ' and for whose needs he cared so liberally that they became a burden not only on his household administration but also on the kingdom itself.[4] (Charles, of course, was prompted largely by the desire to help those who would proclaim his generosity far and wide and increase his ' reputation ')[5] This desire could not be satisfied by escaped evil-doers but only by honourable people, especially of the higher orders, such as the English woman who had made a pilgrimage to Rome with her deaf and dumb son, but who, to Einhard's great satisfaction, only found at Steinbach the cure which the saints of the eternal city had been unable to procure.

There were of course, many honourable people whose journeys through the Frankish dominions were due to other causes than piety. Traders used the pilgrim's garb in order to pass unmolested through the numerous toll barriers;[6] and we have already mentioned those who used pilgrimage as a pretext to exhort new taxes from their peasants.[7] Many clerks undertook journeys without the permission of their superiors, and others

[1] MGH, *Cap.*, i, p. 298, c. 7.
[2] M. Buchner, *Einhard's Künster- und Gelehrtenleben*, Bonn, 1922, pp. 280 sq.
[3] Ibid., p. 302.
[4] Einhard, *Vita Karoli*, c. 21.   [5] Loc. cit.
[6] Alcuin, quoted in AS, ii, p. 509 n. 4.   [7] p. 117.

became mere vagrants who never aimed to reach the holy place which they alleged to be their goal.[1] (Many such clerks misused the clerical dress which made them welcome in every monastery, with the idea of specializing in the theft of relics,) which at that time was an extraordinarily profitable business.[2] Occasionally we hear of strange characters, of ' naked men ' like fakirs. They were in chains and claimed that they were wandering to and fro because of their guilt.[3] Such things are intelligible if we remember the survival, among the common people, of heathen conceptions such as the purifying effect of nakedness and the protective force of iron against demons.[4]

Genuine travellers and pilgrims were under the king's protection. But dubious characters were classed among the ' outlaws ' who ' cheated the people ',[5] with buffoons, jugglers, beggars with fictitious diseases and deformities, vagrant thieves, harlots and highwaymen. According to Alcuin, here and there even the royal judges were in league with the latter.[6] In Aix-la-Chapelle, during the reign of Louis the Pious, it was necessary to search for such rabble in the lodgings of palace servants and of merchants, both Christian and Jewish, and in the houses of the upper classes. There was a regulation that once a week a report was to be made about such folk.[7] The embassies of foreign nations were bound to be most unfavourably impressed if, on their way to the ruler who claimed to be the guardian of peace and justice, they were assaulted and robbed.[8]

Life on the highway was by no means without its dangers, not even for those who managed to circumvent all police regulations. The slave-traders, still officially sanctioned in the reign

---

[1] Quoted in AS, loc. cit., n. 5.

[2] *Translatio s. Severi*, MGH, *Script.*, xv, i, p. 292, where the following statement about Felix, a member of the clergy of Gaul, is made : ' Huic erat consuetudo per diversas vagari provincias et santorum reliquias, ubicumque potuit, furari '. For the whole question of relics, cf. p. 173, below, and H. Fichtenau, *Zum Reliquienwesen im frühen Mittelalter*, MIÖG, 1950, lx.

[3] MGH, *Cap.*, i, p. 60, c. 79 ; p. 104, c. 45.

[4] H. Bächtold-Stäubli ed., *Handwörterbuch des Aberglaubens*, Berlin-Leipzig, 1929 sq., ii, pp. 717 sq. As late as the sixteenth century men went on pilgrimages in the nude ; ibid., vi, p. 870. A ' clericus quidam seminudus ' prayed to be cured of his deafness and muteness in Einhard's church of Seligenstadt ; MGH, *Script.*, xv, p. 249, c. 4.

[5] Ibid., p. 60, c. 79.

[6] MGH, *Poet.*, i, p. 258, No. 45.

[7] MGH, *Cap.*, i, p. 297, No. 146.

[8] Ibid., p. 306, c. 18.

of Louis the Pious, were, of course, supposed to obtain their living merchandise from beyond the frontiers of the realm. They were also supposed to offer them for sale in public, in the presence of a secular or an ecclesiastical official.[1] But it was much quicker and less expensive to kidnap men on the highway. We have already noted Alcuin's suspicion that he may have lost his servant in this manner. Furthermore, all who wanted to rid themselves of their enemies through hired assassins, recruited their willing tools from the highway. Such assassins might themselves be assassinated later in order to forestall confession.[2] It is characteristic that even such a crime as incitement to infanticide, followed by the suffocation of the murderer in a ditch, could be expiated by a money payment,[3] provided that the criminal was a member of the free class. The public penance, demanded in such cases, by the church, was even less of a deterrent; for it was often refused and the bishop himself had no power to enforce it.[4]

The picture revealed by the sources of the life of the poor and of its many dangers, is grim. The poor were constantly threatened both by economic upheavals and by the arbitrary power of the magnates. Life on the roads, which all who had suffered social shipwreck were compelled to lead, was equally hard. We must remember, however, that many of the sources that have come down to us were designed to emphasize the evils of the age rather than more normal conditions. The period, on the whole, was still one of economic prosperity; the realm remained safe from civil war and devastation by foreign enemies; and the administration, if not particularly good, at least functioned after a fashion. To later generations the era of Charles the Great was, in comparison with their own times, a golden age of peace and order.

Measured in terms of the intellectual and material equipment for the work of government that was at the disposal of Charles and his contemporaries, their achievement was by no means

---

[1] *Form. Imp.* 30, MGH, *For.*, p. 309 ; H. Sée, op. cit., p. 53 n. 1.

[2] MGH, *Cap.*, i, p. 257, No. 129.

[3] Loc. cit.

[4] Under Louis the Pious the counts were supposed to help him ; MGH, *Conc.*, ii, p. 595.

inconsiderable. A mere tribe, itself to all appearance already on
the verge of dissolution, had proved capable of furnishing the
basis for an empire which comprised the whole of Europe. An
aristocratic class, long since diluted and corrupted, retaining
mostly the less desirable aspects of its ancient Germanic ideals,
had nevertheless endeavoured to harmonize its style of life with
that of Christianity. That this endeavour had entailed a distortion
of Christianity and had been made possible at all only at the
expense of essential points, was not entirely the fault of those,
lay or clerics, who had themselves only been taught Christianity
in vulgarized and impure form. Just as mere repetition of the
creed and the Lord's Prayer was not enough to make a layman
into a Christian, so also a clerk could not acquire the knowledge
and the moral attitude of a bishop of the late Roman empire simply
by studying in a cathedral school which was often enough no
more than a training centre for reading and singing.[1] His behaviour continued to be determined by the aristocratic customs
of his relatives, who set him an example of how to govern.

Christianity was mostly a matter of theoretical knowledge
without any immediate connection with the task of administration ; and the pastoral office, like the office of the count, was
considered to be essentially a matter of administration. Knowledge of Christianity itself was available only to the few. The
majority of priests were not deeply touched by it. Hence it is
incorrect to speak, in the age of Charles the Great, of ' the
Frankish church ' as though it were a single unit. The lower
clergy, who belonged socially to the servants, to the broad mass
of the middle and the lower classes, were quite distinct from the
higher clergy, who thought of themselves, with their aristocratic
style of life, as part of the *élite*. The life of the lower clergy was
not only parallel to, but actually was a part of the life lived by the
lay poor.

The pressure exercised by the wealthy landlords upon free-
men was experienced also in the ranks of the clergy. It is true
that there were priests who ' owned ' their churches without
obligation to any lord and subject only to the official supervision
of the bishop of the diocese. Usually they had established them-

[1] U. Stutz, *Geschichte des kirchlichen Benefizialwesens*, Berlin, 1895, pp. 144 sq.

selves on land cleared of forest by the labour of their own hands.[1]

But normally a lord would assign a parish on his estates to one of his serfs, much in the same way as he would assign a cottage to one of his peasants. In such case he not only preserved his own power to dispose of the church but also was reasonably sure that his priest would not make a nuisance of himself with spiritual admonitions. In theory, of course, the land, the buildings and the altar were dedicated to a saint and thus separated from the rest of the lord's domain. But in practice this was not the case.[2] The foundation of a new church might sometimes result in a reorganization within the domain; it might become the centre of a larger area, which was turned into a dependency of the parish. But such reorganization did not separate the new church from the lord's domain, any more than the serf who had been ordained priest by the bishop at the request of his lord, was separated from the rest of the lord's serfs. Very often, however, the proprietary churches themselves were simply dependencies attached to a manor or to the lord's residence—mere adjuncts, like the mill or the stables. In either case, the proprietor could dispose of them freely, in part or in full, and we find the conveyance of relics and of livestock mentioned in the same breath.[3]

To every ' proprietary ' church there belonged, so to speak, a ' proprietary ' priest. It was his duty to say mass for his lord on Sunday in the lord's house,[4] to wait upon him at table and to lead the hounds for the hunt.[5] There was hardly anyone of rank in the Frankish kingdom who did not set store on having a ' house-priest ' of his own,[6] and if the latter were disobedient, he risked corporal punishment,[7] or else was simply dismissed. No class of men, said Agobard of Lyons ten years after Charles's death, are so insecure as priests; they never know how long they will be allowed to keep their church or house.[8] When every-

---

[1] A. Stutz, *Geschichte des kirchlichen Benefizialwesens*, Berlin, 1895, pp. 144sq.
[2] U. Stutz, ZSSRk, 1937, xxvi, p. 24.
[3] Ibid., p. 41.
[4] This practice was prohibited in MGH, *Cap.*, i, p. 64, c. 25 (789).
[5] Agobard, cited by U. Stutz, *Geschichte des kirchlichen Benefizialwesens*, Berlin, 1895, p. 238 n. 7.   [6] Loc. cit.
[7] Ibid., p. 277.   [8] Ibid., p. 238.

one of substance had his own priest as servant, some particularly ambitious magnates seem even to have tried to revive the practice of aristocratic ' proprietary bishops ', and it was necessary to draw attention to an old conciliar decree forbidding the appointment of bishops in small villages and manors.[1]

If the prestige of the *potentes* was increased by possessing the largest number possible of servants, it was their particular delight to emphasize their claim to be above the priesthood. This was due not so much to contempt for the class that was not allowed to wear arms and defend itself, as a desire to assert themselves in relation to the very people who were supposed, in spiritual matters, to be their superiors. It was said that a magnate would go to a bishop and say : ' I have a fellow there, a sort of clerk, whom I have brought up and who used to be a serf of mine ; maybe I bought him from someone. I want you to ordain him as a priest for me.'[2] When such a spiritual serf ran away from his master, it was a legal obligation incumbent on all and sundry to arrest him and to deliver him to his rightful owner.[3] Nobody ever asked why the clerk had run away, although in some cases such an escape was nothing more than a protest against the enforced clerical status.

The law prohibited one lord from appointing another's serf as priest without the latter's permission.[4] But the law never considered the serf's own consent as necessary. In his admonition to the clergy in 811 Charles the Great asked the rhetorical question ' where Christ had prescribed, or which of the Apostles had preached, that an ecclesiastical fraternity of canons or monks should be constituted from people who were unwilling and who belonged to a low social order '.[5] But even on the royal domain conditions were no better. The *missi* were simply charged to ensure that no more male and female serfs were turned into clerks and nuns than was compatible with the sound administration of the royal domains ; they were not to be depleted of labour.[6] Charles discharged his Christian duty by remonstrating

---

[1] *Admonitio generalis*, c. 19 ; MGH, *Cap.*, i, p. 55.
[2] Quoted by U. Stutz, op. cit., p. 238 n. 7. The contemptuous expression *clericio* in this passage cannot be rendered in English.
[3] MGH, *Cap.*, i, p. 76, c. 27.
[4] Ibid., p. 55, c. 23.
[5] Ibid., p. 163, c. 10.
[6] Ibid., p. 122, c. 11

with the bishops. He was not really bent upon finding a solution of the conflict between the Germanic and the Christian sense of justice. To ask a serf whether he wanted to become a clerk would have been tantamount to recognizing him as a legal person, to treating him like a free-man. This, in turn, would have entailed a complete revolution in the legal conceptions prevalent among the laity. Canon law, on the other hand, demanded the manumission of the serf before the latter could enter the ranks of the clergy. The lords, however, were not always willing to lose a worker through manumission and to jeopardize their control over the ecclesiastical property with which the priest was invested, by loosening its dependence on themselves. Later on, when Louis the Pious decreed that all priests who were not free were to be removed,[1] the decree remained a dead letter;[2] its enforcement would have interfered too drastically with the whole social system.

It seemed unbecoming for the sons of free-men to belong to an order which numbered so many serfs among its members; the more so as the sons of free-men, upon becoming clerks, were also obliged to renounce their right to bear arms in the army and to sit in the law-courts. We know how much it went against the grain for Charles the Great himself. When a certain Aldrich, a member of the highest aristocracy, with royal blood in his veins, contemplated taking holy orders, he did not hesitate to make attractive offers to restrain the young man from carrying out his plans. Perhaps this story is not to be taken literally, but it is not entirely untrustworthy,[3] and Charles's ideas were shared by Aldrich's family. Indeed, as a result of the conditions described above, the clerical profession was generally the object of contempt.[4] On the other hand, no matter how much it contradicted the old code of honour of the Frankish upper class,

---

[1] Ibid., ii, p. 276 (818–9).
[2] Cf. the quotations in U. Stutz, op. cit., p. 273.
[3] *Gesta Aldrici episcopi Cenomannensis*, c.1 ; MGH, *Script.*, xv, i, p. 308. The account was written in 838, in Aldric's lifetime, perhaps even at his own command (ibid., p. 304) and may therefore be assumed to be true. For a different opinion see F. L. Ganshof's review of the German edition of this book, *Moyen Age*, 1950, lvi, p. 378.
[4] MGH, *Conc.*, ii, p. 594, c. 4 (818–829) : ' Ut sacerdotes . . . tanto despectui non habeantur.'

Charles, because of his sense of responsibility for the Christian guidance of his people, gave way to the influence of the church to the extent of officially expressing the desire that many men, free-men as well as the sons of serfs, should be educated for the priesthood.[1] Even in the days of Louis the Pious, however, Thegan tells us of the nobility's widespread contempt for the priesthood.[2] Later this provoked a reaction among the members of the lower clergy which is illustrated by the many anecdotes in which Notker scourges the weaknesses of nobles and *potentes*.

In this sphere, as in so many others, Charles in his legislation endeavoured to create ' a peaceful harmony between apparently irreconcilable contradictions ',[3] instead of trying to put into practice the rigid distinction between the secular and the ecclesiastical spheres demanded by canon law. Like his predecessors, before him, he opposed specific abuses of the law concerning proprietary churches, but he took no exception to it on principle. Through Charles's intervention the diocesan bishop was at least given a chance of deciding whether a clerk or a priest was entitled ' to be so called ' and whether he was ' blameless '.[4] The social and economic conditions of the minor clergy, however, remained unaltered. Only at the end of his reign did Charles try to secure for the bishops the right to some kind of control when lords wished to dismiss their ecclesiastical servants.[5] But it was only under Louis the Pious that the lord's arbitrary power to appoint and depose his clerks was curtailed and that a minimum income was guaranteed as an economic basis for parish services.[6] The ecclesiastical reform party, however, could not effect more ; not even during those years in which the ruler was their willing tool.

The synod of Frankfort of 794 had recognized the right of the magnates to own proprietary churches[7] and had thus confirmed the lord's control over his clerks. In the same spirit the *capitulare de villis* decreed that only such ecclesiastics as belonged to the royal household, in its widest sense, were to be invested

---

[1] MGH, *Cap.*, i, p. 60, c. 72 (789).
[2] MGH, *Script.*, ii, p. 595, c. 20 : ' Illud sacrum ministerium plerumque a nonnullis valde despicitur.'
[3] U. Stutz, op. cit., p. 235.   [4] MGH, *Cap.*, i, p. 110, c. 12 (802).
[5] U. Stutz, op. cit., p. 229.
[6] Ibid., p .236.   [7] MGH, *Cap.*, i, p. 76, c. 27 ; p. 78, c. 54.

with churches on the royal domain.[1] This exclusive rule, which
the king and the secular magnates exercised over their churches,
was exactly paralleled by that of the major prelates. They too
had their ' proprietary clergy ' of whom they could dispose as a
master disposed of a serf,[2] and whom, ' acting rather as tyrants
than as just rulers ', they taxed at rates far above the dues allowed
to the ecclesiastical superior by canon law.[3] They were able to
do this all the more easily as there existed no permanent authority
to supervise them. The secular magnates, if they went too far,
were, at least, exposed to episcopal admonitions. But the bishops
themselves were free to squeeze money out of their churches
until the arrival of the king's *missi*. And even then it was probably
not easy to find someone to lay a charge and take the risk of
secular as well as of ecclesiastical revenge.

Where ecclesiastical lords confiscated the tithe paid by the
faithful and granted it away or sold it,[4] instead of using it for
the maintenance of their priests and the upkeep of their churches,
the clergy were of necessity prevented from carrying out their
appointed tasks and forced to consider other ways of making
a living. They not only accepted offices in the administration
of the domains of the magnates or in their households ; they also
engaged in usury and money lending, activities strictly prohibited
by the church. ' Many work night and day to acquire, through
usury, worldly possessions such as chattels, slaves, wine and
grain '.[5] The capitularies, though full of indignation at such
practices, were silent about the conditions that caused them,
though these conditions were, of course, no excuse. There
must have been many priests who embarked upon shady transactions in times of want and then continued them even when
conditions had changed for the better. What drove them on
was the desire to make money and to climb socially, which could
not be restrained by ecclesiastical prohibitions. 'After their
ordination, men who previously were poor, buy land and serfs
and other property with the money intended for the upkeep of
divine service. They achieve nothing either in learning or in

[1] Ibid., i, p. 83, c. 6.   [2] U. Stutz, op. cit., p. 236 n. 2.
[3] Quoted ibid., p. 348n. 44.
[4] Cf. the description by H. Sée, op. cit., pp. 115 sq.
[5] MGH, *Cap.*, i, p. 237, c. 2. See also p. 244, c. 16.

M

collecting books or in performing divine service, but spend their time on banquets, oppression and robbery.'[1]

Such was the typical parvenu among the lower clergy. He was numbered among the free-men; possibly he had bought his freedom with the profits from earlier transactions. Owing to lack of supervision by his ecclesiastical superior, he made use of the church property entrusted to his care in order to lord it over others. On many secular estates we find, side by side with a concentration of the lord's rights, developments working in the opposite direction, i.e. a loosening of relationships of dependence and the rise of serfs to the economic status of free-men. In the ecclesiastical sphere developments were analogous. Possession of landed property and serfs, combined with his spiritual authority, enabled a priest to exercise great pressure upon the servile population of his parish. Frequent injunctions against the carrying of arms were directed not only against the higher prelates but also against parish priests of this type.[2] The same was true of the complaint that many ecclesiastics used their spiritual dignity only as a means of collecting together a troop of devoted retainers, and only carried out their ecclesiastical functions in return for payment.[3]

If the conditions in the newly-converted districts of Germany some fifty years earlier are remembered, it will nevertheless be agreed that there had been much improvement by Charles's time. It was certainly bad enough that serfs were forced to become priests. But from the church's point of view, it was better that this should be so than that there should, as Boniface had complained, be no priests at all in many areas.[4] It was easier to put up with priests who failed to commune when saying *mass*,[5] or who gave offence by spitting,[6] than to be confronted, as people had been in 757, with the problem whether sacraments administered by unbaptized priests were valid or not.[7] In spite of the five reforming synods held by St. Boniface, there were at that

---

[1] MGH, *Cap.*, i, p. 238, c. 6.   [2] See pp. 123, 128 above.
[3] Paulus Diaconus, *Alfabetum de malis sacerdotibus*, MGH, *Poet.*, i, pp. 81 sq., No. 52.
[4] MGH, *Epp.*, iii, pp. 376 sq., No. 91.
[5] MGH, *Cap.*, i, p. 54, c. 6.
[6] Thus Amalar of Trier, MGH, *Epp.*, v, p. 264, No. 11.
[7] MGH, *Cap*, i, p. 38, c. 12.

time clergy who sacrificed animals to the gods,[1] or who lived with five or more concubines simultaneously.[2] In our period the problem was merely whether the clergy ought to be able to read a Latin letter,[3] and how to prevent altogether association with women.[4]

In one sphere only, conditions seem to have improved very slowly since the days of Boniface. (It was very difficult to convince the clergy that drunkenness was a vice.) The ritual drinking confraternities of heathenism had been given a Christian veneer. They had not died out. Paul the Deacon, a great figure of the Carolingian Renaissance, was the author of a drinking song the verses of which are very reminiscent of ancient oaths.[5] When drinking feasts were held, it was laid down no priest was to force others to become intoxicated[6]—a deplorable habit which has survived in modern times in clubs and other masculine associations. In those days many a parish priest would drink with his neighbours well into the night and then sleep at the neighbour's house or his own rectory, throughout the following day without holding divine service.[7] When other clergy were present at such gatherings, he would quarrel with them;[8] or even worse, the drinking fellowship (*coniuratio*) would be turned into a conspiracy(*conspiratio*), directed against their ecclesiastical superiors.[9] It was the same tendency as we have already noted among the laity.[10] The young clerks, living as curates and pupils under the guardianship of the parish priests, naturally behaved in a similar fashion.[11] They cultivated popular songs and games,[12] without disguising them in learned Latin, like the clerks at the royal palace.)It was certainly easier for them than for the inmates of nunneries who had to be content with writing out drinking songs and surreptitiously passing them from hand to hand.[13]

---

[1] MGH, *Epp*., iii,. pp. 357 sq., No. 80 (748) ; R. Stachnik, *Die Bildung des Welt-klerus im Frankenreich von Karl Martell bis auf Ludwig den Frommen*, Paderborn, 1926, p. 16. [2] Loc. cit.

[3] E. Weniger, in : *Historische Vierteljahrsschrift*, 1935, xxx, p. 483.

[4] MGH, *Cap*., i, p. 237, No. 120, c. 2.

[5] MGH, *Poet*., i, p. 65, No. 31 : ' Coniurationes convivarum pro potu '. Every time the words ' si non ' occur in this edition, they ought to be followed by a dash.

[6] MGH, *Cap*., i, c. 14, p. 107 (802).   [7] Ibid., p. 238, c. 4.

[8] Ibid., p. 243, c. 6.   [9] Ibid., p. 56, c. 29.

[10] p. 138 above.   [11] MGH, *Cap*., i, p. 96, c. 23.   [12] Loc. cit.

[13] Ibid., p. 63, c. 19. On *winileod* (wine songs) see G. Ehrismann, *Geschichte d. deutschen Literatur bis zum Ausgang d. Mittelalters*, München, 1932, i, pp. 23 sq.

Yet there were advantages in the fact that the lesser clergy were not an exclusive order, clearly distinguished from the ordinary people, but had emerged from their ranks and knew how to get along with them. Feasts and popular songs were a medium through which Christian teaching could be brought to circles which had remained close to heathenism. Alcuin himself encouraged a monk—probably in England—to intersperse edifying Christian speeches at drinking parties.[1] When a heathen uprising at the end of the eighth century prevented the Friesian missionary, Liudger, from continuing his activities, he sent out a bard ' who was well versed in singing the deeds of the ancients and the battles of the kings ', and at the same time was empowered by canon law to perform emergency baptisms.[2] Later on, this Friesian bard also learned to sing psalms, and he probably recited them together with his epics during festivities. All this was in the spirit of the missionary programme which pope Gregory III sent to Boniface : to ' propagate the teachings of the Old and the New Testament in a manner adapted to untutored minds [3]

Since then, it is true, the Frankish clergy had laid more emphasis upon adaptation than upon propagation. They themselves could have done with missionaries ; but there was nobody to carry out such work. The only task which the Frankish clergy, on the whole, was able to discharge fully was the administration of the sacraments—although even this was not always performed according to canonical regulations. Even here, however, there were dangers. Time and again we hear complaints that people abandoned their secular status without wishing to become either secular clergy or canons regular or monks.[4] Satisfied with minor orders, they remained mere clerks for the rest of their lives. Many a young curate, whom the parish priest was supposed to educate, saw a more promising career in the service of a lord or even in an unattached life, in which he was not tied to a diocesan bishop, and in the course of which he could find manifold employment as the clerk or official of a noble or as a courtier and councillor to Charles.

---

[1] MGH, *Epp.*, iv, p. 348, No. 209.   [2] Aetfrid, *Vita Liudgeri*, quoted as AS, ii, p.38.
[3] MGH, *Epp.*, iii, p. 258, No. 12.   [4] MGH, *Cap.*, i, p. 122, c. 10.

Just as the old social order of the Frankish tribe had broken down and given way to fluctuating gradations which no longer corresponded exactly to the old ranks of society, so also an intermediate group gradually grew up between the clergy and the laity. This group was the butt of frequent criticism ; but no serious attempt was ever made to exterminate it. We have met its representatives already when discussing the scholars at the Carolingian court. They alone were capable of initiating a reform movement ; but they were as little interested in reform as Charles himself, who valued the services of these semi-ecclesiastics so highly. Even so, warning voices were heard during his own life-time. Thus Paul the Deacon wrote that the evil conditions among the clergy were destroying the order of the world ; the soil was yielding fewer fruits and the winds were blowing without restraint.[1] This statement adumbrated the future tendency towards a more clear-cut definition of the social hierarchy. Under Louis the Pious the campaign against ' the army of the clergy in the palace, popularly known as chaplains ', was expressly based upon the contention that these people did not belong to any known ecclesiastical *ordo*.[2] The division into spirituality and laity, and inside the spirituality into monks, canons regular and secular clergy, left no place for the inter-mediate group that had been responsible for so many excesses as well as for so many positive achievements, particularly in the literary field.

Even the monks did not always stand for that withdrawal from the world and from secular affairs that had been envisaged by the founders of the monastic orders, Benedict and Columban. In Irish monasteries this withdrawal had been effected by a total separation of the monk from his kith and kin. The follower of Christ had been supposed to be a mere wanderer on earth without a fixed abode. But this system had given rise to the first of the spiritual vagrants, who could not be fitted into any local eccle-siastical organization and whose moral discipline no one could supervise. The Irish monks had entered the pagan parts of the continent as wandering pioneers of the church ; but this task

---

[1] MGH, *Poet.*, i, p. 82, c. 19.
[2] *Vita Walae*, ii, c. 5 ; MGH, *Script.*, ii, p. 550.

now seemed to have been accomplished. Already under Pepin the attempt had been made to attach them to a permanent abode by assigning each to a monastery. The Irish ' wandering bishops ' suffered a similar fate, for their very existence made the creation of a stable ecclesiastical hierarchy difficult. They were turned into ' monastic bishops ', with the ludicrous result that no less than seven such Irish bishops were congregated together in one monastery in the upper Rhineland in Charles the Great's time.[1]

But the monks' desire to wander was by no means dead. The simplest way of avoiding superior discipline was to go wandering about under the pretext of a pilgrimage,[2] or simply to run away from one's abbot. Or else one tried to found a monastery of one's own in which one could order life according to one's own wishes,[3] gathering together a following of one's own. Indeed, the novice's vows to his abbot followed the formulae of the oath of fealty sworn to a lord,[4] and in the monastery of Reichenau, for example, they were administered by way of personal commendation to the abbot.[5]

All this contradicted the spirit of the monastic rule. In fact, there were religious communities in which sometimes the rules of Benedict of Nursia were obeyed, sometimes the rules for canons regular, and sometimes neither. Not only the official visitor but Charles himself must have been profoundly irritated to find that the ' monks ' of Tours passed themselves off, as suited them best, for genuine monks, for canons regular or for a mixture of both.[6] Alcuin, as their abbot, should have seen to this. But he himself lived in the no-man's land between the strict monastic rule, the rule for canons which allowed a separate house and income, and the status of a royal chaplain without a fixed abode. As a result he spoke with much sympathy of the ' third order ' which existed side by side with the monks and canons regular : ' They ought not to be despised, for many people of that sort can be found in the house of God.'[7]

---

[1] H. Frank, *Die Klosterbischöfe des Frankenreichs*, Münster i, W., 1932, pp. 29 sq.
[2] MGH, *Cap.*, i, p. 35, c. 10, etc.
[3] Ibid., p. 111, c. 17 (802).
[4] H. Frank, op. cit., p. 171, after H. Herwegen, *Geschichte d. benediktinischen Prozessformel*, Münster i. W., 1912.
[5] Loc. cit. 			[6] Cf. Charles's letter, MGH, *Epp.*, iv, p. 400, No. 247.
[7] Ibid., p. 416, No. 258.

Already Pepin had decreed, under pain of excommunication, that all who wore the tonsure but had retained their property and lived neither under the disciplinary control of a bishop nor in a monastery, must become either monks or canons regular.[1] But as late as the reign of Charles the Great there were still people who ' availed themselves of the monastic habit in order to confuse spiritual with secular business '. They drifted about from one urban settlement to another,[2] engaged on the most diverse kinds of business, not always of an honest character. At times, for instance, they travelled in the employment of magnates such as Einhard or archbishop Otger of Mayence, who desired to increase their collection of relics either through purchase or through theft.[3] Some members of the regular clergy, of course, were driven on to the streets by bitter hardship rather than by the desire for profit and freedom. It was well known that there were prelates who withheld from their inferiors their due means of existence, and thus forced them to wander about and engage in dishonest transactions.[4]

Thus the social position of the regular clergy of low birth and without private income was very similar to that of the parish clergy and of the poor among the laity. Side by side with monasteries, such as Corbie, the inmates of which were in large part noblemen,[5] there were monasteries which drew recruits from the male and female serfs of the large domains. A monk might be a poor fellow, a vagrant beggar,[6] or he might be a respected ' lord ', as was the case in the famous old abbey of Fulda, where land and grain stores had been divided among the monks so that everybody was free to go about his own business.[7] Some-

---

[1] MGH, *Cap.*, i, p. 35, c. 11 (755).
[2] See p. 166, n. 3.
[3] Einhard, *Translatio ss. Marcellini et Petri*, MGH, *Script.*, xv, pp. 239 sqq. Cf. note 53.
[4] MGH, *Conc.*, ii, p. 402, c. 122 (Aix-la-Chapelle, 816).
[5] There is nothing in the material collected by A. Schulte, *Der Adel und die deutsche Kirche*, 1910, which compels one to believe that there were any monasteries in the reign of Charles the Great which were composed exclusively of nobles. Böhmer maintained that all monks were exclusively of noble blood. This view has been rejected by H. v. Schubert, *Geschichte d. christlichen Kirche*, Tübingen, 1921, pp. 620 sq. For the nobles in Corbie see *Vita Adalhardi*, c. 35 ; but cf. MGH, *Cap.*, i, p. 122, c. 11, for evidence to the contrary.
[6] A. Pöschl, *Bischofsgut und mensa episcopalis*, Bonn, 1909, ii, p. 216 n. 1.
[7] MGH, *Epp.*, iv, p. 550, No. 33 (812).

times, on the other hand, the economic basis of a monastery was too small to support the monks. Vanity and the founder's desire to have people pray for his soul all too often resulted in a poorly endowed new foundation. In such cases, monks were driven to make a living by accepting the office of a bailiff or by concentrating upon trade and usury.[1] Hardship often destroyed the sense of community among the brothers. But even the rich monks of Fulda were wont to quarrel and intrigue with each other about their fields.[2]

If the abbot were a layman, there was probably even less difference between the monastic domain and an ordinary secular estate. On the death of Fardulf, the Lombard who had been granted the abbey of St. Denis as a reward for his betrayal of the conspiracy of the hunchback Pepin, Waldo of Reichenau had to march with armed men into the chapter-house and force the rebellious monks to fulfil their spiritual duties.[3] Even in monasteries which were in sympathy with reform it was debated whether the house might not fare better under an aristocratic abbot than under a member of the lower orders, no matter how pious the latter might be. ' He will defend us against counts and other mighty lords, and his rank will incline even the emperor's favour towards us. Do you know how he can do this? He can do it, because he has relatives in the royal palace '.[4] These were, after all, weighty grounds for not departing from accepted custom.

Just as a lord could force a serf against his will to become a secular priest, so also he could force him to take the tonsure of a monk. There were complaints that the victims of such compulsion frequently tended to become criminals and vicious men.[5] This was not always due to the despair felt at being forced into monastic life. On the contrary, dangerous people were often sent to a monastery as a precaution instead of being put under lock and key : aristocratic conspirators, prisoners of war, hostages[6] as well as ' evil and ill-disposed men who were capable

---

[1] MGH, *Conc.*, ii, p. 630, c. 28 (Paris, 829).
[2] MGH, *Epp.*, iv, p. 550, No. 33.   [3] MGH, *Script.*, iv, p. 447.
[4] Ibid., xv, p. 224, c. 5 (Fulda, 818).   [5] MGH, *Epp.*, iv, p. 549, No. 33.
[6] Thus especially the Saxon nobles who were distributed among the Frankish monasteries and who became monks ; AS, i (2nd ed), p. 361 n. 3.

of any infamous action ',[1] It was unlikely that people's respect for the religious profession would be heightened or that monasteries would attract many honourable people, when they had to live there in daily contact with murderers and bloodshedders, and when whole convict colonies, which soon organized themselves into robber confraternities, were settled upon monastic lands.[1]

It certainly suited the secular authorities to rid themselves in this way of opponents or of those involved in a blood feud. In the case of a man involved in a blood feud, however, there was always the danger that the family of the victim would turn their ancient right of revenge against the whole convent.[2] On the other hand, it was equally profitable for an abbot if he could get a premium for accepting novices without probation,[3] or for giving credence to the lies on the pretext of which they were being enticed into the monastery.[4] It could hardly be expected that people who were longing for the secular life[5] of which they had been deprived by such frauds, should turn into models of monasticism. Many such monks tried to drown their sorrows in drink or in even worse ways.[6]

Charles the Great's legislation was confined to denouncing specific consequences of these conditions. No systematic attempt was made to improve monastic discipline as a whole. The responsibility for this rests less in ' the Emperor's lukewarm interest ' in monasticism[7] than in the fact that any regimentation from above was unlikely to be successful without a corresponding movement for reform among the clergy themselves. Moreover, Charles needed the close support of the aristocracy. Therefore, he always carefully refrained from interfering with the internal administration of both ecclesiastical and secular estates. The condition of the clergy could not, however, be improved without causing, sooner or later, the sharpest conflict over the principles of the proprietary church system, and this would have shattered the established order of the whole realm. At a later date, such an

---

[1] MGH, *Epp.*, iv, p. 549, No. 33.   [2] Loc. cit.
[3] MGH, *Cap.*, i, p. 63, c. 11 and c. 15 ; ibid., p. 76, c. 16.
[4] MGH, *Epp.*, iv, p. 549, No. 33.
[5] Loc. cit.   [6] MGH, *Cap.*, i, p. 94, c. 17 (802).
[7] A. Hauck, *Kirchengeschichte Deutschlands*, ii, (2nd ed.), p. 574.

attack was in fact attempted, with singularly little success by the extreme wing of the reformers, under the leadership of bishop Agobard of Lyons.

As far as the spiritual attitudes of the Frankish clergy of the period is concerned, it is hardly possible to reduce its varied manifestations to a common denominator. One thing, however, is certain. The real danger did not stem so much from a lack of book learning as from the fact that people were not thoroughly imbued with a Christian spirit. The great missionaries had been men of action, heroic warriors of Christ, just judges of truth and falsehood in the sphere of religion. These ideals may have remained valid for the laity, especially for Charles and the leaders of his armies. But when further conquests became impracticable, the initial spark was soon extinguished. And for the present there was nothing with which to replace it. People did not comprehend—as the Christians of the Orient, nourished by rich sources of spiritual exercise, comprehended—that the time had come to transfer the scene of battle from the world to the soul. Instead, they vainly wasted their energy in external organization. They busied themselves with the administration of church property, participated in the running of the state, and delivered ' thundering ' sermons, poor substitutes for the living appeal to the inner man. Men of that age were dependent upon personal example, the place of which could not be taken by books. Perhaps the enormous appeal which the worship of relics made to the people in this time of crisis was due, in part, to the fact that in an age devoid of saints, people desired the bodily presence of the saints of earlier ages.

The religious mood of the people needed saints. When there were none, it created them. There was little reason for worshipping men like Alcuin or Angilbert during their lifetime. But no sooner were they buried than legends began to circulate. They were alleged to have performed miracles, and in the place where they had worked and lived they were considered blessed or were even called saints.[1] Charles, in his legislation, had to oppose the weed-like growth of ' false martyrs and unrecognized saints '

---

[1] *Vita beati Alchuini abbatis*, MGH, *Script.*, xv, pp. 185 sqq. St. Beissel, *Die Verehrung der Heiligen u. ihre Reliquien*, 1890, i, p. 39.

days '. Charles even tried to prohibit altogether the worship of
these new saints, whose monuments were being erected at every
street corner.[1] The survival of local heathen cults was certainly
only a very minor cause of such popular customs ; on the contrary the heathen cults and the rise of Frankish Christian local
saints, were probably due to the same factor. This was the
longing people had to subject themselves, together with their
manor or village, to a divine leader or protector, just as in
worldly affairs they sought the protection of a ' good lord '.
In seeking a patron saint, people considered themselves, much
as in their worldly relationships, as the vassals and followers
of a heavenly magnate. This is proved by the willingness with
which they were ready to defend his ' honour ', and the place
that was due to him in the heavenly hierarchy. One Sunday, the
men of the archbishop of Orléans arrived in St. Martin de Tours
to arrest a fugitive who had placed himself under the protection
of St. Martin. The peasants, who had been drinking wine in
their cottages, rushed out to take up arms : ' There is one thing
which people of all ages and of all places have in common. They
do not suffer their saints to be dishonoured.'[2] In return, it was
taken for granted that the saint would assist his people in times
of want and danger, and this he did by the miracles performed
at his grave or when he was invoked. People were proud when
it could be shown that their own saint was more powerful than
someone else's, to whom pilgrims and the sick had turned in
vain.[3]

These things should not be mistaken for a tendency towards
polytheism. Just as government formed a graded pyramid
between lord and man, which would have been incomplete
without its apex—namely, the ruler's dominion over the whole
state—so a corresponding order obtained in heaven. Every
position, from that of a minor local saint to that of the powerful
' prince ' who had his own house in the heavenly palace, was
strictly graded. The ruler of the universe, Christ-God, whose

[1] MGH, *Cap.*, i, p. 55, c. 16 ; ibid., p. 56, c. 42, (789) ; ibid., p. 77, c. 42 (794).
[2] MGH, *Epp.*, iv, p. 403, No. 249 ; p. 398, No. 246.
[3] People who had prayed in vain ' in many places ' and whom e.g. St. Lambert
of Lüttich had not been able to help, were cured in Seligenstadt. MGH, *Script.*,
xv, i, p. 251, c. 10.

'honour' was enhanced by the number of his saintly followers and vassals, stood at the summit. A small peasant of Tours could no more address a petition directly to the emperor without first seeking justice from his own abbot, than he could dispense with the intercession of the competent saint. He did not worship St. Martin for the saint's sake but in order to reach, through him, the inner springs of the heavenly kingdom.

The emphasis on the legal order inherent in religion caused men to regulate their conduct, so far as possible, according to the commands of the church and to perform good 'works' in large numbers. But, owing to the same legalistic attitude, they rarely embarked upon the struggle for the inner regeneration and sanctification of the individual—a struggle which is as essential for salvation as the performance of good works. Where the inwardness of religion was concerned, the clergy, for the most part, failed to set an example, and in this sphere the saints also were of no avail. They had long since been removed from earthly life and their miraculous intervention, in the form of rewards and punishments, was commonly understood as a sign of their approval or disapproval within the framework of the existing legal system. Popular legends, handed down orally or in writing, offered only slender guidance for self-discipline, for the lives of saints which they recounted were hardly calculated to solve the problems arising in the course of everyday life. Even sacraments were only a very partial help ; for people hardly dared to partake of the flesh and blood of the heavenly King ; and the remaining sacraments, baptism and confession, were conceived of as legal institutions, primarily concerned with external conduct. The penitential books show clearly how much the Germanic sense of justice was preoccupied with the principle that people were responsible for the results of their actions rather than for their intentions ; they never inquire into the inner guilt of a person but always into his actions, which are weighed in terms of unchanging quantitatively assessable penances.

Men judged themselves and others not according to their inner attitudes but according to their overt acts. No law and no sermon, composed on familiar lines, could teach people to lay hold of that inner attitude. The only power able to do so, would have been the constant presence and example of personalities who had achieved their own inner regeneration. The strong but fluid piety of the common people was ready to crystallize around such men. But such men were not available. Hence the Franks sought substitutes by gathering around relics. But relics redirected attention to the sphere of matter and of the senses, and thus turned men away from any preoccupation with the soul, which it was so difficult for ordinary people to comprehend.

Every time a saint was transferred to a new place of worship and every time a church was consecrated,[1] a veritable eruption of popular piety occurred, naively expressed in external actions. ' I can neither pass over in silence nor really describe how great was the rejoicing and the pleasure of the crowd who had assembled along the road.' Thus reported Einhard, adding that on that occasion even a man engaged in a blood feud had been reconciled with the murderer of his father.[2] When the news that the relics had arrived had spread through Aix-la-Chapelle ' everybody abandoned the work in hand and rushed as fast as their legs would carry them to the church '.[3] Physical nearness was what people always longed for. In order to enable people to get as close as possible to the tomb of a saint, special circular crypts were constructed, as for instance in the church of the abbey of Werden.[4] Those who could afford to buy relics, carried them in small bags around their necks.[5]

In all these cases an attitude is apparent which is found in old Germanic religion, in which both the sacred and the demonic had been treated as something like a centre from which operative matter radiated. This conception could be applied to human beings as well as to animate and inanimate nature. In the Carolingian age, people still performed sacrifices in honour of the spirits of trees, stones and springs.[6] Bells were baptized in order to render them capable of warding off demonic power.[7] It is

---

[1] See Candidus' description of the consecration of the church of the abbey of Fulda (819), *Vita Eigilis*, 2, v, 114 sqq., MGH, *Poet.*, ii, pp. 111 sq.
[2] *Translatio ss. Marcellini et Petri*, MGH, *Script.*, xv, p. 247, c. 8.
[3] Ibid., c. 4.
[4] J. Braun, *Der christliche Altar*, München, 1924, i, pp. 577 sqq.
[5] MGH, *Epp.*, iv, p. 448, No. 290.
[6] MGH, *Cap.*, i, p. 59, c. 65 (789).
[7] Ibid., p. 64, c. 34. See also H. Bächtold-Stäubli, op. cit., iii, pp. 869, 873.

true that such practices were waning. The conception that holiness was confined to human beings, even though dead, was gaining ground. And similarly, (the idea that evil occurrences were caused by people real or imaginary, was becoming more common.) Such explanations of evil occurrences appeared absurd to Agobard of Lyons, but they were at least more rational than earlier beliefs. (Thus, for example, people punctually paid fees to weather-wizards who protected them against thunderstorms, while the clergy had to wait for their tithes.) In the vicinity of Lyons four people, three men and one woman, about to gather fruit in fields devastated by a gale, had been arrested. It was said that they had fallen down to earth from ' airships '. They were sentenced to be stoned ; but the wrath of the people was directed even more against the people who were alleged to have commissioned them, namely magicians in the country of ' Magonia ', who were supposed to have sent the aviators and who had planned, after the completion of the expedition, to buy the loot they had collected. Agobard writes with displeasure of this ' false belief which has gained such an ascendancy over practically everyone in this region '.[2] Similarly, emissaries of the duke of Benevento were held responsible for an epidemic among the cattle. They were alleged to have scattered a poisonous powder on the pastures, and a number of strangers, believed to be the emissaries in question, were captured and forced to confess their guilt. According to the treatment customarily meted out to poisoners, they were tied to boards which were floated down the river until the men were drowned.[3]

Such events show that people were eager to fasten the responsibility for all evil happenings upon actual persons, just as they supposed that saints were the authors of all good things.) Just as they conceived the state to be an association of persons, and law to be personal law, so also they thought that natural events were determined by natural or supernatural persons. It was impossible for the clergy who themselves—with rare exceptions, such as Agobard of Lyons—were deeply immersed in popular

---

[1] Agobard, *Contra insulsam vulgi opinionem de grandine et tonitruis*, MPL, civ, col. 157, c. 15.

[2] Ibid., col. 148, c. 3.　　　　　[3] Ibid., col. 158, c. 16.

superstitions, to enlighten them. They merely tried, so far as possible, to prevent people from having deailngs with men who boasted of supernatural powers. That this ktas was taken seriously is shown by the fact that, in the penitential books, those who consulted a soothsayer were subjected to the same penance as people guilty of manslaughter.[1]

Popular imagination was more familiar with sorcerers, soothsayers, witches and other magical powers such as demons in animal shape and haunted places, than with the figure of Satan, their master. The widespread belief in an hierarchical order required that all the demonic powers be subject to a single common head. But (the prince of hell always acted through his creatures.) He very rarely appeared himself in person. (People believed in God but prayed to His saints ; they believed in the devil, but protected themselves against his agents) Thus people were relieved in everyday life of the necessity of operating with the difficult, because comprehensive, concepts of ‘ God ’ and ‘ Devil ’. It was easier to think in terms of a plurality of single beings each of which had a definite agency for good or evil.

To this relatively peaceful coexistence of saints and sorcerers or goblins in the external world, there corresponded a coexistence of good and evil in the soul of man. In this respect people did not work out consistent attitudes ; they lived from occasion to occasion rather than according to the requirements of a single principle. They confessed major sins of commission rather than the attitudes and thoughts that had caused such sins. They even held that a pilgrimage sufficed to cancel all guilt.[2] These attitudes were not due to what, among us moderns, might be called indifference. They were due to the coexistence of a large variety of rules of conduct which had not yet been subjected to a unifying and regulating principle. It might be thought that in so thoroughly religious an age a unification of the principles of conduct ought to have been within the realm of possibilities. Thus, knowledge of God might have become experience of God and gathered, like a magnet, all the scattered elements of piety. Or conversely, people might have realized that behind the threat of total annihila-

---

[1] A. Hauck, op. cit., ii, p. 762.
[2] MGH, *Conc.*, ii, p. 282, c. 45 (813).

tion, there emerged the figure of Antichrist and the Last Judgement.

In fact, such a transformation of the spiritual attitude actually took place. But it occurred not in the reign of Charles the Great but in that of Louis the Pious. Only a relatively small section of his contemporaries were affected, and it was a very gradual process; but the effects of the transformation were nevertheless so great that they not only coloured the outlook of a whole generation but also shook the very foundations of the Carolingian empire. The Christian ' radicals ' who began this transformation were not sufficiently powerful to put an end to the old conditions ; in the end, they were captured by social and political factions and their interests. But, in the first place, their very existence caused a deep rift. The conservatives looked upon the reformers as utopian doctrinaires ; while the reformers saw in the conservatives no more than corrupt opportunists.

In the generation after Charles the Great we thus find, separated (as it were) under an X-ray screen, what had appeared earlier as the solid, if not entirely healthy, structure of a single body. It is possible to debate what, in the first place, had caused the separation of the different elements ; whether it was the inner stirrings of the monastic reforms inaugurated by Benedict of Aniane, or the increasing poverty and the incompetence of the ruling classes, which led to a more radical type of Christianity. What is certain, however, is that this radicalism would not have had such profound effects upon the structure of the state, unless there had been deep-seated tensions in the structure itself. The age of prosperity was bound to retard the growth of this radicalism ; while the increasing poverty of the subsequent years tended to favour it. But sooner or later this radicalism would have manifested itself even without economic causes—for a serious, if ultimately inadequate, attempt to transform a religion (whose external forms had long since been accepted) into a consistent inner attitude, and to mould a way of life that correspond to it, was bound to be made.

CHAPTER VII

THE LAST YEARS OF CHARLES THE GREAT

Charles the Great once dreamt that he was approached by a man who handed him a sword, a present from God. Four words were written on its blade : *raht, radoleiba, nasg, enti.* Charles recorded the dream that very night[1] and attempted to interpret it the following day. The sword signified the power of dominion ; ' now, after the subjection of our enemies there is more abundance than in the days of our fathers. This fact is indicated by the first word, *raht. Raht* means abundance of all things. The word written in the second place signifies what will, we believe, happen after our death, in the times of our sons : the abundant crops will diminish and some of the newly-conquered nations will rebel. This means *radoleiba* in everything, a rapid decrease. When the sons die and their sons in turn begin to rule, there will happen what is indicated in the third place, *nasg.* For they will increase the taxes for the sake of sordid profit. . . . They will not care with how much confusion and ignominy they collect their wealth. . . . But that which was written near the point of the sword, *enti*, means end. It can be understood in two senses : either the end of the world or the end of our dynasty. . . .'[2]

This story was spread by Hrabanus Maurus who alleged that he had heard it from Einhard. Was it, perhaps, invented in the middle of the ninth century when dark shadows were falling over the Carolingian empire and the prevailing mood was very similar to that in the quoted text? Or did Charles who, following tradition, was fond of propounding and solving riddles, think of them even in his dreams? Whatever the answer, it is fairly certain that a prophecy composed after the event would have contained some

---

[1] People who (like Charles) were unable to write with any degree of accomplishment in the ordinary way, could well have made a few notes on *tabulae*. As a matter of fact, Einhard's report that Charles was unable to write has been described as a fairy tale. E. Weniger, in : *Historische Vierteljahrsschrift*, 1935, xxx, p. 486.

[2] *Visio Caroli Magni*, P. Jaffé, ed., *Bibliotheca rerum Germanicarum*, iv, pp. 702 sqq.

reference to the greatest misfortune that could befall any ruling
dynasty, to the fact that son took up arms against father and
brother against brother. It would hardly have been confined
to mentioning the rebellion of a few frontier tribes in the reign
of Louis the Pious.

The political and financial prosperity of which we have
spoken above, is insolubly linked with the prevailing picture of
Charles's reign. But during the last years of that reign we can
discern a slowing down, and the beginnings of the regression
which was to become very much more obvious during the reign
of his son Louis. Charles the Great seemed to have been abandoned by the good fortune which had attended his earlier years
and which, in the mind of his contemporaries, was connected
with abundance in all things. He was by no means unaware of
this lack of good fortune—in spite of Einhard's story that Charles,
' either for appearance's sake or through genuine contempt ', took
no notice of evil omens.[1] Perhaps he had to face in his dreams
the thoughts which he was not eager to talk about during the
day.

At the age of sixty-four, in February 806, Charles provided
for the succession of his three sons to the Empire. In that year
a failing harvest caused a famine, and the capitulary of March
of the same year was the first to lay down comprehensive measures
against usury and for the care of vagrant beggars.[2] In the following year and again at the beginning of 808 detailed orders regarding military service were drafted, and an investigation was
ordered of all cases where, contrary to these orders, men had
failed to participate in the campaign in western Francia.[3] At
the same time it appears that the nuisance of robbers had increased, for the agenda for Charles's consultations with the
magnates of the Empire were headed by measures against that
danger.[4] A mild winter brought the pest,[5] and was followed
in spring by the news that the Danes had stirred up rebellion
among the Slav tribes on the frontier and were threatening the

---

[1] Einhard, *Vita Karoli*, c. 32.
[2] MGH, *Cap.*, i, p. 132 ; only MGH, *Cap.*, i, p. 74, c. 4 (794), is in any way
comparable.   [3] Ibid., pp. 134 sqq.
[4] Ibid., p. 138, c. 1.
[5] *Annales Regni Francorum*, MGH, *Ger.*, vi, p. 125

Saxons.[1] Two years later the Danish king boasted that he would
soon march with his army into Aix-la-Chapelle. We know from
Einhard that people in Aix took these threats seriously,[2] and
this is corroborated by the fact that Charles awaited the Danish
army in his camp near Verden on the Aller. Times had changed
since the days when Charles used to take the offensive.

In the end, all danger was removed by the assassination of
the Danish king, Guthrödr. But earlier, while Charles was
waiting for the Danish attack, he had an experience which
seemed to indicate the sinking of his star even more clearly than
did the unusual number of solar and lunar eclipses in one year,
which Einhard mentions.[3] A ball of fire traversed the sky and
frightened his charger. He was thrown off and lay on the ground
without arms and cloak, the symbols of his authority, and had
to be picked up by his servants. With the buckle of his cloak
broken and his baldric torn[4]—how much longer was his rule to
last? A successor seemed to be wanting to take his place :
Guthrödr, who was already ' confident of dominion over the
whole of Germany '.[5]

For medieval people the health and well-being of the ruling
dynasty indicated God's favour. Disease and death were har-
bingers of the ' devil's age '.[6] It seems that Charles suffered from
frequent attacks of fever from the beginning of the year 810.[7]
Pepin, his son, died in the middle of the same year, and was
followed to the grave in April 811 by Charles, the emperor's
eldest son. Only Louis, the least warlike of the three, remained ;
and it was at this very moment that on a Spanish expedition he
proved his incompetence as a military leader. To these calamities
there was added, in June 810, the death of Charles's eldest
daughter, Rotrud. A little later, during the expedition against
the Danish king—so Einhard tells us, and it is a characteristic
juxtaposition, even if it makes us smile—there occurred the death

---

[1] Loc. cit.   [2] Op. cit., c. 14.
[3] *Annales Regni Francorum*, MGH, *Ger.*, vi, p. 123 (807). In his *Vita Karoli*,
Einhard related the eclipse of the sun, together with Mercury's transit across the
face of the sun in 807, as a sign of Charles's approaching death.
[4] *Vita Karoli*, c. 32.   [5] Op. cit., c. 14.
[6] E. Bernheim, *Mittelalterliche Zeitanschauungen*, Tübingen, 1918, p. 90.
[7] Einhard, op. cit., c. 22.

N 2

of Charles's beloved elephant,[1] which accompanied him on all his travels and even on military campaigns.

Charles did not use the opportunity of Guthrödr's sudden death to go over to the attack. Perhaps the outbreak of a deadly cattle epidemic would have made an offensive difficult.[2] Instead, he concluded peace with the Danes, came to terms with the emir of Cordova, and halted the aggressive policy of his deceased son Pepin in Italy, where the Frankish conquests were abandoned. Byzantine officials returned once more to Venetia and Dalmatia. The peace treaties were drafted in the palace at Aix-la-Chapelle, and here also directives for the *missi* were issued, from which we gather, for the first time, that there had been deserters from Charles's army[3] and that many men who owed military service had stayed at home altogether. We also hear of fugitives from justice who had been kept in hiding, of robbers and of men 'with evil intentions' whom many people supported rather than opposed.[4]

The fire, it is evident, was already smouldering. Civil disobedience was on the increase and, what is more, the *missi* occasionally met with the resistance of armed bands which sometimes were led by the emperor's own rebellious vassals.[5] The ultimate cause of the increasing litigation and of resistance to military service on frontiers and in the army[6] may well have been a growing shortage of what we to-day would call consumer goods. The increasing economic difficulties are clearly indicated by the refusal in some quarters to accept the imperial coins, in spite of the fact that they contained the full weight of silver.[7] Only the well-to-do, of course, could afford to adopt this attitude. Many small peasants, on the other hand, were forced, long before harvest-time, to sell their crops standing in the fields, and were ruined by doing so.

In the year 811 Charles instituted an inquiry into the causes of ever-increasing desertion. The findings have come down to

---

[1] *Annales Regni Francorum*, MGH, *Ger.*, vi, p. 131 (810).
[2] Ibid., p. 132. It was at that time that people were looking for the Duke of Benevento's 'poisoners'; see p. 175 above and MGH, *Cap.*, i, p. 153, c. 4.
[3] MGH, *Cap.*, i, p. 153, c. 13. [4] Ibid., p. 154, c. 19.
[5] Ibid., p. 153, c. 17; p. 160, c. 1.
[6] Ibid., p. 161, c. 2 (811). [7] Ibid., p. 152, c. 7 (809).

us, and strikingly illuminate the situation at the time. Thus we are told how (' the poorer people complain that they are being deprived of their property.) This complaint is directed equally against bishops and abbots and their *advocati*, as well as counts and their subordinates. Those who refuse to surrender their property to a bishop, or abbot, or judge or even a minor official—so they maintain—are convicted on any pretext and compelled to render almost continuous military service, until they are completely impoverished and forced to surrender or sell their property. Others, who have already done so, are left quietly at home. . . . The counts themselves report that part of the men in their countries refuse to obey them and refuse to pay the fine for ignoring the emperor's orders. . . . Even if they put these people's houses under the ban, they cannot exact obedience '.[2] All these things pointed to the conclusion ' that the men of the county show less obedience to counts and *missi* in all respects than they used to '.[3] When people went so far as to kill their own relatives in order to avoid being called up,[4] we may well ask whether such an attitude did not, from the very start, make the outcome of any military expedition extremely questionable. (The people were tired of war.) They longed for a ruler who loved peace and social justice, such as, for a while, they believed they had found in the person of Louis the Pious.

In the meantime the ageing emperor was forced to continue to govern with the help of the nobility who had made his rise to power and greatness possible. There was no change in personnel—the basic condition of all reform. He tried to strengthen the loosened ties between ruler and ruled through a renewal of the imperial oath. He thus hoped to brand, before God, all recalcitrant men as perjurers.[5] In addition there was one spiritual weapon, which Charles recognized and had already tried to use during the first part of the crisis : it was to win back the grace of an enraged God through fasting and prayer. In the autumn of 807, at an assembly of secular and ecclesiastical magnates, it was decreed that an ' imperial fast ' be held for three days. The

---

[1] Ibid., p. 152, c. 12.   [2] Ibid., p. 165, c. 2, 3, 6.
[3] Ibid., p. 165, c. 9.   [4] Ibid., p. 165, c. 10.
[5] Ibid., p. 177, c. 13.

decree and the reasons for it were communicated to all the bishops with the order to pass it on to all parish churches and monasteries. ' We know from the reports of our faithful servants from various parts of the Empire ', so the decree ran, ' that the soil is everywhere losing its fertility abnormally and more rapidly than one might expect and that a famine is threatening ; that gales are damaging the crops ; that epidemics are raging ; that there is continuous warfare with heathen tribes on our fron-tiers. . . . From these external events we can infer beyond all doubt that, inwardly, we are not finding favour with the Lord ; for we are compelled to undergo so many external sufferings. Therefore it seems to us fitting that every one of us should truly seek to humble his heart and . . . do penance '.[1]

The style of this letter is such that it is unlikely to have been composed by the emperor himself. But this does not mean that the matter was of no personal concern to Charles. Once again, in the year 810, when the misfortunes had reached their climax, similar three-day fasts were ordered ' to beg God to show us the things in regard to which we must improve our conduct before Him'.[2] A memorandum concerning the points 'we want to discuss with our bishops and abbots and on which we want to admonish them with reference to the common weal of our people ',[3] clearly shows the result of these meditations. And on this occasion the hypocrisy and egotism of the clergy were shown up in a manner that is unusual for Charles's official documents. A series of effective rhetorical questions was put to the clergy sharply contrasting the Christian ideals and the sad realities, in such a way that they were bound to condemn themselves in their answers. The reproaches were directed against the superficiality of the regiment which these mere administrators exercised over the church—a superficiality which meant that any real change of heart was neglected, to the manifest disadvantage of the church of Christ. An ecclesiastical dignitary who was interested only in increasing the number of those subject to him, and not in their moral improvement, was as objectionable as one who cared only for church building and the chant without attempting to

[1] Ibid., pp. 244 sqq.
[2] Ibid., p. 162, c. 1.
[3] Ibid., p. 162, preamble.

raise the moral level of the clergy. 'If we ourselves desire, in ecclesiastical matters, to follow Christ, the Apostles and their true followers, we must alter our conduct in many things, give up much that is customary and do much that we have not been wont to do '.[1]

And yet Charles himself, again and again, had urged his clergy to care for the building of churches and for the choral chant, without making any attempt to reform their inner attitude. Every one of the bishops to whom the above words were addressed, was bound to recognize in them a confession of guilt by Charles himself. If Charles himself, the guardian of law and justice, publicly admitted that he had made mistakes, that fact alone is proof of how much the times were changing. We have reached a point from which a straight line leads to Louis the Pious's confessions of guilt and to his attempt to conform not only in external conduct, but also in his inward attitudes, to the image of a Christian man.

The decrees of the Synod of Châlon-sur-Saône over which Charles presided in 813, were characterized by the same desire to advance from the sphere of the external world into the unchartered territory of the soul. The decrees dealt with the meaning of fasts and of almsgiving, with the concept of the worthiness of the recipient of the sacraments, and especially with the question of sins committed in thought only. These, and not only overtly committed sins, were now to be the object of confession.[2] Compared with the decrees of the subsequent age of reform, these were small beginnings.[3] They show, nevertheless, that the emperor as well as the clergy were conscious of the need for a higher conception of Christian duty than had prevailed so far.

It is from the last years of Charles's reign, also, that the poems of Theodulf of Orléans are to be dated which show him no longer as a humanist devoted to the arts, and a mocking court-poet, but as an acid critic of his contemporaries, living in expectation of a just punishment for the sins of man. There can be little doubt that these poems were read out to Charles. There was, for instance, the poem about the old age of the world, in

[1] Ibid., p. 164, c. 11. [2] MGH, *Conc.*, ii, p. 279, c. 32.
[3] MGH, *Cap.*, i, pp. 161 sq., c. 12.

which Theodulf's earlier cheerfulness and vitality were notably missing. ' The wall, so firm and artistically decorated in the days of my youth, is showing cracks, and signs of approaching decay. As an old man is loath to sing . . . and to talk pleasantries . . . everything sweet has fled from the ageing world and nothing is left of its former strength '.[1] The fact that many of these words were borrowed from ancient writers, does not alter their significance. The mood they express corresponded to that monkish manner which not only became so marked with Theodulf personally during those years, but also replaced the earlier levity in the court of the ageing emperor.

Although there is no proof, we may surmise that Charles, under the impact of the crisis in the empire and of his personal misfortunes, began at this time to consult not only his customary councillors, but also members of the clergy from the ' radical ' Christian wing which was developing in Aquitaine under the influence of Benedict of Aniane.[2] Benedict himself had appeared once at the imperial court to rebut charges levelled against him by the nobility. He had been well received and the emperor had offered the cup with his own hands to the man who, as a youth, had been his own and Pepin's cup-bearer.[3] But the courtiers and the court-clergy, who had denounced Benedict to Charles as a greedy robber of secular goods,[4] formed too firm a barrier against all outsiders for any effective change of personnel in Charles's council to be possible. Nevertheless the changes which took place at the accession of Louis the Pious do not appear quite so revolutionary when we remember that even the ageing Charles had not been totally insensitive to the new trends that were to assert themselves fully after his death.

In 811, when the crisis had reached its zenith, the emperor

[1] Theodulf, *Quod multis indiciis finis proximus esse monstretur*, MGH, *Poet.*, i, p. 468, No. 14, lines 31 sqq.

[2] F. L. Ganshof (*La fin du règne de Charlemagne, Zeitschrift f. schweizerische Geschichte*, 1948, xxviii, p. 451) has argued that, most probably, Wala was Charles's councillor during the last years and was therefore responsible for the nomination of Louis as emperor. Together with Wala's influence, he suspects the advice of Adalhard, Einhard and Fridugis. It is certainly possible that both Wala and Adalhard, in opposition to the courtiers of the Palace, were active on behalf of the reform movement and did what Wala was to do in the winter of 828–9. Charles may also have been influenced by Einhard's strong and simple religiosity.

[3] *Vita Benedicti Aniani*, 41 ; MGH, *Script.*, xv, p. 211.　　　　　　[4] Loc. cit.

made a last will disposing of the treasures and other belongings stored up in his palaces. Three-quarters of the precious metals were left to the main churches of the empire.[1] A donation of such enormous value was intended to stimulate prayers throughout the realm for the welfare of Charles's soul, and this seemed more important to Charles than the need to provide the heirs of his body with gold and silver. His heirs, in fact, were given little more than eight per cent of the total treasure, no more than was given to the men and women servants of the palace. In his last decrees, too, the emperor sought to turn men's minds from earthly riches to the care for their own souls. One clause of his will, in particular, has aroused historians' speculation. That is the reference not only to Charles's impending death but also to the possibility of 'voluntary withdrawal from secular life'. Must we assume that the emperor had in mind the example of his uncle Carlman who, 'for unknown reasons, but apparently through love of spiritual contemplation', had become a monk on Mount Soracte and later retired to Monte Cassino?[2]

If Charles had resigned his throne, it would certainly have been impossible for him to lead the life of a secular private person in the midst of his subjects. Even Carlman, the monk, had been continuously interrupted in his meditations by the visits of his magnates. It was perhaps conceivable that Charles might have withdrawn as a lay-abbot to one of the imperial abbeys, just as earlier he had been in nominal charge of the abbeys of Murbach and Echternach.[3] But all speculation as to the possibilities that may have occurred to Charles during those last, bitter years of his rule, are idle.

The recognition of his imperial position by the Greeks was the one ray of light during those years. Now that God, through the death of two of his sons, had decided that there was to be one ruler only,[4] Charles raised Louis the Pious to the dignity of co-

---

[1] To be quite exact, two-thirds and one-fourth of that third which had been set aside for Charles's use while he was alive. Einard, op. cit., c. 33.

[2] Ibid., c. 2.

[3] K. Voigt, *Die karolingische Klosterpolitik*, Stuttgart, 1917, p. 33.

[4] The *ordinatio* of 806 had envisaged a single dominion for the whole realm divided into separate administrative units for the three brothers. Such a dominion was meant to heighten the power and unity of the dynasty rather than to diminish it, even as the divine Trinity did, about which people were then speculating so much.

Emperor, using exactly the same ceremonial forms as had been employed when the Byzantine Emperor Michael I made his son Theophylact his co-regent.[1] Thus Charles had ordered his dynastic affairs as became the head of a family. Then the man who formerly complained that fasting was bad for him, died, on January 28th, 814, during a voluntary fast designed to put a stop to his attacks of fever.[2]

Charles the Great had lived a worldly life. The transformation that took place during the last years of his life was typical of many aristocratic laymen of the Middle Ages. As long as they were vigorious, they served God with the sword; with the approach of old age they did penance for the sins which they had not been able to avoid. What is remarkable is not that Charles's life should exhibit this common pattern, but the fact that its stages corresponded so closely to those of the development of the Frankish empire. In his thirties and forties he had led the *regnum Francorum* to its climax. His imperial coronation at the age of 58 was a fitting epilogue to that period. Six years later a number of events foreshadowed the coming crisis. In 811, Charles, as became a man of almost seventy, laid down his arms; but his son, although much younger, only took them up again in exceptional emergencies. The Carolingian empire, itself a late manifestation of the *regnum francorum*, seemed to enter the period of old age. Its small ruling class either turned away from the world to otherworldly objectives, or exhausted itself in jealous party strife.

It is impossible to understand the political history of the

See H. Mittels, in: Th. Mayer, ed., *Der Vertrag von Verdun*, 843, 1943, pp. 67 sqq. The parts which Charles gave to Bernard of Italy and those which he planned to give to the children he had had from his concubines (Einhard, op. cit., c. 33), were also meant to be subordinate administrative units. He did not mean them to endanger the unity of the whole. It is remarkable that there is no mention in the *ordinatio* of the *imperium*. It has been suggested that this is due to the fact that Charles had a very personal conception of the imperial dignity. (F. L. Ganshof, op. cit., p. 444). It may also possibly be due to the fact that at that time the imperial dignity had not yet been recognised by Byzantium. F. L. Ganshof believes that by 806 Charles had lost much interest in the idea of a spiritual empire which had been so much in the foreground in 802. He explains the lack of interest as due to the hostility and lack of understanding on the part of the lay nobility and the younger sons of the emperor. The imperial idea did not regain its interest until the very last years of Charles (ibid., p. 446).

[1] F. Dölger, in: Th. Mayer, ed., op. cit., p. 220.
[2] Einhard, op. cit., c. 30; cf. c. 24.

following reign and the personality of Louis the Pious himself, unless one has grasped the twofold current which is so characteristic of Louis' reign. On the one hand, there was the nobility's descent from the heights of prosperity and success. This descent, retarded at first by a few peaceful years, was soon accelerated by the urgent question as to who was, and who was not, to enjoy the ever diminishing capital laid up by earlier generations. On the other hand, there was the ever-increasing desire to salvage, from among the many ephemeral goods of this world, the only thing that really mattered : a knowledge of the ultimate principles of the cosmic order and of the corresponding principles of the human soul. For the world was bound to remain in disorder as long as the microcosm of man stood in need of regeneration.

It is certainly true that the last phase of Charles's reign contained within itself the seeds of new developments. Decline was at the same time, a gathering of forces for the future; and the foundations were being laid for the independent life of the succession-states. We have drawn a picture of the empire of Charles the Great, of its ideals and of the men with whose help an attempt was made to put these ideals into practice. It would be the task of another book to show how the breakdown of the universal empire under Louis the Pious and his sons made it possible for healthy forces to find a new sphere of activity in the separate provinces of that empire. The very diversity of the provinces and of the men who governed them, and the incompatibility of earlier Germanic notions with Christian universalism, had been a constant source of weakness to the empire as a whole. But these same factors also had their positive aspects. Thrown back upon their own resources, the local nobility, in each province, responded to the challenge. They resisted the new invasions and, their strength once aroused, gave birth to new political societies in place of the old empire.[1] Europe has never since formed a political unit, and all later attempts to bring about political unity have ended in failure. But, because of the common historical and cultural inheritance from the Carolingian age, the resulting disunity has never dissolved into complete anarchy.

[1] G. Barraclough, *The Origins of Modern Germany*, Oxford, 1946, pp. 5 sqq.

The Roman empire continued to live, after its fall, in the realm of dreams and ideas which, in turn, became historical forces. Charles the Great, like the Christian emperors Theodosius and Constantine, was not forgotten. All later European rulers were proud to have Carolingian blood in their veins, even though only very indirectly, and particularly when it was a matter of claiming a universal authority. They did so not only in France but also in the new empire set up by the Saxon rulers of Germany and their successors. That new empire was to comprise only central Europe and parts of Italy. But the old ideas continued to live in it, and its emperors made pilgrimages to the tomb of Charles the Great who was venerated as a saint by the Hohenstaufen emperor, Frederick I, and his bishops. In the east, Charles's name came to signify ' ruler ' ; the Slavonic word ' kral ' was used not for ' Charles', but to designate the ' king ' in general.

Thus the empire of the Franks and its mighty emperor became the symbols of splendour and greatness. The darker aspects were consigned to oblivion. It is human to overlook what is all too human.

INDEX

Abbots,
corruption of, 168
duties of, 122
royal service of, 168
Adalhard, 184 n. 2
Adallindis, 40
Advocati, 139, 140, 142
Agobard of Lyons, xxii, 34, 157, 170, 174
Aix-la-Chapelle,
accumulation of treasures in, 80–1
arrival of relics in, 173
imperial buildings of, 151
building plans of Charles in, 68–9
crime in, 154
culture of, 83
exposure to Danish threats of, 179
palace chapel of, 54–5
poverty in, 153
residence of Charles, 67
' new Rome ' in, 72
synod of, 88, 119
Alcuin, xx
acquisitiveness of, 86
ethical advice of, 118, 119, 120–2
conception of new Athens of, 84
as collector of information, 95
attitude to corruption of, 116
creativeness of, 95
and monastic discipline, 166
and education, 90–1
egotism of, 96
views on exploitation of, 152
friendships of, 94
imitativeness of, 99
conception of *imperium chris-tianum* of, 64–5, 71–2

encyclopaedic knowledge of, 96
and profane knowledge ,102
praise of poverty of, 85
quarrel with Theodulf of, 123, 171
love of quotations of, 96
relations with Charles of, 29, 30
religiosity of, 97
views on salvation of, 101
and school of palace, 91
sensuousness of, 94
sentimentality of, 96
teaching of, 87, 93
religious tears of, 86
worldliness of, 92
Angilbert, 84, 95, 124
Angilram of Metz, 129
Annales Laureshamenses, xix, 74, 74 n. 1
Anthropology,
History and, xvii
Arno of Salzburg, 108, 116, 127
Arnulf, 10 sq.
Arquillière, H.-X., xx sq.
Art,
official nature of, 83
Arts, liberal, 88
Astronomy, 88
Attigny,
synod of, 124
St. Augustine, xx, 64
Augustinism, political, xx
Austrasia, 110
emergence of, 8
Avars, 79–80, 115
and Byzantium, 80

Ban,
degrees of, 105
delegation of, 104
king's power of, 104

Franks,
  poverty of, 79
  tribe of, 1
    catholicism of, 3
    and heritage of *populus Romanus*, 24
    mission of, 63 n. 1
    propaganda of, 3
    reputation of, 5
Free-men, 7, 114, 140
  church and, 140
  descent in social scale of, 146
  flight into monastery of, 146
  economic hardships of, 135
  poverty of, 144
  and priesthood, 159
  progressive subjection of, 135
  surrender of property, 145
Fridugis, 184 n. 2
Fulda,
  consecration of abbey of, 173 n. 1

Ganshof, F. L., vi, xix, 159 n. 3
Gaskoin, C. J. B., xiii
Gaul,
  Frankish administration of, 5
  Frankish conquest of, 1–2
  Frankish occupation of, 4
Gersuinda, 40
God,
  influence of Arianism on conception of, 48–9
  and Christ, 48
  popular conception of, 48, 50, 175
  and kingship, 105
  provisions for government by, 48
  as source of political power, 104
Gregory the Great, 15, 96 n. 3
  and Anglo-Saxons, 15
  sacramentary of, 88

Grimoald, 11
Guilds, 139
Guthrödr, 179–180

Hadrian, 88
Halphen, L., vi, xiii, xiv, xx, 85 n. 1
Harnack, A., xvii
Hauck, A., xxii
Hildebold of Cologne, 129
Hildegard, 39
Himiltrude, 39
Hodgkin, Th., xiii
Hrabanus Maurus, 99, 127, 177
Hundredmen, 139

Iconoclasm, 70
Imperial dignity,
  personal conception of, 185 n. 4
Imperium, 104
Imperium christianum, 62–3, 65, 118
  renovation of, 89
Ingelheim,
  paintings at, 83 n. 6
Irene,
  Charles and enemies of, 73
  and Constantine IV, 72
  and iconoclasm, 70
  planned marriage to Charles of, 76
  succession of, 66
  and imperial title, 66–7
Islam,
  threat of, 13

Jonas of Orléans, 127

King,
  spiritual functions of, 61
  Pope and, 60
Kingdom,
  division of, 185 n. 4
Kingship and *imperium*, 63
Kleinclausz, A., ix, xiv, xx, xxi